AFTER THE WAR ZONE

DR. MATTHEW J. FRIEDMAN, MD, PHD, is the Executive Director of the U.S. Department of Veterans Affairs' National Center for Posttraumatic Stress Disorder (VA National Center for PTSD), established in 1989. He began to assist Vietnam veterans while that war was winding down and is currently working within Veterans Affairs (VA) and with military colleagues to assist troops returning from Iraq and Afghanistan. He has worked with PTSD patients as a clinician and researcher for thirty-four years. Dr. Friedman is a professor of psychiatry and pharmacology and toxicology at Dartmouth Medical School and is recognized as a world leader in the field of traumatic stress studies. He has written or co-edited over 200 publications, including scientific research articles and nineteen books. Listed in *The Best Doctors in America,* he is a Distinguished Lifetime Fellow of the American Psychiatric Association. He is the son of a World War II Navy veteran, and his wife, Gayle Smith, is a nurse and Vietnam veteran who worked in the Third Surgical Hospital in Binh Thuy, Vietnam from 1970 to 1971. **DR. LAURIE B. SLONE, PHD,** is a researcher and the Associate Director for Research and Education at the National Center for PTSD. She is an experimental social psychologist with a faculty appointment at Dartmouth Medical School. She codirects the National Center for PTSD's extensive educational Web site (www.ncptsd.vo.gov). Her sister, brother-in-law, uncle, and grandfather have served in the U.S. Army, and her nephew currently serves in the Army Reserves.

Together, Drs. Friedman and Slone have been intimately involved in working with those who have served in the current wars in the Middle East. They have worked at the national level with military and VA colleagues to improve methods of preventing, assessing, and treating traumatic stress reactions. In addition, in Vermont and the surrounding region, they have worked locally to promote better reintegration for returning troops and families. This initiative, called the Vermont Military, Family and Community Network (MFCNetwork), consists of a partnership between the Vermont National Guard, the VA Medical Center, and the Vermont Agency of Human Services, as well as many other collaborators.

The MFCNetwork's mission is to make reintegration into civilian life as smooth as possible. It's dedicated to increasing awareness about the many deployment-related issues that might affect troops and their families. It works to help service members, veterans, and all family members cope with these challenges as successfully as possible. It seeks to educate all community service providers, as well as members of the general community, about the cycle of deployment, potential re-entry problems, the best interventions, and available local and national services and resources. This entails education, training, and collaboration between the troops, families, health care providers, other community resources, family programs, and all interested parties.

AFTER THE WAR ZONE

A PRACTICAL GUIDE FOR RETURNING TROOPS AND THEIR FAMILIES

LAURIE B. SLONE, PhD
and
MATTHEW J. FRIEDMAN, MD, PhD

Da Capo
LIFE
LONG

A MEMBER OF THE PERSEUS BOOKS GROUP

Copyright © 2008 by Laurie B. Slone, PhD, and Matthew J. Friedman, MD, PhD
All rights reserved. No part of this publication may be reproduced, stored in a retrieval system, or transmitted, in any form or by any means, electronic, mechanical, photocopying, recording, or otherwise, without the prior written permission of the publisher. Printed in the United States of America.

Designed by Linda Harper
Set in 12.5 point Perpetua by the Perseus Books Group

Library of Congress Cataloging-in-Publication Data

Slone, Laurie B.
After the war zone : a practical guide for returning troops and their families / Laurie B. Slone and Matthew J. Friedman.
    p. cm.
  Includes bibliographical references and index.
  ISBN 978-1-60094-054-5 (alk. paper)
  1. Veterans—Mental health. 2. War neuroses—Prevention. 3. Post-traumatic stress disorder. I. Friedman, Matthew J. II. Title.
  RC550.S548 2008
  616.85'212—dc22
                                                                                2008005555
Published by Da Capo Press
A Member of the Perseus Books Group
www.dacapopress.com

Note: The information in this book is true and complete to the best of our knowledge. This book is intended only as an informative guide for those wishing to know more about health issues. It consists entirely of our personal views and does not represent official policy of the U.S. Department of Veterans Affairs or its National Center for PTSD. In no way is this book intended to replace, countermand, or conflict with the advice given to you by your own physician. The ultimate decision concerning care should be made between you and your doctor. We strongly recommend you follow his or her advice. Information in this book is general and is offered with no guarantees on the part of the authors or Da Capo Press. The authors and publisher disclaim all liability in connection with the use of this book. The names and identifying details of people associated with events described in this book have been changed. Any similarity to actual persons is coincidental.

Da Capo Press books are available at special discounts for bulk purchases in the United States by corporations, institutions, and other organizations. For more information, please contact the Special Markets Department at the Perseus Books Group, 2300 Chestnut Street, Suite 200, Philadelphia, PA 19103, or call (800) 810-4145, extension 5000, or e-mail special.markets@perseusbooks.com.

1 2 3 4 5 6 7 8 9

*This book is dedicated to all of
the brave women and men who have been,
will be, or are deployed to the Middle East
during the Operation Enduring Freedom and
Operation Iraqi Freedom conflicts, and
their families who have also sacrificed.
We hope the advice we offer
will help.*

CONTENTS

Introduction   *ix*

1 Understanding the Emotional Cycle of Deployment   1

2 During Deployment: Setting the Stage for Homecoming   19

3 Homecoming: Separating Myth from Reality   39

4 Understanding Battlemind   56

5 Common Reactions to the Trauma of War   65

6 Anger and the Adrenaline Train   83

7 Guilt and Moral Dilemmas   96

8 Handling Grief   106

9 Reconnecting with Your Partner, Children, Family, and Friends   116

10 Overcoming Barriers to Care   136

11 Posttraumatic Stress Disorder   150

12 Recognizing Other Mental Health Issues   171

13 Dealing with Injury   187

14 Community Support   199

15 For Those Facing Unique Challenges   213

A Final Note   223

Glossary   *227*

References   *233*

Resources for Troops and Their Families   *241*

Acknowledgments   *263*

Index   *267*

INTRODUCTION

The impact of war extends far beyond the battlefield. As a service member in a war zone, you are forever changed by your experiences. The lives of your family and friends, who were left behind during deployment, have also changed. You've all had to make compromises and readjust your lives so things can run smoothly during deployment. Then, once deployment ends, everyone faces further challenges and readjustments as you reintegrate into life at home. The military requires you to go through intensive training and preparation before going into battle, but they offer little, if any, preparation for your return home. Not surprisingly, many troops find this transition more challenging than adjusting to the war zone. Thankfully, human beings are extremely resilient, and most troops and families will make it through this reintegration successfully. However, although it will be easy for some, others will encounter difficulties. A small but significant percentage will need professional help in order to make it through this tough time.

You may be surprised to learn that you need to prepare for life at home after the war zone. Most people expect that homecoming will be a wonderful experience. After all, you've survived the dangers of battle and are returning home to be with your family and friends once again. Why would that be difficult? In fact, there *is* usually a "honeymoon" phase that occurs shortly after demobilization, when everything seems right in the world. But the honeymoon never lasts. Both you and members of your family have changed during deployment. You'll need to get reacquainted with one another and very likely renegotiate some of your roles now that you're home. This is why being prepared for homecoming is so important.

We recognize that you may not think this applies to you. It's easy to believe that such difficulties might affect the other guy, but not you. Even if you're one of the lucky ones who do have a smooth readjustment, we believe that it's always better to prepare for the worst and hope for the best. Even if *you* don't experience any difficulties, what you learn in these pages will enable you to help someone else.

WHO THIS BOOK IS FOR

We wrote *After the War Zone* to help service members and their families. We wrote it in the hope that it will educate and guide a wide range of people. First and foremost, we wrote it for troops who are experiencing any degree of difficulty readjusting to life at home after deployment in a war zone. It's for the unmarried Reservist who has seen far more than she ever bargained for when she signed up for service. It's for the married Airman who left behind a wife, two small children, and a baby who was born during his absence. It's for the many women who found themselves experiencing more danger and combat in a war zone than ever before.

We also wrote this book for the partners, children, parents, and friends who must first cope with separation from their service member during deployment, and then with new challenges after he or she has returned home. This book is for the parents of service members who can't sleep at night because of constant worries about the dangers their children are facing in the war zone. It's for partners at home who fear for their loved one's life and are exhausted from having to function as the head of the household, a single parent and a full-time employee. It's for the twin sister of a Soldier, the mother of a Marine who lost a leg, and the friend who wants to know how to be there for someone when he or she returns from the war zone.

There are also lessons in this book for our communities. We offer information and advice to neighbors, coworkers, employers, and service providers who assist returning veterans and their families—every single member of each of the communities in which service members live. There's a lot that community members can do to ease troops through their transition from the war zone to the home front. Really, *After the War Zone* is for anyone who wonders what to expect when a service member returns home from a war zone and how they can help when the going gets tough.

WHY WE WROTE THIS BOOK

Our desire to ease the reintegration process for all concerned, our experience with the Vermont Military, Family and Community Network (see About the Authors on page ii for a full description as well as Chapter 14, page 208), our research and clinical expertise on traumatic stress, and our personal experiences with troops and their families were major driving forces that led to the creation of this book. By translating scientific and clinical knowledge into useful, practical advice for service members and their families, we believe *After the War Zone* fills an important gap. There are other good books out there that discuss the reintegration challenges that follow deployment. Almost all of these books are written from the personal perspective of someone who has been through deployment. Because each service member and family member's experience is different, we believe that a more general overview is in order. Therefore, we present many different perspectives with respect to both troops and their families. Based on our work with a broad spectrum of individuals, we have drawn from our expertise and experiences to provide you with the most research-based coping advice we can muster.

Ultimately, we wrote this book because we want you and your family to be as well prepared for homecoming as you were for deployment. This involves educating yourself on what to expect during reintegration and learning useful tools and effective coping mechanisms to help you overcome any difficulties. You may face some tough emotional and psychological challenges, such as anger, guilt, grief, or difficulty reconnecting with your loved ones. You may also face barriers that could prevent you from getting the services and resources you deserve. This book seeks to demystify these challenges and barriers so they no longer need stand in your way during reintegration. By drawing your attention to reintegration challenges, we hope to help you and your family achieve the smoothest possible readjustment and show you that *you are not alone in your struggles.* Many troops wrestle with these reintegration issues. Time spent in a war zone changes people. It also changes those who wait for them and then have to watch them go through a troubling reintegration process. There are many who also feel the pain of no longer fitting in, the despair of no longer knowing their loved ones, or the incongruity of not being the same people they used to be.

HOW TO USE THIS BOOK

After the War Zone is designed to be read from beginning to end, but it also allows you to easily locate and read about topics as they pertain to you. We begin by describing the entire "emotional cycle" of deployment and how it generally affects both you and your family and friends. We then set the stage for homecoming by describing some of the characteristic experiences that occur both in the war zone and at home during deployment. We do this so service members can appreciate the sacrifices that their families have made, and families can gain a better understanding of what happens to a loved one when fighting a war. We discuss the expectations and myths troops and their families often hold about homecoming and explain what really occurs. We also explain Battlemind, or the mindset troops need for survival in a war zone, as well as the problems it can cause after homecoming.

We then shift our focus to the ten most common challenges troops face during their first year home. We discuss the common reactions that service members experience when they return from the war zone, such as anger, overprotectiveness, avoidance, guilt, depression, and PTSD. We describe the emotional difficulties of dealing with both physical and psychological injuries. We also discuss other common problems that can disrupt family life, such as financial and employment issues. We provide coping strategies to help you manage these issues and advice on when you should consider seeking professional help to successfully deal with them.

We've also included a resource section, which offers a wealth of information on the services available to you and your family, should you need them (See page 241). This will allow you to get started in your search for further information and services on a variety of topics. We've organized it by topic to make it easier for you to find what you need.

We've also included a glossary to help with any unfamiliar terms you encounter. Any **boldface** term you see in the book is defined in the glossary on page (See page 227).

THE STRONG AND THE BRAVE

The "strong and the brave" is a term that exemplifies all of you who have joined the military. Given the strength and courage that you repeatedly demonstrated in the war zone, it may be hard for you to accept that you might need help with readjustment. It might cause you to mistakenly believe that such problems are a sign of weakness. The truth is that some of the most successful and effective warriors, officers, and enlisted personnel—both men and women, Soldiers and Marines—experience reintegration problems. In some cases, they even require mental health treatment for problems such as posttraumatic stress disorder (PTSD), depression, alcoholism, and substance abuse. Research has been unable to tell us why some people have trouble readjusting after traumatic situations and others do not. It may be genetic, it may be circumstantial, or it may simply be bad luck. Whatever the reason, it's important that you realize that emotional or psychological problems are *not* a sign of weakness. Experience in a war zone can cause both physical and psychological injuries. The more severe the traumatic experience, the higher the likelihood it will cause psychological problems or psychiatric symptoms. Actually, the stronger and braver you are, the more likely you are to place yourself in the most dangerous—and potentially traumatic—situations. The reality is that injuries, including psychological injuries, affect the strong and the brave just like everyone else.

KNOW THAT THERE *IS* HELP AVAILABLE

The stigma surrounding mental health issues can be a huge barrier for those in need of professional help. This is especially true for troops, who often believe that their strength and bravery should be enough to get them through tough times. This can make it very hard to both admit you have a problem and to request information or seek assistance for psychological or interpersonal issues. The challenges involved in reintegration can seem overwhelming, especially if you feel that there's nothing you can do about them. That's why it's so important for you to know that there are many services and resources available that are designed to help you readjust to home life successfully. You can find assistance through the military, the VA, and in virtually every community. There are effective treatments to help you manage and/or overcome all the emotional and psychological problems you may encounter, including PTSD, depression, alcoholism, and excessive anger. This book will show you how to tap into those resources and connect with people and services that can help you both locate resources near you and also cut through the red tape.

You and your family have made great sacrifices for the rest of us. We honor that commitment by providing you information that will help you identify and understand any problems you may be having and empower you to seek solutions. Our hope is that these pages will be a useful resource that will help you improve the quality of your life as well as that of your family and enable you to move forward to the next phase of your life. We offer *After the War Zone* as a small part of the support you deserve from your community and nation.

1

UNDERSTANDING THE
EMOTIONAL CYCLE
OF DEPLOYMENT

The members of our platoon have been on high alert, sleeping very little, taking each day as it comes, and trying to survive for the past eleven months. You wouldn't believe the heat, especially with body armor on. We have to be on guard each and every minute, prepared for an ambush, incoming fire, or other bad stuff. You even take your weapon with you to the bathroom. Last week, I saw a suicide bomber kill two U.S. Soldiers and four Iraqi children while the Soldiers were handing out candy to the innocent kids.

It's great to be able to email and talk to the folks back home, but it's also really hard. My cell phone rang one time last week when we were patrolling. (I had forgotten to turn it off!) It was my wife's sister telling me that Sue has been sobbing every day again and she's really worried about her. It's hard to hear those things and not to be able to do a darn thing about it. Our son has been having some troubles at school, too . . .

Deployment is a difficult and stressful time for everyone involved. As you struggle to come to terms with going to war and leaving your loved ones behind, strong emotions are evoked. Your family must prepare for life at home without you. When you're in **theater**, the war takes over your life. Surviving in the war zone is a full-time job. Meanwhile, your family makes some serious life adjustments in order to function well while you're gone. Once you return home, you and your family must acknowledge and accept your separate experiences and find a way to live together again. In this initial chapter we discuss the "emotional cycle of deployment," or the feelings and experiences you and your family may have immediately before, during, and several months after your deployment, and offer strategies to help you cope. Being aware of the entire emotional cycle is helpful in understanding the homecoming process. As you'll soon see, all stages of the emotional cycle of deployment have a direct effect on your reintegration to life after you return home.

THE EMOTIONAL CYCLE OF DEPLOYMENT

The emotional cycle of deployment, acknowledged in all military circles and by all branches of the armed forces, consists of three separate stages: pre-deployment, deployment, and post-deployment. **Pre-deployment** is the period between the day you receive the deployment warning order and the day you leave for your post. It usually begins with feelings of anticipation and even excitement about departure, mixed with feelings of distress over the disruption and physical separation from your family that deployment will cause. During the **deployment** stage, you are required to effectively execute complex tasks in a very dangerous environment, while your family must adopt new attitudes and skills to keep the family functional and intact. During deployment, everyone is affected but in different ways. Yet, all of you experience loneliness and miss the daily presence of the people who are no longer with you. Finally, **post-deployment**, the six to twelve months or more after you return home from war, is the time during which you and your family must readjust to life at home together. Your plans for the future, dreams, and expectations may need to be re-examined because of personal changes that occurred in the war zone, at home, or both. You and each member of your family will have unique experiences during the deployment cycle. Appreciating what it's like to be in each other's shoes will help you be more understanding and patient with one another as you adjust to family life once again.

THE PRE-DEPLOYMENT STAGE

Joe has been serving in the Guard for almost twenty years now. They just notified him that they are sending him over to Iraq; his first war zone deployment. He is concerned for his daughter. His wife passed away a few years ago, so he'll have to leave his eleven-year-old daughter with his folks while he's away. As though being a single parent was not already hard enough. Joe wishes he had time before he leaves to take his daughter to Disney; they've always wanted to go.

As soon as deployment orders have been issued, the waiting begins for specific word about when you will have to report for duty. This is a time of uncertainty for both you and your loved ones. The wait may be long and drawn out or it may be very brief, leaving either too much or too little time for you to prepare. Like most families, you'll likely spend the pre-deployment stage trying to be together as much as possible and enjoying each other's company to the utmost. At the same time, you must also make practical preparations for your departure.

We recommend that you create a household management plan before you're deployed. Even minor household or financial matters that go wrong or are unexpected can create overwhelming distress at home while you're away. Having such a plan in place enables those at home to deal with problems more effectively and eases your mind so that you can focus on your military mission. Single service members as well as partnered couples need to make sure to consider the following issues and responsibilities. This should be a joint process involving parents, siblings, friends, neighbors, and other important people in your life.

For couples, developing a plan during the pre-deployment stage can be difficult, especially because of the anger and avoidance issues we discuss later in this chapter (see page 7) and throughout the book. (See especially Chapter 9 on reconnecting.) Feelings of anxiety and uncertainty may also make it difficult for you to create a plan or discuss details for items such as wills and living wills. Financial matters are often the most difficult to discuss and, unfortunately, many couples avoid them as a result. As hard as it may be to tackle these topics, keep in mind that effective communication and development of a household and financial management plan will better enable you and your family to cope with the difficulties of deployment and the subsequent challenges of homecoming. If either you or your partner is having trouble approaching this conversation, try setting a specific time in the near future to do so. Making a date to create a plan can help you overcome the natural tendency to avoid such issues. It's important to mention that these types of discussions might also extend to the homecoming. We discuss this matter further in Chapter 3.

PLANNING FOR DEPLOYMENT

Things that should be considered include:

- All day-to-day aspects of managing household maintenance
- All routine tasks performed throughout the week
- Children's daily routines
- Discipline for children
- If you are a Reservist, how to handle absence from your civilian job
- Pet care
- Contingency plans for solving household problems that might arise (If the roof begins to leak, who do you call?)
- Contingency plans for taking care of family members when unexpected things occur (If your daughter has a stomach ache at school and your partner at home has a big meeting that day, who can you rely on to pick her up?)
- Plan out how seasonal tasks will be done (Who will shovel the snow or take the car to the garage for a tune-up?)
- Plan out your bills and finances (How should the bills be managed?)
- Contingency plans for medical emergencies (Do you need to change your emergency contact on your medical forms?)

- Educational needs (Do you need to pay tuitions or fill out financial forms?)
- Legal issues (Have you updated your wills? Have you designated powers of attorney or considered signing a **health care proxy** in case one of you is injured?)

The Impact on Troops

My twenty-year-old son, Christopher, just learned that he's being deployed to Kuwait in three weeks. He just moved out of our house and has only lived on his own for the past seven months. Now my little boy will be sent into a foreign country at war. He insists that he's ready and eager to go. I'm worried sick about it. How will we make it through?

Most troops are understandably conflicted once they're notified that they're being deployed. On the one hand, you might be excited that you're finally going to do what you have trained for. You are also likely motivated by a sense of patriotic duty. On the other hand, it's hard to not be there for the people at home who rely on you. Troops often have mixed feelings about deployment because they are leaving family and friends behind. This internal conflict may be even more complicated for **Reserve Component** troops in the **National Guard** or **Military Reserve**. Most of these service members and their families never expected to have to deal with deployment to a war zone when they enlisted—especially with extended deployment times—even though they knew that going to war was a possibility as part of the deal. You may be leaving a job in which you have clientele whom you work with regularly who will need someone else's services during your absence. You may need to reestablish new clientele once you return. You may be a business owner who needs to find a temporary replacement or may need to close down. Some troops may also be less than enthusiastic about deployment to the current conflicts in Afghanistan and Iraq if they do not support the reasons for the war, but they also recognize that you "can't pick your war."

The high number of redeployments happening in this current conflict makes the pre-deployment stage even more complicated. If you have previously served in the war zone and are now being redeployed, the mix of emotions generally experienced during pre-deployment will be complicated by reactions to your previous tour, such as memories of death and destruction experienced. Some troops welcome redeployment, eager to return to finish the job, while others do not want to go back. In either case the initial enthusiasm you experienced before your first deployment will undoubtedly be different this time. See the box on page 11 for more information on multiple deployments.

Instead of taking steps to cope with their pre-deployment feelings, many troops adopt the attitude that "this is how it is, so let's get on with it." The best thing Soldiers, Marines, Airmen, and Sailors alike can do to handle the emotional side of pre-deployment is to be prepared to expect this wide range of emotions. It's also helpful to discuss and plan out what will happen during your absence. (See the list of suggested discussion items on page 4.)

THE IMPACT ON FAMILY

Family members must try to anticipate how life will change while their loved one is gone and prepare to pick up the slack, accepting all of his or her responsibilities during the deployment period. As we mentioned (see box on page 4), partners will have to be responsible for all household management, and may need to take on tasks that they have never done before. Walter, anticipating his Reservist wife's departure, stated, "My wife always drives the kids to all of their after school activities. Now that she's deploying, I need to learn the entire schedule, all the kids involved, all the details I never needed to know. Not only the phone numbers of other parents who will carpool, but their *names*." Balancing household finances, home maintenance, child care, and holding down a full-time job is very stressful and can sometimes be overwhelming for your family members.

Pre-deployment is also the time during which families must prepare themselves for the separation and loneliness to come. This can be extremely difficult. In order to protect themselves, people oftentimes express their sadness as anger and avoidance. Service members begin to focus more on the mission that lies ahead. Family members may start to detach emotionally. Because it's far easier to separate when you are angry with someone, you may actually find yourselves picking fights with one another. These angry reactions may be misguided, but they are a normal human reaction to the fear of the loneliness ahead. If and when they happen, try to be as patient and understanding as you can. Know that your loved one is simply trying to shield him or herself from getting hurt, and he or she isn't really mad at you.

THE DEPLOYMENT STAGE

The second stage of the emotional cycle of deployment begins the day you leave for Active Duty. The deployment stage consists of three distinct steps: the first month, recovery and stabilization, and the anticipation of return.

THE FIRST MONTH

The first month of deployment can be a roller coaster of emotions for both you and your loved ones at home. You all may experience relief that the anticipated departure has finally happened, although worries about one another will also set in quickly. Are the children going to be okay? Will everything be handled smoothly in your absence? Although everyone is busy adjusting to new responsibilities, you will all miss the daily presence of those whom you love and who are normally present. Anger is also frequently experienced in the first month, often as a mask for other emotions. This is because anger is readily available. You may not even know why you are angry.

THE IMPACT ON FAMILY

Family members might be angry with the government or the military for forcing this separation and putting their loved one in danger. Partners, parents and other family members will live in constant fear for the safety of their loved one who is deployed to the war zone. They will become emotionally drained because of the constant worry over whether you will return, as they constantly worry about your safety and well-being. They will experience loneliness and sadness, and may have insomnia or other sleep problems. In addition, they will worry about children and finances.

Sometimes partners also become angry because they feel that their loved one is skipping out of all the family responsibilities. They may think that you are hanging out with your buddies while they have to deal with all of the issues of running the household on their own. Whatever state your relationship was in before you received your deployment papers— close, conflicted, explosive, and so on—is usually magnified by deployment. During this stage, family members at home can become overwhelmed with the new responsibilities they must handle on their own. They may be exhausted from added responsibilities, sometimes even to the point of desperation.

Many partners experience something called **anticipatory grief,** where they try to emotionally prepare for the possibility that their loved one will not return alive. Each day may contain desperately sad moments, crying in the shower, feeling like you can't get out of bed. Sometimes the intensity of these emotions is so unbearable that people "numb out," or shut off their capacity to experience any feelings. To cope with anticipatory grief, social support is critical, so having a plan in place about who you can turn to is helpful. You can connect with others who are experiencing the same thing through your service member's unit or your nearest Family Assistance Center (www.guardfamily.org). Different coping strategies work for different people and what works also depends on how flustered, disorganized, or debilitated you become. These feelings will not completely go away until your loved one is safely home, but they will become more manageable and bearable with time. If you continue to feel overwhelmed or find yourself unable to function, consider turning to a chaplain or a mental health care provider for help.

It may also help if you do things that remind you of your loved one and make you feel close or stay busy by volunteering. You should also avoid things that intensify your fear, such as paying attention to media reports and gossip. Remember that you're not the only one who's feeling this way and that anticipatory grief is a common reaction.

Every morning I would turn on CNN and watch the text scroll ominously across the bottom of the television screen. It made me crazy, but I had to do it. One time my husband and I were talking on-line and he said he had to go because he heard bombs. After that I didn't hear from him for three days.

Media coverage can intensify a family's concerns about their service member's life and well-being during deployment, and we recommend that you minimize the amount of media to which you are exposed. Sensationalism in the media can sometimes lead troops to minimize the dangers they've faced in an effort to alleviate their families' fears. Some troops and families may want to talk about what is happening during deployment and others may not. Not all family members want to hear about the realities their service member is experiencing during deployment. If you and your service member do not want the same amount of communication, try to acknowledge one another's method of coping and the differences that exist. Know that these behaviors and emotions are all normal, and be careful not to force your needs on each other. If your coping styles differ, try to find someone else who's in your same shoes with whom you can discuss your concerns (i.e. discussing the realities of deployment with a friend whose partner is also deployed can satisfy your need to talk and take the pressure to talk off your partner).

The Impact on Troops

It's quite different when you're the one who has been deployed. You too will likely feel relieved that your deployment has finally started, but at the same time might feel guilty over the fact that you will not be there to support your family at home. You may worry about children, finances, and household management during your absence.

However, when you reach the war zone, you enter a different world. There are many new things to get used to, from the extreme heat of the desert sun and the mind-numbing dullness of repetitive tasks to being assigned to dangerous convoys with the ever-present threat of roadside bombs—or **improvised explosive devices (IEDs)**—and lethal contact with the enemy. You're embedded in an unfamiliar culture without any of the luxuries of home life. Because of the ever-present danger, tours of duty are relentlessly taxing and life altering. Violent death is a fact of life. Since there is no predictable letup in the violence, many troops must be on guard twenty-four hours a day, seven days a week. Such hypervigilance takes its toll, causing exhaustion that makes you more emotionally susceptible.

As a result of these factors, troops in the field tend to draw together and become very close. Your combat unit becomes a new family in which members depend on each other for physical protection and emotional support. For some, the intensity of the trust and loyalty felt for their comrades in arms exceeds what they previously felt for their partners back home. For others, the intensity of these feelings in the immediacy of the war zone might make them forget the strength of their love for their partner in the hazy recollections of what life was like before deployment.

Troops also experience concern over how their families are handling things without them, and sometimes guilt over not being there to provide assistance and support. At the same time, all service members naturally experience some level of fear about known and unknown dangers of the war zone, and are in a constant struggle to survive. To do so, you need to keep your energy focused on the tasks at hand. This can create family tension when loved ones at home want your input on family problems at a time when your major concern is staying alive. Both parties need to take each other's perspective into account.

RECOVERY AND STABILIZATION

Although devastatingly lonely at first, one sergeant's partner eventually took pride in her newfound sense of independence at home. She discovered that she could handle things without him. Now, as his homecoming approaches, she's worried about how things will be. She knows that she's changed as much, if not more, than he has, even though he was the one faced with constant dangers in the war zone.

Meanwhile back at home, approximately two to five months after deployment, something unexpected often occurs. Life for your family members begins to settle into a comfortable pattern. New support systems develop and a new sense of pride emerges as your family realizes that it can continue to function effectively without you. In essence, your family has recovered from your departure, and life has stabilized for them, at least somewhat. With this newly won confidence usually comes a more positive outlook. Your family learns how to handle new routines and can even have fun in the process. They may feel a sense of accomplishment because they are able to handle everything. Each member learns to handle crises that come up and recognizes that there are others on whom they can rely for help when necessary.

However, this newfound confidence and independence doesn't erase the emotional toll of the persistent concern, worry, and loneliness they feel while you're gone. These emotions do not subside, and dealing with them can be a constant and exhausting struggle. During this time it's important to make use of your social supports. In addition to your family and friends, you can find support in church or local community organizations. There are also support groups on military bases, people who share your plight at National Guard Family Assistance Centers, and many military family programs that can help family members make it through this challenging period.

Multiple Deployments

A unique aspect of the wars in Afghanistan and Iraq is that many troops experience **multiple deployments** and are required to return to the war in a shorter time frame than ever before. You might expect that with each deployment, each stage of this emotional cycle would become easier, but in truth things may actually become more difficult. This is especially the case if you have any unresolved issues or lingering problems from previous separations and reunions. Each deployment is also different from the last, making it somewhat unpredictable. Although those who have gone through a previous deployment have learned how to deal with it, new challenges often arise. You may not have had enough time to recoup from the previous deployment. In addition, if soon after you have returned from a deployment you find out you are going to be redeploying for another tour of duty, you may never mentally return home during your time back. Perhaps your first deployment was devastating for your partner from start to finish, but during your next deployment your partner began to enjoy this new freedom and independence. Or perhaps your first deployment was short in duration and your family found that it was actually not as hard as expected so that your partner was not adequately prepared to cope with a subsequent deployment that was longer and more emotionally taxing. It's hard to know what to expect.

One service member found that following his first deployment he experienced a quick, smooth reunification and picked up right where he left off with his wife and teenage daughter, without a hitch. When returning from his second deployment, he and his family thought they knew what to anticipate. However, during his second tour, one of his close comrades was killed. Although he had previously experienced death among members of his unit, this was different, possibly because he felt that it was his fault that his friend had died. Upon his return he was a changed man. He was sullen and short-tempered, and he spent most of his time going out with his buddies. His family was completely unprepared for his withdrawn and distant demeanor. In another case, a service member returned home following her second deployment expecting things to go smoothly with warm welcomes, but things were a mess at home. While she was away, her seven-year-old son had behavioral issues at school, getting in fights, bullying, and falling behind in his classes. Her partner, who could no longer cope with all of the daily household activities, a full-time job, and a problematic child, was ready to walk away.

It's important to be prepared for differences following each deployment. In addition, multiple deployments that are spaced too close together can often lead to **burnout** for both the troops and family because there isn't enough time or opportunity to recover from the burden of responsibility or emotional toll that everyone experienced during the previous separation. This is particularly a problem when the time period at home is short. This can prevent normal recovery and stabilization when you get home.

Anticipation of Return

The next major challenge occurs in the final month of your deployment. At home things are usually chaotic and full of excitement during this time. Everyone is thrilled about the impending reunion and the fact that you'll be returning home safely. Yet at the same time there's also some fear about what to expect. You may worry about how much each other has changed. You may worry about whether you will still be needed or loved. You may believe that your loved ones will never understand what you've been through during the war, and your loved ones may think you'll never understand how hard it was to manage things at home without you. Your family may be afraid of your reaction to how the family has changed during your absence. In order to get through this time of anticipation, it's extremely important for you and your family to have open lines of communication.

Everyone should be aware that their expectations of each other and how life will be when you return home may differ greatly. As stated above, family members may fear their service member's reaction to how the family has changed during his or her absence. Do your best to be clear and honest about your feelings, and if you have any concerns or requests regarding your impending homecoming, make them known. For instance, many families want to throw their service member a big party when they return home from the war. If your family wants to do this but you don't want to see anyone except close family, don't hesitate to tell them this. (See Chapter 3 for more discussion on homecoming expectations.)

THE POST-DEPLOYMENT STAGE

After long flights, handshakes of thanks, and hugs and kisses, all the troops really want for the first few months when they come home is beer, sex, and pizza.

Homecoming is an emotional time filled with joy and tears of relief, hugs and handshakes, and welcome homes. This joyous occasion often leads to a **honeymoon period**. Couples are extremely happy to see one another. Things may seem like they are just perfect. You are separated

SPECIAL ISSUES FOR RESERVISTS

Reserve troops consist of both the National Guard and Military Reserves, and in the current conflict they make up about 50 percent of all deployed troops. They face many unique challenges during deployment that can have a serious effect on their emotional state.

- Reservists may be assigned or inserted into units in which they know no other personnel.
- Deployment may result in the loss of their job and/or a financial penalty.
- Deployment (and therefore separation from family) is usually less anticipated.
- Reserve forces don't live on military bases, so they and their families are not surrounded by others who share their plight.

In addition to causing difficulty during deployment, these factors may make returning to the civilian world harder for Reservists than for Active Duty troops. Recent research shows that six months after deployment, Reserve Soldiers are at a higher risk for both physical and mental health problems than their Active Duty counterparts.

from real world issues and responsibilities. But just like a honeymoon, this has to end, and usually the honeymoon balloon is punctured with the first argument. Once the initial elation wears off, reality begins to set in. Your reintegration with the family takes time, and varies from family to family, Soldier to Soldier, and person to person. If you're returning to a military base, this transition may be a little easier than if you're not, as everyone around you is very familiar with the emotional cycle of deployment and therefore more sensitive to your feelings and needs. If you're a Reservist who must rejoin the civilian community, homecoming can be much more difficult.

The impact on troops and family members

Before he was deployed, he used to do little things like leave love notes, or send me flowers at work. Now he seems like a completely different person.

I don't understand what the big deal is. Sure, I still love my wife. But flowers don't help keep her and the kids safe! Why is it that no one back here in America seems to get it? They're all just wrapped up in their trivial lives.

Homecoming is essentially a time of **readjustment and renegotiation**. You've all been through an immense change, and when you arrive home you may feel like you hardly know one another anymore. It takes time and effort to rebuild intimacy and to relearn how to rely on one another for support. You and your family will need to reexamine your common goals, as they may need to be readjusted. You may also need to renegotiate roles that have changed during your absence. For instance, your partner may not want to relinquish the independence he or she fought so hard to achieve while you were deployed. You may feel like a fifth wheel that's left out of things and therefore no longer needed.

Now that I'm home following my tour in Afghanistan, my husband informed me that there's no way I'm taking back the check book!

You must also work to find a balance between spending time together and honoring everyone's need for personal space and time to be alone. It takes time and work, but eventually this period of readjustment will settle back into a normal pattern of daily life. After this, you will have successfully made it through reintegration and stabilization, the final stage of the emotional cycle of deployment.

Certain events can complicate this final stage. For example, following deployment, Active Duty families are sometimes ordered to move from their current home to a new military base. Such reassignment interferes with the final stage of the emotional cycle because the family has been separated from the friends and neighbors who have provided the social support that is so vital for the reintegration process. Another possible situation that might complicate reintegration and stabilization is when back-to-back deployments interrupt the resolution of major family problems.

LESSONS LEARNED

While I was back in Watertown last month for two weeks of leave, I was pleasantly surprised to have the elderly couple at the next table buy me and my buddies a round of drinks. They thanked us for sacrificing for our country. When I told my dad about this, his eyes welled up with tears. He served in Vietnam for two years.

We've learned some important lessons following previous conflicts in which our military has taken part. One major implication of research following Vietnam and the first Gulf War involves the importance of social support; the understanding and support of family, friends, coworkers, and the community. Greater social support makes it less likely that returning service members will experience emotional and mental distress. The following is a list of lessons we have learned from prior experiences of returnees:

- Difficult living and working environments add to war zone stress.
- Preparation for the psychological impact of war and preparation for what to expect following return from a deployment is necessary, the same way that tough conditioning for the physical demands of war is required.
- Community and government agencies can help troops and families through readjustment by working together to prevent family breakdown, social withdrawal, isolation, employment problems, and issues with alcohol and substance abuse.
- Making our troops outcasts or marginal members of society is unacceptable. Societal support of troops must remain as high as it is today, no matter what political viewpoints are held.
- Constant perceived threat twenty-four hours a day, seven days a week, no downtime, and no front lines are new elements in current warfare that can sometimes take as great a toll on troops as direct combat. This is a new reality in the current wars and one that must be taken very seriously when preparing newly returned troops for readjustment to civilian life.

Post-deployment Can Be Hard on Your Children

Children often display a range of responses when they are reunited with their parent after deployment. These reactions vary for children of different ages. If you have an infant or toddler, he or she may not remember you and may wonder why this stranger is now staying in his or her house. During the deployment, children often learn to rely more on the caregiver that remains, and it can take awhile for them to act as though they "need" you again. If you have an older child or a teenager, he or she may resent the changed family dynamic your deployment caused or may react negatively to the imposition of new rules or authority when you return. These behaviors can be hurtful and often lead to arguments and conflict that further complicate your homecoming. We discuss more about reconnecting with children in Chapter 9.

Moving Beyond the Cycle of Deployment

Now that you're familiar with the typical emotions and reactions that can accompany the cycle of deployment, you and your family will be better equipped to begin to negotiate pre-deployment, deployment, and homecoming stressors successfully. The remainder of this book is to help you through the most common challenges that occur once you return home.

It's also important to understand that almost everyone returning from a war zone will have some symptoms that families may find disruptive, such as nightmares, edginess, hyperalertness, and overprotective behaviors. (This is discussed further in Chapter 5.) You and your family and friends at home need to be prepared to deal with these kinds of common stress reactions that occur following deployment to a war zone. You also need to understand that such predictable readjustment problems do not, in themselves, indicate that you have a psychiatric problem, such as **posttraumatic stress disorder (PTSD)**, which requires professional attention. (See Chapter 10.)

I have a cousin who was deployed to Iraq. He's been back for almost a year. My aunt said he's having a real hard time, can't sleep, won't talk to her, is only working sporadically, and never sees his friends. None of us are sure how to help him.

The bottom line is that *everyone* goes through a period of readjustment in varying degrees when they return home from deployment. Sometimes it may take over a year for life to return to normal again. That's why patience and understanding are so important. If reactions or symptoms are causing problems in your family, work, or social life at all, get some early assistance. This can help prevent things from becoming worse and creating disruption in your life. You do not need to be an emotional mess in order to benefit. In the next chapter, we'll look at the experience of deployment from both the troops' and the families' perspective to help you understand the ways in which deployment can affect you all after you return home from the war.

2

DURING DEPLOYMENT

SETTING THE STAGE
FOR HOMECOMING

During wartime, everyone makes sacrifices, both in the war zone and at home. Both sides have their stories. Understanding each others' perspectives and experiences will help you cope more successfully with the challenges you'll face when you return home from war. In this chapter, we discuss what troops typically endure during deployment as well as what their families experience back at home, and whenever possible we offer advice for coping.

WHAT'S IT LIKE TO BE AT WAR?

Any Soldier, Marine, Airman, or Sailor who has served in a war zone knows what deployment is like in a way no ordinary citizen will ever fully understand. However, each conflict, each location, each experience differs. We know you each have your own personal experiences. At the same time, there are many commonalities that occur across individuals. The

---

WHO MAKES UP OUR ARMED FORCES?

The average age of American Active Duty enlisted members is twenty-seven years and officers' average age is thirty-five years. Reserve Component members are slightly older with enlisted averaging thirty-one and officers forty-one years of age. A little over 50 percent of U.S. service members are married and about 43 percent have children. Forty percent are single with no children. Of those deployed to Iraq and Afghanistan, almost 50 percent have been Reserve Component members and 50 percent Active Duty. Women are playing a larger role in our U.S. military today than ever before, making up 14 percent of the troops. Although women are still not officially allowed in "combat" positions, the nature of current-day warfare often puts them in some of the most dangerous situations.

---

following stories will give you a glimpse into the lives and experiences of troops during deployment. (Please note that Alex C., Kathleen B., and Tony K.'s stories are not real. They're composite case histories we follow throughout the book that help illustrate different kinds of experiences faced by troops coping with the challenges of reintegration.)

ALEX C.

Twenty-year-old Alex C., from Boise, Maryland, is a football player and B+ student in accounting at the University of Maryland. Following his high school graduation, he continued to live with his mother and his seventeen-year-old sister, Michele, who is a junior in high school. His father abandoned the family shortly after they moved to the United States from Mexico, when the kids were small, so their mom raised three children alone by working the night shift as a nurse. Alex's older brother, Sam, lives in a townhouse across town with his wife and two small children. Following the 9/11 terrorist attacks on the World Trade Center and Pentagon, Alex felt a strong desire to do something to help protect our nation. Unsure about his personal career goals and thinking it an opportune time to consider his future before settling into something permanent, he joined the U.S. Marine Forces Reserve. His decision to enlist was also influenced by the pride and self-esteem he associated with being a Marine and the fact that it would enable him to pay for college expenses without having to get student loans. Also, since he wasn't involved in a serious relationship, the prospect of deployment was less complicated. His best friend, John, joined the Air National Guard a few years back, a move that also helped inspire Alex to enlist. Alex is strong, optimistic, conscientious, independent, and very family oriented. He's been like a second father to his young nephew and niece. After finishing basic training and returning to Maryland for the summer, Alex was called up in mid-August to go to Kuwait for eight months, assigned as a member of a units' artillery division / striker force. They were to take daily trips over the border into Iraq.

KATHLEEN B.

Kathleen B. is a full-time Multichannel Transmission Systems Operator-Maintainer in the U.S. Army, a communications specialty. She will turn twenty-four next month. During that time, instead of being the guest of honor at her own wedding shower, she'll be back in Iraq. She's engaged to Isaac, a third-year medical student. This is her second deployment, and she has been in Iraq this time around for eight months. Although her **military occupation specialty (MOS)** doesn't involve direct combat, for this tour she's been assigned to dangerous areas and has witnessed bloodshed and casualties among military personnel and Iraqi civilians, including the bombing of her own convoy, in which several U.S. Soldiers were killed or injured along with dozens of Iraqis. Now she's wrestling with emotionally troublesome thoughts and memories of combat scenes and experiences she has witnessed. Kathleen is tough and smart, yet she's also kindhearted and doing her best to help the local people.

TONY K.

Major Tony K., a thirty-eight-year-old Army National Guard Soldier, is on his first deployment to the Sunni Triangle in Iraq, where he had his first exposure to combat in his eleven years of National Guard duty. Before deployment, Tony worked successfully as an automobile salesman, was a happily married father with children aged ten and twelve years old, and was socially outgoing, with a large circle of friends and active in civic as well as church activities.

While in Iraq he has experienced extensive combat exposure. His platoon was heavily shelled, often resulting in death or injury to his buddies. Following their first severe attack, Tony and others in his unit sat around in a daze, saying little *and feeling nothing. He now realizes that attacks like this occur almost every day. On several occasions his patrol encountered roadside bombs, which destroyed vehicles and killed or severely wounded people with whom he had become close.*

Understanding the experiences that occur during wartime can help all members of a family anticipate and understand the reactions and issues that may arise following the return home. Military families all become familiar with the structure, rigor, and lack of predictability of military life. Family life needs to be balanced with military life, even during peacetime. During times of war, however, it can become even more complicated. This is particularly true for families of reserve troops who are not always as prepared as full-time military families.

Military leaders train their troops to be prepared for the many challenges and uncertainties of combat—to do what it takes to fight and win battles. There's a strict chain of command, and individuals are held responsible for their actions. Troops do what they're told to do, and this is what they need to do in order to function effectively and stay alive. The structure of the military and the chain of command allows for no back talk. You must follow orders, and you are accountable for getting things done. Control is essential. It's important to contain your emotions, never showing any sign of weakness. You are focused on the mission at hand, ready to protect yourself and the lives of your buddies at any moment.

Unlike some conflicts of the past, this is a guerilla war with no front lines; it consists of fierce urban warfare, risky patrols, and long treks across the desert in danger-filled convoys. Every hour, twenty-four hours a day, seven days a week, troops hear or are threatened by explosions. Troops are always on high alert, constantly scanning the next corner, the next roof, or anyplace from which there might be an attack, an IED, or a suicide bomber. There's always the fear that the same Iraqis whom Alex, Kathleen, Tony, or other troops help during the day might be trying to kill them at night.

Driving on a patrol or in a convoy is one of the most dangerous assignments in this current conflict. Crossfire can come from anywhere at any moment. In Iraq and Afghanistan, the troops own the road. The safest way for convoys to move is at high speeds, and you can't stop because doing so makes you an even easier target for the enemy. The troops are on constant alert, never knowing if an IED is hidden in the next pile of trash

Frequent Combat Experiences Reported by Members of the U.S. Army and Marines

	Afghanistan	Iraq
Being attacked or ambushed	58%	89%
Receiving incoming fire	84%	86%
Being shot at	66%	93%
Discharged weapon	6%	18%
Seeing dead bodies or remains	39%	95%
Knowing someone seriously injured or killed	43%	86%
Felt in great danger of being killed	25%	50%

that you pass. When unknown vehicles approach, they automatically worry that it might be a **VBIED (Vehicle Born IED)**. There's an unspoken understanding that oncoming traffic is supposed to move off the road and stop to let the convoy continue through, though sometimes civilians will deliberately drive or step out in front of a military vehicle to try to make it stop. The troops, however, are under direct orders that, for the safety of the convoy, you are not to stop.

Suicide bombers are rampant, unleashing their vengeance at busy marketplaces, police stations, religious gatherings, and other public places, wounding dozens and taking many lives. Service members are constantly dealing with dead bodies and remains. You can't help but become numb to the grisly and threatening reality of it.

Many service members find that their mission is confined to a "secure" **forward operating base (FOB)** or **logistical supply area (LSA)**, such as LSA Anaconda in Balad. Although you're not out on the roads or out in the neighborhoods, you still face real dangers that many tend to minimize because of the relative perceived sense of security and "comforts" available on FOBs or LSAs. These dangers include random, incoming, indirect fire that can occur many times a day, more days than not. Dining facilities, post exchanges, living areas, and R&R (rest and relaxation) facilities have all been hit by mortars. VBIEDs have also charged the gates of these bases. Inside "the wire," you have little visibility of what's being done tactically outside the wire to neutralize the threat to you. This reduces your sense of control and security regarding your own personal safety. Troops who spend most of their time on secure bases live inside a maze of concrete barriers, unsure about when the next mortar might fall and possibly hit something or someone.

You may also have feelings of relief mixed with feelings of guilt and frustration because you're not out on the road, kicking in doors, or participating in the tactical campaign. You might be surprised to find yourself struggling with reintegration when you get home because you infrequently left the base and never saw anyone shot or killed. The perceived daily threat that exists inside the wire, although relatively low compared to outside the wire, can still take its toll on individuals, especially over time.

LIVING CONDITIONS

The Middle East environment includes dry, desolate deserts intensely baked in unbearably high temperatures. The unimaginable hot temperatures are magnified when you're dressed in full gear, sitting inside a Humvee with its bulletproof windows closed tight. Even the drinking water can be over 90 degrees. Dust is everywhere and the insects are huge. This is what Alex had to say about his arrival in Kuwait:

> After training and staging for deployment at Camp Lejeune, NC, we were off. The plane ride there was endless, hours and hours and hours on a plane. Then we were actually there, Al Abraq, in Kuwait. It was daytime and oh my God the desert heat. It was 130 degrees in the sun. Everything was dry and flat and dust was everywhere. Our first assignment was to find our personal gear amongst hundreds of green army duffel bags lined up along the airstrip. Welcome to the war on terror!

CULTURAL DIFFERENCES AND SOCIETAL UPHEAVAL

In addition to the difficulties of being away from familiar places and conveniences, deployment to Iraq, Afghanistan, Kuwait, and other surrounding locations involves a change in culture that can be confusing and distressing. You may find you're dealing with different languages, different customs, and differences in food, sounds, and smells. This only adds to the stressful atmosphere.

Operation Enduring Freedom/Operation Iraqi Freedom

Here are some facts about the current conflicts in the Gulf:

- Over one and a half million U.S. troops have been deployed in this second Gulf war as of January 2008.
- As of October 2007, 3,856 U.S. troops have died, over 28,400 have been wounded, and many times this number of Iraqi and other civilians have perished.
- Fourteen percent of troops are women. Although they're often assigned to non-combat ("combat support") roles, such a designation has become meaningless since one of the most dangerous jobs in Iraq is driving a truck in a convoy where there is great risk of attack or lethal contact with IEDs.
- Unlike the Vietnam War when the draft meant that most Americans were directly affected by the conflict, the modern "all volunteer" military has left participating families feeling a sense of isolation from the rest of society.
- Multiple deployments are the norm, and nearly one third of the troops who have served in Iraq and Afghanistan have done more than one tour of duty. Rather than having one to two years between deployments, some troops are returning within nine or fewer months.
- The survival rate for those wounded in action has increased from 75 percent during previous wars to 90 percent. However, while more troops are surviving serious wounds than ever before, these survivors are at the greatest risk for psychological problems later on.
- The top two reasons returning troops seek care at Department of Veterans Affairs Medical Centers are musculoskeletal problems (e.g. pain) and mental health issues.

A bomb has landed in the middle of the town where Kathleen's communication base is set up. As she struggles to help the wounded civilians, Kathleen is frustrated over the language barriers she faces. Communication is her area of expertise. However, prior to her trips overseas, she and her unit were taught nothing about the culture they were going to be working within; no

basic phrases or cultural norms. During this deployment, she tried to pro-
vide the most basic education to all service members she came to meet.
Simple things like "hello" and "goodbye" can cause grave results if miscon-
strued by the local population. For instance, she knew that Soldiers often
hold up a hand as a signal to halt approaching civilians. What they didn't
understand is that this gesture, rather than meaning "stop," is a hello greet-
ing to Iraqis.

In addition to these cultural barriers, more and more educated civilians are fleeing these countries. Three years since the war in Iraq started, an exodus is occurring, particularly in the more dangerous areas of the country. Many people that have the ability to flee to a safer place are headed across the borders with their families. This has led to a shortage of local doctors, teachers, and other professionals, which is causing even more upheaval. Those who remain find themselves trying to lead normal lives in the middle of a war zone with dwindling resources.

WHAT'S IT LIKE TO BE
A LOVED ONE LEFT AT HOME?

We described the deployment stage of the emotional cycle of deployment in Chapter 1. These elements become reality for family members once their service member leaves. Initially, family members may experience some relief that the anticipated departure has finally happened, so it can be over with sooner. Then loneliness and sadness, which can be overwhelming for some, begin to set in.

DEALING WITH LONELINESS AND WORRY

Tony's wife, Laura, found herself crying frequently. Just prior to Tony's leav-
ing, they found out that Laura was pregnant. She felt alone, abandoned,
and even angry when she let herself admit it. Following a tip from a fellow
military spouse, she'd cry in the shower so that her boys couldn't see how
upset she was.

Although these feelings of loneliness will never disappear completely, they usually subside somewhat over time. Simple strategies such as allowing yourself to feel sad at certain times or exercising regularly can often help. The most important thing to do is to maintain your social supports. Make efforts to talk with friends, share your feelings with someone who can relate to what you're going through, and stay involved in church and other social gatherings. Be sure to actually schedule in fun activities, otherwise you'll find you're always "too busy." In addition to lonely and sad feelings, you and other family members may experience constant worry and fear for the safety of your loved one who is at war.

> *Kathleen's mother, Mrs. Bassette, lay next to her husband, unable to sleep again. Her child was off to war—her sweet daughter at war. And she could do nothing to protect her, but could only lie in bed, wondering if Kathleen had made it safely through the week, and wishing that she had a way to find out. No matter that Kathleen was twenty-four and getting married; she was still her little girl.*

The protective instincts of parents don't disappear just because their children grow up. It can be very hard on parents whose kids are on the front because often they don't have immediate access to information about their children's well-being. In Mrs. Bassette's case, while she was in touch with Kathleen during her deployment, she had to rely much of the time on updates from Kathleen's fiancé, Isaac, which she found frustrating. (See page 28, Issues for the Extended Family, for more on this.)

Again, to help prevent excessive worry, limit the amount of time you spend absorbing media reports on TV, in the paper, or online. Know that you're not alone and that you may find solace in talking with others who are in your similar situation. Contact your local military family program or a Family Assistance Center, a nearby Family Readiness Group, or Lifelines to connect with others. (See the end of this chapter and the Resources on page 248 for contact information.)

Feeling Overwhelmed

Hopefully, prior to deployment you've discussed taking over your absent family member's responsibilities. It helps greatly if together you compose a list of the things that might come up during your absence and develop a plan for dealing with them. (See list on page 4.) If you're staying home while your loved one is deployed, you will undoubtedly have to learn to do things that you might never have had to handle before, such as balancing the checkbook, getting the oil changed in the car, or being the tough disciplinarian for the kids. Balancing household finances, children's, schedules, home and yard maintenance, and so forth can be overwhelming, especially in the beginning. Preparing yourself to take on these new tasks is the best way to avoid feeling overwhelmed. However, even with the best preparations, doing everything can take its toll.

> Given all the responsibilities at home, not feeling well due to morning sickness, and the schedules of both of the boys, Tony's wife, Laura, had to give up her job at the advertising company when her husband got deployed. This was a bitter pill for her to swallow because she really enjoyed her work. As a working mother, she always knew that it would be difficult to balance career and home life, but she never expected that she'd have to give up her job and be the sole caregiver for an entire year. That was never in her life plan. However, she had felt completely overwhelmed trying to balance her demanding job with all of the child and household responsibilities. It was just too much!

After some time has passed, family members will begin to learn to handle things on their own. This successful shift in roles, while necessary during deployment, may become problematic upon homecoming. Your returning service member may feel unneeded or cut out of things. Keep in mind that you'll have to renegotiate tasks again once your loved one has returned.

> Tony has had a chance to phone Laura from Iraq. While they're on the phone, he hears the doorbell ring and she tells him that the repairman has arrived. Laura's email yesterday described her trouble with the broken furnace. He's relieved that she's located a repairman, but also feels guilty that he's not home to fix the problem himself.

ISSUES FOR THE EXTENDED FAMILY

When service members are deployed, they're often fairly free to communicate with as many family members and friends as they want as often as they can. However, troops need to provide specific points of contact to their command for notification purposes, for both primary and secondary next of kin. The military created this system in order to help simplify the process of providing loved ones with information about their service member, particularly about safety issues, information about homecoming, or notification about casualties. For married troops, their primary contact is almost always their partner. So when news about a married service member needs to be passed along by the military, or when direct communication with a service member is restricted, parents and other extended family may have to rely on the partner for information about their loved one. This can be very frustrating, especially for those who don't have a good or close relationship with their service member's primary contact.

Support for a deployed service member's extended family is also somewhat lacking. Many of the military family support programs that currently exist focus primarily on the partner or primary contact of the service member, leaving parents, siblings, cousins, and other extended family to fend for themselves. Services that take parents and other extended family members' perspectives into account are scarce.

At times, various family members may have difficulty dealing with one another, and they experience conflicts as a direct result of issues about the communication of information or the absence created by their loved one's deployment. Some family members may be jealous of others or feel that they're not being kept in the loop. Explaining how communication will work with your loved ones before you're deployed and troubleshooting any anticipated family conflicts over this issue may help things run more smoothly for those left at home. We also suggest that the extended family establish their own family phone tree in order to communicate important messages and regular phone calls to keep everyone updated.

Kathleen had named her fiancé, Isaac, as her primary contact, which meant that the military couldn't give Mr. and Mrs. Bassette certain information about Kathleen without her explicit permission. In the turmoil and rush of deployment, Kathleen hadn't realized that she would have to complete that particular form with both her parents' and Isaac's names. In fact, the form only provided one space for a primary contact. Now that she was in Iraq, the form could not easily be changed. Kathleen knew her mother was upset, but she felt justified in choosing Isaac, even though they were not married yet. Isaac was going to be her husband and he lived near her unit's armory in North Carolina, while her parents lived back in Missouri. Furthermore, her mother had often been strongwilled and meddlesome in the past. Mrs. Bassette could not put her mind to rest. She was unhappy that she had to rely on updates from Isaac and did not believe that such communication was frequent enough. She could hardly wait until Kathleen was back home safely.

Mrs. Bassette was driving Isaac crazy with her constant calls, requesting updates on Kathleen's safety under the pretense of trying to involve him in planning for the wedding. These calls continuously interrupted his studies and prompted him to avoid speaking with her whenever possible. Kathleen's absence was clearly not helping the relationship between her future husband and her mother.

All family members are important. Most want to be kept informed, and they have strong feelings about the absence and dangerous circumstances of their deployed loved one. Family support services have started to realize that parents, siblings, and other family members also need help coping with deployment and handling reintegration. As a result, they are beginning to take this more into consideration. The National Guard Family Program provides **Family Assistance Centers (FACs)** that serve *any* military family member of any branch of service. This means that a mother in Vermont who has a son who's deployed out of California can go to her local Vermont FAC for information and support to help her through her emotional turmoil and to connect with others in the same situation. (See page 36 for more information on family support.)

HELPING CHILDREN COPE WITH DEPLOYMENT

In order to understand how your kids may react to your homecoming, you must first understand how the separation of deployment influences kids. The impact of military deployment on children differs for various age groups. School-age kids, like Tony's son, Ben, sometimes hear negative things about the war from other children at school, or sometimes are even bullied. Although our society has made progress and adults seem to recognize the distinction between political support for the war and community

support for the troops, children often find this distinction much more difficult to understand. It's important that teachers and school officials address
this potential problem so that they can help children when it occurs and
can also watch what they say in front of kids.

Adults in the school system should know which children have parents
who are deployed. Teachers, principals, guidance and school counselors
as well as school nurses should be briefed on how war can impact children of various ages so they can be on the lookout for signs that a child of
a deployed parent is having trouble adjusting. This is especially important
for families of the Guard and Reserves, who live in civilian rather than
military communities. In rural areas, the child of a deployed Reservist
may be the only one at school trying to cope with the absence of a deployed parent. All school personnel should also be aware of how sensitive
the children of deployed parents can be to hearing negative things about
the war. They should watch carefully for any kind of bullying or nasty
comments about the war or the troops from other kids—or adults—and
stop it as quickly as possible.

> Laura needed Tony's calming voice today because her ten-year-old, Ben, had
> been pushed around by some of the other kids at school. They told him that
> their parents said we had no business in Iraq and that his father was killing
> innocent children. They taunted him and called his father a "baby killer."

Some children act out or develop problems at school as a result of
their parent or loved one's deployment. Such problems include poor
grades from a child who had been an excellent student, frequent visits to
the nurse's office for stomachaches or other health complaints, or disruptive behavior from a child who had previously been a pleasure to have in
the classroom. Because this war involves only a small percentage of the
American population, most Americans (including teachers and other
school officials) don't think about the family impact of military service
unless it's called to their attention. For Guard and Reserve children who
live in our civilian neighborhoods this can be even more problematic. If
your child is exhibiting any of the problems we mentioned above or is
showing signs of any other behavioral or health issue, contact his teacher
immediately if you haven't already done so. Discuss the possibility that
your partner's deployment may be the culprit, and come up with a plan

to manage your child's problems for the duration. Military family programs also employ youth program staff who can help you communicate with school officials.

> Alex was very close to his four-year-old twin niece and nephew and saw them very frequently before deployment. Both became clingy and whiny after Alex left.

Younger children may suffer separation anxiety. Some can't understand why an important adult has suddenly disappeared and will not return for a long time. You can help by offering them love and reassurance and by understanding that whining and clinging behaviors may be the children's expression of loss and uncertainty. Children have trouble understanding and communicating these complex feelings. You can also help by taking care of yourself and seeking out emotional support when *you* need it. This will make it easier for you to focus on your children's needs.

During a long separation from a young child, the normal bonding that occurs between parents and children is disrupted. For very young children, keeping connections open in creative ways can help maintain this bond. For example, Tony's wife, Laura, gave birth to her baby girl while Tony was still overseas.

> Little Marie is eight months old and has not even set eyes on her father. Laura makes sure that pictures of Tony are in every room. Over time, as Marie grows, Laura is determined to make sure that Marie knows her father's voice and can identify his picture. Tony taped himself reading some bedtime stories that Laura plays while putting Marie to bed.

Older children and adolescents may withdraw emotionally and not want to communicate with the missing parent. They may react negatively against attempts at authority from abroad. They may feel that only the parent at home has any authority or knowledge about their lives. It's easy to feel hurt or angered by such behavior, but it's important to understand that these are common reactions that usually run their course at this volatile age. As these different reactions of children and adolescents play out during the deployment, children of all ages begin to rely more on the caregiver at home and to distance themselves from the parent who is gone.

THE NEED FOR SOCIAL SUPPORT

While your loved one is deployed, it's important for you to take the time to share your own concerns and fears with other adults, loved ones, friends, or counselors so you are sure not to overburden yourself or your children. Seeking social support from other adults outside your family is one way to manage your own stress. You want to protect children from unwarranted worries and concerns and provide them with a sense of safety and security. Research has revealed that parents who are able to handle troubling, traumatic, or conflicting issues can cushion their children against too much anxiety and distress.

> In contrast to what Isaac perceived as intrusive attention from Kathleen's parents, Tony's wife, Laura, would have loved to have closer contact with her in-laws. She was hoping that they might help her care for their two grandsons and new granddaughter during this time, to make it easier for her to manage the household by herself.

COMMUNICATING WITH HOME

Distance from family can create low morale in troops, and the military knows that communication with loved ones during deployment is essential. Research shows that keeping connected during separation helps maintain stronger relationships. Wartime communication in the twenty-first century is vastly different than during earlier conflicts. Recent technology has brought the frequency and quality of communication to new levels. Cell phones, media coverage, Web blogs—all of these mediums have placed information at our fingertips, eyes, and ears as never before. Email has also changed the face of communication from afar.

> Late one night, Tony called Laura at home. His two boys, Ben and Zak, were already off to school. Earlier that day, Laura had emailed Tony some photos from Ben's recent birthday party. Although he was delighted to see Ben's face, full of smiles—even if it was only in photos—he also felt quite guilty about not being there to celebrate with his son. The email made him simultaneously glad to see his son and sad to be so far away from his family.

CREATING A COMMUNICATION PLAN

At first, you might think that so many opportunities for communication are a wonderful bonus—no more going months and months waiting by the mailbox for the slightest word. But this increased communication puts service members in a position where they are constantly faced with the problems and challenges happening at home. Because of the frequent communication, it's more tempting to want to share with them all aspects of your life as they are occurring. There is increased intermingling of two worlds: the horrors of war and the realities of home. Keep the following advice in mind as you consider how much and what kind of communication it's best to have during deployment:

- Create a communication plan for the deployment. Discuss what should and should not be conveyed, and what types of communication might be preferred. This conversation should continue and evolve during the deployment cycle.
- Although handwritten letters in the mail have become more and more obsolete, know that care packages and physical words on paper can last long after the "call" is over and are still cherished forms of communication.

The deployed partner cannot help solve problems at home. His or her energy needs to be focused on the military mission and staying alive. Family should use supports at home to help them cope with immediate problems and, whenever possible, share information with deployed troops after things are okay, after the problems are resolved. This keeps everyone emotionally connected while not creating unnecessary distress about things that can't be solved over the phone or through email.

- When you communicate, assure your family that you are okay. At home everyone is inundated by news stories about what's happening in the war. Every moment you're away they live in fear that you will never return.

- Turn off the news at home. Worrying will not help things.

Isaac spoke with Kathleen almost every day, though it wasn't always easy. To keep the costs down as well as to accommodate her unpredictable schedule, Kathleen had to call Isaac, and the time difference was somewhat problematic. Their wedding had been postponed because of Kathleen's extended deployment. They had planned to get married the previous spring, but now had to wait another year. They were upset about this delay but had adjusted reasonably well. Even though they communicated often, Isaac missed Kathleen every moment of every day.

As you can see from Tony and Kathleen's stories, unlike wars from the past, there's usually a great deal of communication going on between troops and their loved ones at home. However, it's unclear how this new level of communication is affecting the performance of troops during deployment or facilitating their readjustment when they return home. On the positive side, communication eases the separation and provides reassurance to families that things are okay. On the negative side, bad news travels faster than ever, and the distraction of problems at home, which the service member cannot help with, may interfere with his or her focus on military duties.

Laura carried her cell phone with her at all times to make sure that Tony could reach her day or night. As much as she looked forward to his emails, it wasn't the same as hearing his voice on the phone, even though she knew he was minimizing the dangers of the day. She too had to keep herself in check about what she told him on the phone. She tried to be careful to share problems with him only after they had been resolved. He did not need to be burdened with troubles at home while he was dealing with the war.

FEAR OF THE WORST KIND OF NEWS

Every family member who has someone they love deployed to a war zone lives each day with some level of fear. They fear that they'll hear that their husband, girlfriend, brother, sister, or uncle has become a **casualty**; that he or she has been seriously injured—or even killed. A military family's greatest nightmare is seeing uniformed personnel approach their home to deliver unwanted news or getting a phone call with unbearable news that they'll need to withstand. To help reduce these worries, try to limit the amount of news exposure you experience, seek the support of others who know what you're going through, and keep communication with your loved one as open and regular as possible.

Alex's mother stands holding the phone, shocked at what she is hearing. A suicide bomber penetrated the base where his unit was posted. Alex has been seriously wounded. He is stable now, but authorities report that he may need to have his left leg amputated. Two others are in serious condition, one dead.

ACTIVE DUTY AND RESERVE COMPONENT FAMILY SUPPORT

Your partner, like Laura, or parents, like the Bassettes or Alex's mother, often need somewhere to turn for information and support while you're on active deployment. Family support groups were created to assist all family members during deployment: spouses, siblings, parents, and children alike. All branches of the armed forces realize the strain that deployment places on families and communities. The military knows that to retain service members and assure their optimal performance, they must take care of your families. As a result, specific personnel are assigned to assist families, many of whom understand these problems very well from personal experience. Their goal is to help provide support for family members throughout the deployment cycle.

Although many Active Duty members and their families live on military bases or in military housing, over 40 percent do not. In addition, unlike Active Duty military members, the families of members of the National Guard and Reserve Troops are not enmeshed in a community that shares their common plight. The following services exist for service members and their families on or off base, to help tie them together and provide them with needed communication and support. They're available both to the families living on military bases as well as those out in the community:

Army Community Services (ACS) and **U.S. Air Force Services Agency:** These services exist within the respective armed forces to provide family support and readiness, thereby helping families to meet the challenges of separations due to deployments, new assignments, and other disruptions associated with military life. Visit the ACS Web site at www.armymwr.com or the Air Force Services Agency at www-p.afsv.af.mil for more information.

Navy Family Ombudsman: This is an appointed person whose job is to maintain the well-being and morale of sea service families when troops are away from home. A Navy Family Ombudsman is assigned once the unit knows of a pending deployment and should contact your family. If not, you should be able to locate him or her through your unit's command.

Coast Guard Ombudsman: This is a Coast Guard partner or other volunteer who serves as the family's liaison. An ombudsman understands and supports command policy and works with command, the Active Duty Coast Guard members, and families to keep communication open. The ombudsman will usually contact your family. If not, you should be able to locate him or her through your unit's command.

Army Family Team Building (AFTB): This is a volunteer-led organization that helps empower Army families through family preparedness training. AFTB helps families adapt to Army life by providing information about the resources available to both Soldiers as well as their family members. Visit their Web site at www.myarmylifetoo.com for more information.

Family Readiness Groups (FRG): These groups began in the Army with the mission to bond Guard families together. Units have groups of volunteers dedicated to facilitate communication to the families of deployed troops. Their primary concern is the National Guard because those families are dispersed geographically. FRGs use phone trees to assure open communication between command

and families. Your FRG should contact your family, but if not, you can locate them through your service member's unit.

LIFElines: These groups are the family support groups of the Navy and Marines. They too provide deployment readiness, family support, transition assistance, and Morale, Welfare and Recreation (MWR) for both Active as well as Reserve members. MWR involves a varied program of recreation, social, and community support activities for military members and their families. For more information, visit www.lifelines.navy.mil/lifelines.

Air Force Reserve Family Readiness: This organization provides deployment assistance services to Air Force Reserve families, such as family support groups, reunion information, and volunteer opportunities. You can contact them by phone at 800-223-1784, ext. 7-1243 (7 a.m.–5 p.m.) (ext. 7-0089 after duty hours) or through their Web site at www.afrc.af.mil/library/family.asp.

Marine Corps Reserve Community Services (MCCS): MCCS exists to help Marine families wherever they may be stationed. It developed from merging the Corps old Morale, Welfare, and Recreation and Human Resources programs to help with family readiness. Visit www.usmc-mccs.org for more information.

Rear Detachment Officer (RDO): This is a service member who is not deployed and is appointed to work with the FRG while a unit is deployed. FRGs and RDOs are formed when a unit's deployment is pending.

Family Assistance Centers (FAC): Located at armories across the states, these centers were created by the National Guard Bureau, but they exist to assist all service members and their families in all branches of military. For instance, if your son or daughter is deployed from Arkansas but you live in Miami, you can still go to any Florida FAC and receive assistance. To find the location nearest you, visit www.guardfamily.org.

Military OneSource (MOS): Around the clock information and referral service supporting service members and their families. Visit www.militaryonesource.com, or call 1-800-342-9647.

3

HOMECOMING

SEPARATING MYTH
FROM REALITY

Following months of continual vigilance and constant alert, your deployment is over. The time has come to return home. Your loved ones can now breathe a collective sigh of relief because you're on your way home, safe and sound. Although reunion is a happy time, it can also be a time of considerable stress for both you and your family. In order to get through homecoming and the months that follow as smoothly as possible, you need to know what kinds of issues you might face, and make sure your expectations are realistic.

Both you and your family have been through a great deal of change over the past months. War experiences generally have a significant effect on those who have been deployed to a war zone. You may have seen death and destruction, felt your own life was in danger, been through harsh living conditions, survived explosions, been shot at, and handled dead bodies and remains. These experiences may affect you for the rest of your life. You've likely been surrounded by a completely different culture than the one at home. Because you are in a completely different mindset when you're deployed to a war zone, it can be difficult to transition back to a "civilian" mindset once you get back home. Furthermore, while you were gone your partner or other family members may have established new friendships, taken on more responsibilities, and established new roles for themselves in your family. Your children have grown and matured. Everyone will need to recognize such changed circumstances and make an effort to adjust to these new family realities.

We all have fantasies about emotional homecomings after separation from loved ones; lovers embracing romantically, children full of excitement, parents with tears of relief. Although initial welcoming receptions may include some of these elements, there are many myths about homecoming that you need to be prepared for.

TONY'S HOMECOMING REALITY

Tony is on his way back to the States; sitting listening to the hum of the jet engine, feeling sort of odd about his return home. Like many of his comrades, he is relieved that each new day won't be a struggle to stay alive. However, it seems strange to be going back to the "regular" world. After all that he has seen and experienced during deployment, his old life at home now seems so distant and unfamiliar. Although he is looking forward to reunion with his wife, and, now, three children whom he knows are waiting to greet him with open arms, he is also torn by mixed feelings about going back.

His happiness about leaving Iraq is partially dampened by his regret that he hasn't finished the job he was sent to do. There's a big piece of him that wishes he were staying longer to help finish what was started. He knows that a part of him will miss the thrill of combat, the intense sense of feeling alive when on constant alert and at the top of his game as an effective Soldier. He also wonders if the nightmares will stop once he's back sleeping in his own bed.

Despite these concerns, Tony is eagerly looking forward to his leave. He wants to do nothing but "veg out," watch TV, flip through the channels, and snuggle on the couch with Laura and the kids. He wants to remember what it feels like to slow down. Now that the family is being reunited, he expects that things will go back to normal again.

A few weeks later, following his time in demobilization, Tony is met at the base by his wife, Laura, his new daughter, Marie, and the boys. A small band is playing celebratory music and the initial homecoming is all that he expected. He feels appreciated and proud, as well as exhausted.

After that first day, instead of things going back to normal, he feels he has walked into another foreign world. Things with Laura are strained, not happy as he had expected. Why wasn't she just glad to have him back? Why didn't she stop quizzing him and trying to get him to talk about everything that had happened in Iraq? He just wants to forget all of it. The nightmares have not stopped. He can't sleep. The new baby cries every time he tries to hold her and he is even irritated with the boys. They won't leave him alone and can't seem to get enough of his attention. Why can't they appreciate how good a life they already have instead of complaining that they are bored? He cannot believe he is feeling resentful because his own children seem to be acting like spoiled brats.

From Laura's perspective, things also seem to be a mess. She hardly recognizes her own husband. He used to be outgoing, always wanting to have friends over for dinners and barbeques. Now, he doesn't want to see anyone. He is aloof and sullen, spending hours of time all alone, unwilling to tell her anything that's on his mind or in his heart. He's short with the boys and hasn't started to take care of anything around the house. She continues to feel overwhelmed and in addition is now hurt by the lack of communication between them. She wonders whether this has something to do with that final incident over in Iraq when a VBIED blew up a truck and killed his friend in the convoy. She wishes he would speak to her about it so she could help him get over it. She can't understand. Why won't he talk to his own wife about it?

MYTH 1: "MY RELATIONSHIP WITH MY PARTNER AND FAMILY WILL BE THE SAME WHEN I GET HOME FROM WAR"

Many troops mistakenly assume that once they return home, their relationships with their partner and family will be the same as it was before they left for deployment. It's important to understand that the closeness you shared with your partner and family will not automatically reappear. You've been apart for a long time and have had to learn to live without each other. It takes some time for the trust and bonds to be reestablished before you and your family can again rely on each other. The separation and varied experiences that occurred during deployment may have created some understandable distancing that you and many of your loved ones will need some time to get over. In Chapter 9, we focus on specific strategies for getting past these difficulties and reestablishing trust and intimacy.

Family members should try to keep in mind how hard homecoming can be for their service member. Troops deployed to a war zone often experience and witness terrible things that make them perceive themselves as different from regular civilians when they get home. The lifestyle in which they've been embedded for months is extremely different from daily life in the United States. Coming home can actually be *more* difficult than going to war.

Life has changed for your loved ones at home as well. The experiences they had during your deployment, such as Laura's pregnancy and the birth of their child while Tony was away, may have made life different for them in a way similar to the way that your experiences during deployment have changed your life. Granted it's not the same kind of life-threatening or traumatic experience, but nonetheless everyone has undergone stress and changes. It's also important to note that these changes may be physical (such as injury or a new child) as well as emotional, particularly for troops returning home.

ALEX'S HOMECOMING REALITY

*Homecoming for Alex was marked by a frustrating series of events. The blast had shattered his left leg so badly that he was immediately flown out of Kuwait to the United States, where he was placed in a **Medical Holding Company (MHC)** at Brooke Army Medical Center, San Antonio, Texas. Although the orthopedic surgical team managed to save his upper leg, his left leg had to be amputated from the knee down. The Amputee Care Center was taking good care of him and attending to his injury.*

*Alex's mother had been able to take some leave from work in order to fly to Texas and be with him through the first stages of his recovery. She was issued **Invitational Travel Orders (ITOs)** to go to San Antonio, so her travel was covered by the service and she was provided with lodging at the nearby **Fisher House,** a "home away from* *home" made available to families of military patients. Being uprooted from her two jobs, as a mother and at work, was stressful, frustrating, and inconvenient, but all this was nothing compared to her worry and concern over Alex.*

Alex didn't want to be a burden to his mother. He didn't want her spending time in Texas to be with him. He knew how vital her presence was back at home to his younger sister Michele and that his mother also couldn't afford to miss more work without pay. As it was, he was in a perpetually gloomy mood and didn't want her to be saddled with the additional responsibility and burden of trying to cheer him up.

Finally, Alex is discharged from the hospital and allowed to return home. At his request, he's not greeted with a big ceremony, but does receive a warm welcome from his mom, sister, brother, and family. Although he's come far in learning to use his **prosthesis**, *artificial leg, he's now in a wheelchair, weary from travel. Alex approaches his young niece and nephew for hugs, expecting them to jump all over him as usual. Instead, they hide behind his brother Sam, and stare at him with large frightened eyes. He's hurt because they obviously don't recognize him. It's as if all the joyful times they spent together during the months and years preceding his deployment meant nothing.*

The months ahead are full of stress and disappointments for Alex and his mother. His mom is trying to be helpful but is frustrated because he always refuses her help. She really doesn't understand how much Alex wants to do things on his own. From Alex's perspective, she's overbearing and seems to be treating him like a kid again. They get into heated arguments over minor disagreements.

His brother Sam continues to help with making the house more wheelchair accessible so that, until Alex can walk again and is fully recovered, he'll be able to safely navigate their mother's two-story home. When Sam goes to move some furniture in Alex's room, he notices that Alex has a gun under the bed. He's very concerned about the dangers of having a loaded firearm in their mother's house. When Sam tries to confront Alex about it, Alex is belligerent and refuses to relinquish it.

MYTH 2: "MY LIFE WILL BE THE SAME AS IT WAS BEFORE I LEFT FOR WAR"

Everyone's homecoming is different, and some are easier than others, but it's safe to say that your life will *not* be the same as it was before you left for deployment. In order to get through this difficult period of reintegration, many changes need to be made at home. You and your family have been apart for some time, and as we mentioned above, you've all been through a lot. As we've seen with Tony, your partner has had to take on all of your domestic responsibilities while you were gone, and he or she may or may not want to simply give them all back to you upon your return. You may need to renegotiate these roles so both of you are happy. We address these complicated issues many times, and in great detail, in future chapters.

If you sustained a serious injury during your time on the front, it will certainly add to the stress of reunion. Your family may not know how to handle your injury. They may feel devastated seeing you hurt or overwhelmed by the job of caring for you. Your children, or other young children in your family, may be frightened or confused by your changed appearance and initially shy away from you. If this happens, be patient and, difficult as it may be, try not to take these reactions personally. Remember that it will take some time to reestablish your closeness and get used to living together again.

When you get home, you and your family will definitely need to rework the way that daily activities unfold. (See Chapter 4 for more about weapons at home.) It's not unusual for family members to note new or unusual behaviors in each other, such as Alex's "need" for a weapon close at hand. It's also good to keep in mind that emotional and relationship changes can be more taxing and draining than readjusting to physical and behavioral changes. Some of these changes occur due to "Battlemind," which we discuss in Chapter 4. Battlemind is an acronym used to describe how the mindset that military members need to adopt in order to succeed in a war zone can cause problems when used at home.

For Alex, his mother's reaction to his amputation and temporary dependency is most unwelcome. It's been difficult enough for him to undergo physical rehabilitation and learn to use his prosthesis so that he can move forward with his life. Unfortunately, the flood of misguided motherly behavior has made matters much worse. His mother, misperceiving his physical disability as a sign that he needs the kind of care and attention that she provided when he was much younger, has done more harm than good. As Alex needs to overcome his disability on his own terms, he feels that he has no choice but to push her away. This serious breach in his relationship with his mother is only compounding his medical problems.

Communication between Alex and his mother is failing. They need to talk about how they are treating and reacting to one another; if they don't, things will only get worse. If you find yourself in this kind of situation, it might be helpful to ask someone to play the role of a mediator between you and your loved one. For instance, Alex's brother Sam might be able to fill this role. Sam could talk to each of them individually and then bring them together and help them each listen to what the other needs and is trying to convey.

KATHLEEN'S HOMECOMING REALITY

Kathleen can't wait to be back in Isaac's arms. But she's also fearful about returning home this time. She knows that once she's home she'll be surrounded by people who have not shared her experiences and don't understand what she's been through. This deployment was so different than her previous one. She fears that even Isaac will not really be able to understand. She longs to be reunited with him yet is afraid of seeing him again face to face. Will Isaac even want to marry her still? She senses that the transition back home will be harder than it was to go to war. Little does she realize that at the same time, Isaac is asking himself, "Will I still know and like this person who has now gone through so much and seen so much?"

After almost two weeks at the demobilization site, Kathleen arrives home. She feels nervous but can see Isaac standing in the armory, smiling broadly in her direction. Then across the room she recognizes her mom waving emphatically, standing with her dad and sister. She's surprised that they're not all waiting together. As she climbs down the stairs of the bus, both parties rush toward her. Isaac reaches her first but their embrace is cut short because her mother pushes herself into the middle of things. Her mother is not shy about the fact that she feels she should be the first to hold her daughter now that she has safely returned.

MYTH 3: "ALL I NEED IS THE LOVE AND SUPPORT OF MY FAMILY TO GET THROUGH ANY POST-DEPLOYMENT DIFFICULTIES"

Both Kathleen's and Alex's mothers are trying to express their love and concern for their child. Their intentions are nothing but good. However, Alex's mother is not recognizing his need to maintain his identity as a strong and useful individual, and she is being overly attentive and pampering him beyond what he desires. Kathleen's mother is not acknowledging Kathleen or Isaac's needs; instead, she's putting her own needs first. This type of situation can be tricky to maneuver through unless each person can clearly communicate his or her needs. In addition, these situations are often emotionally charged, making them even more difficult to handle.

The returning service member is often the head of the family, the one who's always been in charge, the strong one. When it happens that he or she is the one who needs special attention, it may be difficult for his or her family to know how to react. It's not unusual for other family members to stick with old patterns and put their own needs first rather than recognizing and responding to their service member's needs. Kathleen's mother is forgetting that the needs of her daughter might be more important than her own right now. In the past Kathleen has had the energy to put her mother in her place and keep her from standing between Isaac and herself. Right now, however, she needs her entire family's support and consideration and is in no shape to take on the mediator role.

These types of scenarios occur frequently among military families. When the "strong one" needs help, things become complicated. Family members need to try to put their personal needs and differences aside during your reintegration, and this is not always easy. Sometimes it's necessary for family members to join forces to give you the help you need. The key to moving beyond this myth is good communication. You need to acknowledge your needs and make use of the supports around you. You're surrounded with people who care and are more than willing to help, but it's up to you to reach out and accept their assistance.

Kathleen's mother continues to be pushy as she insists that Kathleen and Isaac follow her and Kathleen's father back to the hotel for dinner. Isaac is instantly irritated by this request. Although he's trying very hard to be accepted into this family, he's troubled by Kathleen's domineering parents. He and Kathleen had spoken at length about what she wanted homecoming to be like, and he worries that her parents, in spite of good intentions, have insisted on planning a little surprise party that he knew Kathleen did not want. They arrive at the hotel and to his dismay are loudly welcomed by a small party of relatives from Missouri who have traveled down with Kathleen's parents.

Kathleen thinks to herself, "It is so nice that Aunt Kelly and Uncle Jim, Aunt Marjorie and my cousins took the time to come this distance to greet me home . . . ," but at the same time she's upset because it's so unexpected and contrary to her wishes. All Kathleen really wants is to go home alone with Isaac. They join the excited and animated group to order dinner. The family is noisily chatting away as at a typical family gathering. They act as if she's never been away.

Suddenly Kathleen is irritated and angry. The noise level in the room is too much. She feels panicky and stands up telling Isaac that they must leave, now.

MYTH 4: "EVERY RETURNING SERVICE MEMBER WANTS A LARGE WELCOME HOME PARTY"

Families are often so excited, happy, and proud that their loved one is coming home that they feel only a huge party can do the event justice. However, not every service member wants a large welcome home party. Many returning troops feel out of place when they first get back and need time to readjust. They may prefer to have a very quiet homecoming with just their partner and immediate family and ease into seeing extended family and friends over a span of days or even weeks. It's important that you be honest and open with your family about what you need when you first come home. Don't worry about disappointing them or not living up to their expectation of what your homecoming "should" be like. It's far more important that you feel as comfortable as you can when you arrive home.

It's also not unusual for parents and partners to be jealous of each others' role in your life during this time. In other words, your parents might be upset that they're not more involved in your homecoming or your partner may feel that your parents are *too* involved. They may need to be reminded that they have all missed you greatly and need to cooperate to make homecoming as comfortable and happy as possible for you.

DEMOBILIZATION

Before you even get home, most troops are required to go through demobilization, or spend a few days or a week at a special demobilization site between leaving their country of deployment and returning home. (Just to be clear, although most troops enter a demobilization site following deployment, some do not. Air Force Reserve members often experience short deployments lasting only a few months. They often return directly to their homes instead of going through any form of demobilization process. This can create problems. Even though their deployments are shorter, they still go through the emotional cycle of deployment and will experience reintegration challenges. They too could benefit from this period of readjustment.) Experience has shown the armed forces that troops need some down time to make the transition from a war zone to the home front. No matter how much you just wish you were home, the demobilization process is important.

You'll spend this time out-processing, completing paperwork, updating records, returning equipment, servicing medical needs, and being debriefed by command. Vet Center counselors, VA eligibility personnel, chaplains, and others are there to provide information about military benefits, financial and legal issues, and services such as religious and family support and counseling. You will go through briefings ad nauseam. The military, working harder than ever before to care for their service members, has also initiated a **Post Deployment Health Assessment (PDHA)** that all returning troops are to complete. It assesses the physical and mental health status of returning members (see box on page 50 for more information).

The reality is that coming home from war can require as much readjustment as going to war. However, unlike the training and preparation for warfare, you and your family are not adequately trained about homecoming. Even if during demobilization you are briefed on some of these issues, your overwhelming desire to get back to your family can prevent you from absorbing this information. Family members don't always attend family briefings either. It is important for your family's successful reintegration that you all know what to expect upon homecoming and how to find the resources and services you (or others you know) need. We are aware that this information does not always get communicated, and that is one reason why we wrote this book.

In the first month home, Kathleen seems to be easily angered by almost any-
thing. For example, before her deployment to Iraq she and Isaac agreed to re-
distribute some of their household tasks so that bill paying would now be

Isaac's responsibility. He was happy to continue to do this job following her homecoming, but now she's constantly accusing him of messing things up and insists she can do a better job. He's irritated by this criticism because he feels he's doing just fine and likes having this responsibility and control. At times Kathleen seems to be glad to see him, but at other times she looks right through him. Isaac notices that she shies away from his attempts to be intimate. She has a sad look in her eyes that, without notice, turns into flashes of anger. She has stubbornly refused to talk to her parents at all. She also seems to be having constant headaches and is not sleeping well. Perhaps worst of all, she has been drinking almost every day.

In the past few years, the military has made a greater effort to prepare troops for re-entry to civilian life. Each branch of the military has their own version of the Battlemind approach developed by the Army. The various branches use their own models, based on these same Battlemind ideas, to help service members be aware of and understand how the military mindset in which they have been immersed needs to be recalibrated when they return home. (See Chapter 4 for more information on Battlemind.)

The problem with the demobilization period is that, by its very nature, it occurs just prior to homecoming. The only thing that service members want to do at this time is go home. They numbly go through the routine of completing forms and other demobilization procedures. They just want to get them over with because it gets them one step closer to being home. Although we know that this isn't going to change, we want to emphasize that demobilization time is really crucial. It's a time for decompression and preparation for the transition to come. Even if you only absorb a little information, it's still worthwhile.

HOMECOMING: WHAT TO EXPECT

Preparation for homecoming is an essential part of family readiness, for service members, family, and even our communities. Being prepared and knowing what to expect can go a long way in helping you to assure successful reintegration. It's important to remember that war changes everyone. Readjustment will take time. Homecoming is not all rainbows

POST DEPLOYMENT HEALTH ASSESSMENT (PDHA)

We learned a very important lesson during the Vietnam War at the expense of the brave men and women who had risked their lives in service to our country. Americans confused the war with the warrior and demonstrated against troops when they arrived home. We now know better. Most Americans do not want anything like that to happen again. In general, American citizens today want our returning troops to feel accepted and supported, not abandoned. They want to make sure you receive the best care you can get in return for the sacrifices that you and other service members have made.

Another lesson we learned from the Vietnam War was that a significant minority of war zone veterans will develop PTSD or some other chronic psychiatric problem as a result of their war zone experience. One precautionary measure that the military has put in place to help assure that military members with emotional or mental problems get the help they need is the mandatory screening of all returning service members.

This screening instrument is called the Post Deployment Health Assessment, or PDHA. Using what we've learned from previous conflicts, this measure was created to assess the physical and mental well-being of all returning troops. All service members are required to complete this measure, when they return from deployment, during the demobilization processing. Obtaining certain scores on this measure indicates that you will be referred to appropriate mental health care providers, who will complete a more thorough assessment.

Although this screen is mandatory, it is acknowledged that once service members are back in the States, just about the only thing you want to do is go home. You are also bombarded with information and paperwork during this time period. This makes the results of the PDHA somewhat hard to interpret. Some returning troops will deny any problems on the PDHA because, if they admit to them, they believe their return home may be delayed. This is *not* the case. Although you may be referred to mental health assistance, you do not need to delay your homecoming, and usually can choose to seek services at your convenience. Honest completion of the PDHA does not have a major influence on time in demobilization.

Recognition by the military that PDHA information may be of limited usefulness has led to the implementation of follow-up screenings called **PDHRAs (Post Deployment Health Re-Assessment)**. These screens are administered three to six months after demobilization. It's expected that, in addition to issues that arose during deployment, if problems have emerged during the months at home, troops will be more likely to provide truthful answers on the PDHRA. This will help ensure that those in need of services are identified and referred. The first study looking at how the two assessments compare shows that more Soldiers are screening positive for mental health concerns during the second assessment.

and happy endings. It often involves increased conflict within your family. This period of readjustment is difficult for many, and often requires time and effort to get through successfully.

You've just learned about some of the most common myths about homecoming and how to avoid falling victim to them. Following are some other common issues that can complicate homecoming and advice to help you work through them.

EMPLOYMENT

Although many service members will return to military assignments, most Reserve Component troops will return to civilian jobs, and some Active Duty troops will be discharged out of the service and need to find other work. If you run your own company or have an established set of customers or clients that you deal with, the time you're deployed may have a massive impact on your business. Small business owners may have to close down. Those who are accountants or hold similar client-based businesses may have to start over again to reestablish their customer base. Some may find it difficult to know how to reapply the skills they've learned in the military to a civilian job, and they will need help with this transition. The labor involved in searching for a job is compounded by the stress and emotional upheaval that usually accompany homecoming.

For those with jobs waiting for them at home, returning to work has its challenges. Following the fast-paced, hypervigilant, life-or-death environment of the war zone, your workplace back home may pale by comparison. You may find you're no longer interested in what you used to do, or are bored or find no meaning in the work. Many of the post-war reactions you will learn about in this book may cause you to feel detached and unable to work easily with others. If you're feeling this way, discuss the situation with your boss or supervisor. You may need to make some adjustments to get through the first few weeks or months after your return. No matter what your situation, we urge you to occupy yourself in some way during this transitional period, even if it's with volunteer work. The military is committed to assuring a smooth transition to the civilian workplace for its members, so many resources exist to help troops once they return home. (See Chapter 13 and the Resources section on page 247 for more details.)

FINANCES

Many military families experience financial issues once a deployment is over. For some, in fact, financial issues begin during deployment. Some families see a decrease in take-home pay when a service member is deployed, which adds to the emotional strain and overwhelming responsibility that they already have. Reserve Component troops who are self-employed may find themselves without a job to come home to if their business has had to close its doors during their deployment.

Although some may experience decreased income, others may actually receive a higher salary during deployment than the take-home pay from their job back home. This surplus of money can lead some to spend too lavishly and eventually find themselves in debt. Some people don't budget properly and take on debt that the family cannot afford. Often, returning service members will purchase motorcycles, boats, or other items that can place the family in difficult financial situations. These items are often purchased following deployment to help fill the void created by the change in lifestyle or to replace the excitement and adrenaline rush of war.

Be sure to stick to the budget that you and your partner established before you left for deployment to avoid such problems. Take advantage of various means of financial assistance provided by the military and other organizations to help you through. Family Programs can point you to avenues of assistance, and Military OneSource also offers information. In addition, each U.S. state has its own State Department of Veterans Affairs that offers a variety of services to veterans, including financial assistance. Check your local phone book for contact information. You and your family do not need the added stress of conflict over finances. Avoid making any radical expenditures for at least a few months after your return, when everyone is feeling more settled.

RELATIONSHIPS

As we mentioned earlier, many troops initially feel disconnected or detached from their partner and family. Sometimes this has to do with feeling unable to tell your family about what happened, not wanting to intrude on them by speaking about the war, or just thinking that no one will be able to understand. Sometimes it's related to having difficulty in feeling or showing positive feelings, which can make loved ones feel like they did something wrong or are not wanted anymore. Sexual closeness may be awkward for a while. Common reactions to war tend to change how a person feels and acts, and such changes will affect your entire family. As you and your family try to reestablish family relationships, your family will naturally react to the fact that you have gone through a trauma and try to help you as much as they can. Don't be surprised if they are overly cautious around you or overly attentive. At the same time, you may be experiencing symptoms following deployment that make you difficult to get along with or cause you to withdraw from loved ones. It can be very hurtful and confusing for everyone in the family when this happens.

The best way to overcome feelings of detachment and confusion is to recognize that it will take time to reconnect. Remind yourself that you need to relearn how to feel safe, comfortable, and trusting again with your family. You essentially must become reacquainted with one another, and good communication with your partner, children, parents, siblings, friends, coworkers, and others is the key to doing so. It's fine for you to spend some time alone, but be aware that spending too much time alone or avoiding family gatherings isolates you from your family and friends. You need the support of these people for a healthy adjustment. Be sure to spend individual time with your partner, kids, other family members, and friends, as this will help the reconnection process. Family and friends should also be mindful to include you back into regular activities.

FAMILY UNDERSTANDING AND PATIENCE

Patience during homecoming is essential, especially for your family at home. Since normal readjustment takes time, your family should not pressure you to talk about your experiences. Instead, they need to provide opportunities for you to speak when you are ready and refrain from being judgmental or negative. Your family also needs to understand that you may be more comfortable talking with your buddies about your time at war. You've formed a bond with your unit members that may not be replicable at home. You have endured life and death situations with one another. At the same time, confiding in someone is a sign of trust and closeness, and your family may be hurt if you do not share anything. If you're having trouble sharing the details of war experiences with your family, you should speak with a counselor *before* things get out of hand. He or she can help you work through your issues and also provide you with an opportunity to discuss your experiences until you're ready to share them with your family. Your family and friends need to remember not to take signs of withdrawal personally and be patient. At the same time, they should offer an ear when you are ready. Some who return from a war zone believe that loved ones, friends, and others don't want to hear about what they have been through. Reassuring your returning service member that it's okay to talk when he or she is ready—that you want to listen—can be very helpful.

RECOGNIZE YOUR FAMILY'S SACRIFICES

It's important for you to remember that those who have waited at home had to face their own challenges. It hasn't been easy on them, and they also need your understanding and patience. While you were deployed they probably had to take on extra responsibilities, had to deal with problems without your help, and may have felt overwhelmed and lonely. It will take time for them to readjust as well. Although you may want to take back all of the responsibilities you had before you left, your family may now be feeling so independent and self-sufficient that they don't want to relinquish their new responsibilities or control. On the other hand, they may be very angry that they had to do so much on their own and they may impatiently ask for you to take back your previous responsibilities before you're ready to do so. Have an open and honest discussion with your partner or family about responsibilities and how they should be split up now that you're home. A gradual transition back into your old respon- sibilities is usually best, where you take on a few tasks at first and then additional ones as you grow accustomed to being home again. Be willing to compromise so that both of you feel your needs are understood and respected. Again, open communication will help ease this transition of responsibilities and readjusting to new roles (or taking back old roles).

RECOGNIZING NORMAL REACTIONS

Sometimes the everyday stresses of family life can feel overwhelming when you first arrive home. You may become more irritated or react more strongly to common family issues. Anger and aggression are common com- bat stress reactions, but they may frighten your partner and children, even you as well. In the following chapter we discuss common war zone stress reactions, such as anger, and offer advice on coping with them. Following any traumatic event, such as time in a war zone, it's normal for you to expe- rience a range of reactions, such as trouble sleeping or nightmares; feeling like no one can understand what you have been through; or feeling con- stantly on guard and always alert. In fact, if you didn't have some type of reaction, that would be abnormal! However, under some circumstances, feelings and behaviors, including some of these same symptoms, might indi- cate that you are at risk for developing a more serious condition like post- traumatic stress disorder (PTSD). We want to be absolutely clear that having post-deployment emotional or readjustment difficulties *does not automatically mean* that you have PTSD. The following chapters will clarify this point so that you'll learn what common reactions to expect, and you'll know when you should seek out additional—or even professional—assistance.

4

UNDERSTANDING
BATTLEMIND

All branches of the military train members to succeed and survive during war by teaching them a range of skills. The problem is that the mindset necessary for survival in a war zone is usually quite different from the mindset that makes things go smoothly at home. In fact, if you can't switch gears from a war zone to a home front mindset, you'll almost certainly have problems readjusting to life when you get home.

All of the branches of the U.S. Armed Forces understand how the mindset used during war can carry over into the home front inappropriately and create problems. Although each branch—Marines, Army, Air Force, Navy, etc.—has developed its own trainings to help troops understand this, they generally emphasize similar issues. We focus here on the Army's "Battlemind" training, with the understanding that other military branches approach these concerns somewhat differently. Such programs also use service-specific lingo to help troops understand how a wartime mindset is useful at war but not at home.

Battlemind was created through the guidance and efforts of Colonel Carl Castro, PhD, of the Walter Reed Army Institute of Research, and colleagues. Materials used in Battlemind trainings, including brochures, PowerPoint presentations, and videos, are available to the public at www.battlemind.org. The trainings can be viewed online, but are often presented to service members by military command at briefings or by Vet Center counselors or Family Program personnel. The program encourages troops to periodically do a Battlemind check, for themselves and for their comrades. It's also important for your family and friends to understand Battlemind, as knowing how and why certain patterns develop can help them be more patient and understanding.

Each letter in the acronym "BATTLEMIND" represents a different mental skill that troops are taught to help them survive in combat, but that can be problematic when carried over to life at home. Battlemind can help you to see how thinking a different way can change your thoughts, feelings, behaviors, and the way you get along with others. In this chapter we describe Battlemind in detail and offer advice for avoiding the problems it can create when you get home.

BATTLEMIND	
B =	BUDDIES (COHESION) VS. WITHDRAWAL
A =	ACCOUNTABILITY VS. CONTROLLING
T =	TARGETED VS. INAPPROPRIATE AGGRESSION
T =	TACTICAL AWARENESS VS. HYPERVIGILANCE
L =	LETHALLY ARMED VS. LOCKED AND LOADED
E =	EMOTIONAL CONTROL VS. DETACHMENT
M =	MISSION OPERATIONAL SECURITY VS. SECRETIVENESS
I =	INDIVIDUAL RESPONSIBILITY VS. GUILT
N =	NON-DEFENSIVE DRIVING (COMBAT) VS. AGGRESSIVE DRIVING
D =	DISCIPLINE AND ORDERING VS. CONFLICT

B-A-T-T-L-E-M-I-N-D

B

"B" stands for buddies. Many service members feel that their buddies are the only ones that understand what they went through. During wartime, troops in each unit must rely on one another for their lives. Consequently, bonds form in the war zone that are different from all your other relationships. Once home, your buddies may be the only ones whom you feel you can talk to, both because they shared your experiences and because you may have reservations about sharing information with your family. Service members often miss their war buddies deeply, especially during the initial homecoming transition period. This is a normal reaction to separation after the intense bonding that has taken place during war. Ordinarily, your family need not be concerned or feel jealous about these close relationships because missing buddies is a normal part of readjustment. However, this mindset can create problems at home if you are clinging to your wartime relationships and make little effort to reconnect with your loved ones. Make an effort to engage with your friends and family when you get home, even if it feels awkward or strained at first. Family and friends should also be sure to include you in all their normal activities. In Chapter 9 we discuss reconnecting with loved ones and offer further advice.

A

"A"ccountability versus control is the second concept included in the Battlemind acronym. Every individual is accountable for his or her own actions in a military setting. Troops are accountable for their gear, weapons, actions, and fellow comrades. This can lead to conflict about control and responsibility after you return to family life. You may find that you are irritated if someone messes with any of your stuff, or you may not want to let anyone else do things because you believe no one cares enough about making sure the job is done right. Keep in mind that the strict chain of command necessary in the military is not the way that most healthy families function. In order to work through any issues regarding accountability and control when you get home, both you and your family will need to compromise. In cases where "it doesn't really matter," it's usually best to let things go. Again, in Chapter 9 we talk more about how control can impact your relationships. In addition, Chapter 6 discusses handling angry and aggressive feelings that can come from feeling a lack of control.

T-T

Military personnel are taught "T"argeted aggression as well as "T"actical awareness, making up the two "T"s of Battlemind. You're taught that you must be aggressive, forceful, and ready to act in an environment where the focus is to kill or be killed. You're required to always be on the alert, watchful twenty-four hours a day, seven days a week, and ready to respond at any moment. While these behaviors are adaptive and helpful in keeping you alive, once you're at home and no longer in harm's way, inappropriate aggression and arousal can surface. You may feel anxious or "keyed up," and unable to calm down. Minor incidents can lead to severe overreactions. A wide range of potentially problematic behaviors can result, such as a short temper and continual snapping at your partner, kids, or others; self-destructive or overly risky actions; heated arguments; or even assaults or domestic violence. You may be jumpy and easy to startle, always on edge. Upon initial return, some veterans may be hypervigilant, always on guard, excessively concerned about safety and security, and overprotective of their families. Chapter 9 offers ways to better cope with the hypervigilance, irritability, and aggressiveness that can have a negative impact on your relationships. Inappropriate aggression can lead to feelings of guilt, which we discuss in Chapter 7, or to anger and conflict (discussed in Chapter 6).

L

The "L" stands for lethally armed, which is appropriate in a war zone, versus locked and loaded at home where this security is unnecessary. While in a war zone, military personnel are armed at all times. They don't even go to the bathroom without their weapons. Carrying weapons is mandatory and essential. Once home, you may feel that you're vulnerable without your weapon. You may continue to want to have your weapon with you wherever you go. However, back at home, being armed all of the time is inappropriate and can be dangerous. Leave the weapons locked up at home. Remind yourself that you're no longer in a war zone but rather back in your hometown, and you don't need this type of extreme protection.

E

"E"motional control is another critical skill that becomes embedded in the behavior and mindset of all troops. In a war zone you can show no weakness. Emotional expression is discouraged while mental toughness is considered necessary. This mindset, when carried over at home, can have detrimental effects on family (and other) relationships. It makes you appear to be emotionally detached, numb, or uncaring. Your friends and family may feel they no longer know you. Remember that hesitating to display emotions will hurt your relationships. Positive emotions may be hard to experience or express, especially at first, but it's important to be close and open with your family and friends. Planning and participating in activities you enjoy on a regular basis is a good way to help give up your need for emotional control and to express yourself more freely. We discuss preventing emotional withdrawal and staying connected more in Chapter 9, and in Chapters 11 and 12 we show how to identify whether numbing and avoidance are indications of worse problems.

M-I-N-D

The last four letters, "M-I-N-D," stand for mission security, individual responsibility, non-defensive driving, and discipline. "M"ission security requires that you only talk about the mission with those who need to know. It's easy to see why this is an important procedure to obey in the war zone. However, at home this can lead to secretiveness. It may cause you to avoid speaking about your deployment experiences with your loved ones. It may also cause you to become angry when people ask you about the things that happened while you were deployed. We offer some advice about talking about your experiences in Chapter 9 and how to deal with angry feelings in Chapter 6.

Individuals in the military during a time of war are responsible for their own lives as well as the lives of their buddies. The "I" in "M-I-N-D" represents this individual responsibility. Each military member is held responsible for her or his duties. However, individual responsibility sometimes carries over in places where it's unwarranted. For instance, everyone experiences thoughts or memories about those wounded or killed in action. Survivors often feel responsible, that they have somehow failed their buddies. Such guilty feelings may persist after deployment ends, and they may become very disruptive if they have not been addressed. Almost everyone returning from a war zone will experience some feelings of guilt and responsibility over actions or inactions during their tour. We discuss coping with guilty feelings in detail in Chapter 7, but for now, if you find you're unable to work things through and forgive yourself, consider speaking with a military chaplain. They have front line experience dealing with this issue.

Don't mistake individual responsibility for being able to handle everything on your own. One major issue that occurs following deployment is that military personnel often think that they should be able to handle their problems and emotions by themselves. In Chapter 10 we discuss this issue and the many barriers to seeking care that troops face. Knowing when you need help to handle a situation is not just brave; it's smart problem solving. You shouldn't wait until your life is a mess to get help. Early intervention can keep your life from falling apart.

"N"on-defensive driving is the type of driving that occurs in theater. Non-defensive driving is full speed ahead, unpredictable, and deliberate in order to avoid IEDS and VBIEDS. This type of driving is not safe or responsible when it continues back at home. It creates speeding tickets and accidents and frightens passengers. It can also make your family afraid to be in the car when you are driving. Aggressive driving is extremely common among troops returning from the current conflicts in the Middle East. It may be wise for you to hold off on driving for a few weeks until you've adjusted a bit to being home and feel capable of defensive driving. Chapter 6 offers some further advice on handling angry and aggressive feelings.

The final letter in the Battlemind program, "D," represents discipline. The hierarchical structure of the military is necessary to instill order, especially under adverse circumstances where there is no time to ask questions. Discipline and obeying orders are essential for survival and for working together effectively. Rigid discipline may be necessary during wartime, but it can cause you to be inflexible and demanding when you return home to civilian life. Within families there's always a legitimate need to discuss rules and share in decisions. Without such flexibility, conflict will almost always occur. You'll find more ways to cope with the conflicts that might occur in Chapters 6, 9, and also 14, which addresses life in the community. When talking as a family, be careful to listen to one another. Keep in mind that families work best when there is respect for one another, clear communication, a willingness to be open, and when everyone is receptive to considering alternatives. Cooperation is far more effective than self-discipline at home. If you take the time to explain your reasons for decisions you're making, you have a better chance of getting your family on board. Remember, now that you're removed from the dangers of the war zone, there's plenty of time to answer questions.

Transitioning from the war zone to the home front can be much smoother if both you and your family understand the Battlemind mindsets. Recognizing when Battlemind sneaks into everyday behaviors will help you keep things in check.

The Battlemind acronym and overall concept have been expanded to include versions for leaders and partners of military members regarding pre- and post-deployment scenarios. Although we don't thoroughly cover these other versions, here are some highlights of what the Battlemind for partners entails. You can visit www.battlemind.org for more information on all the different versions of Battlemind.

"SPOUSE" BATTLEMIND

The Army has developed a version of Battlemind for spouses or partners, which aims to increase resiliency in military families and smooth the reintegration process. Not surprisingly, partners at home develop their own "Battlemind" in response to handling everything on their own. Just as your partner, family, and friends will benefit from understanding your "battle" mind, it's good for you to understand how your partner's mindset may change while you're away. The same BATTLEMIND letters are used but represent different concepts.

While you were deployed and strengthening your bond with your buddies, your partner may have developed new friendships or may have become more involved in new groups or communities. The "B"uddies mindset refers to the fact that during deployment both of you must rely on social supports other than your partner. Because you're having fewer shared experiences, this may mean you have fewer meaningful communications and less intimacy. Once you're reunited, a balance between time spent with family versus friends needs to be reached. Remember that all forms of social support are needed. Don't hide any of the activities that either one of you are participating in, and try to introduce one another to new friends you've made. Set aside time just for the two of you, but also be mindful that you may each need some of your own time with buddies.

Your roles have also changed, so you'll need to work together to resume joint decision-making and shared roles, "A"dding some and subtracting others. For instance, you may have been responsible for paying bills prior to deployment, but while you were deployed your partner paid the bills. Once the deployment is over, you need to know who will now play this role. We suggest you create a plan ahead of time

SPOUSE/PARTNER BATTLEMIND	
B =	Buddies (Social Support)
A =	Adding/Subtracting Family Roles
T =	Taking Control
T =	Talking it Out
L =	Loyalty and Commitment
E =	Emotional Balance
M =	Mental Health and Readiness
I =	Independence
N =	Navigating the Army (military) system
D =	Denial of Self (Self-Sacrifice)

to divvy up household responsibilities upon your return, but some role changes will be unforeseen and will need to be renegotiated following homecoming. You and your partner should be careful not to let these changes cause you to withdraw from each other. Instead discuss things and practice give and take, respecting the other's sacrifices.

The first "T" of partner Battlemind involves the "T"aking control that has occurred, both for you in the war zone and for your partner who took over as head of the household back home. As we discussed above, this control needs to be renegotiated. The other "T" stands for talking it out. You may have trouble talking about your deployment experiences. Your partner needs to understand that this can take time to come out. Both of you will benefit from realizing that neither of you will ever understand everything the other went through, but that sharing stories is essential to maintain intimacy and closeness. You need to make an effort to keep communication open.

"L"oyalty and commitment should be voiced and practiced by both partners. You both (but especially the returning service member) may need some reassurance about each other's commitment to the relationship. Don't hesitate to get help if issues of mistrust arise. "E"motional balance is also vital, so again, be sure to spend time together, expressing your feelings and sharing emotional intimacy.

"M-I-N-D" represents mental health, independence, navigating the military system, and denial of self. "M"ental health and well-being is essential, and partners need to remember that they're not always the ones who can provide their service member the help that he or she might need and that seeking care can be difficult. In addition, partners at home have gone through a period of increased "I"ndependence and self-sacrifice; running a household and family all on their own for months and perhaps "D"enying many of their own needs. You should both be sure to express your appreciation for each other and what you've been through. Remember that many of these issues can be addressed with the help of military, VA, and other resources. Continue to learn about "N"avigating the military and VA systems so that you are aware of services and resources should any needs develop. We also provide an extensive Resources section in the back of this book.

Your partner may have gained a new sense of independence during your absence when he or she had to take on all of the household responsibilities. It's important for your partner to be aware of this change and how it can affect your relationship when you get home. Try to respect and appreciate your partner's newfound independence; he or she found the strength to make decisions in your absence. However, you both need to be involved in decision making once you return. You also both need to understand that things will not be the same as they were before deployment. Be careful about criticizing how things were done at home while you were away because this can lead to resentment from your partner.

Remember that the effects of deployment vary from service member to service member as well as family member to family member. Deployment is stressful, but it can also have a positive effect and bring you closer to your partner. Knowing what to expect and effective ways of coping will help to create a successful reintegration for everyone. Also keep in mind that many of these issues can be addressed with the help of military, VA, and other resources we describe throughout this book. We encourage military partners to educate themselves about the military and VA systems so that they're aware of services and resources should any needs develop.

5

COMMON REACTIONS
TO THE TRAUMA OF WAR

Living in a war zone is an experience that leaves no one untouched. There are a wide range of reactions that commonly occur after you've lived through the trauma of war. Once you're home again, you are likely to face some or many of them. In this chapter, we discuss these issues and offer advice on how to successfully manage your way through them.

During war, especially if you served in theater, you may have been shot at or witnessed the death or injury of friends or other military personnel, civilians, or enemy combatants. IEDs are common; units and convoys are confronted with blasts on a regular basis. Troops are on alert twenty-four hours a day, seven days a week. You may have been injured as a result of a bombing, mine blast, weapon, or accident. You may have survived an attack with very serious physical injuries, like Alex. Being in an unfamiliar setting and an unfamiliar culture complicates these experiences even further.

You and your family should be aware of the common responses that normally affect almost everyone who has undergone traumatic war zone experiences, experiences such as those discussed in Chapter 2 and above. Traumatic experiences, by definition, involve actual, or the threat of, death or serious injury. These experiences often produce feelings of fear, helplessness, and even horror. During the trauma of war, service members may also feel angry. Sometimes they're not aware of any specific emotions, but rather feel that their training "kicked in." Now that we have discussed common war zone experiences, we will describe the common reactions that may occur as a result. These same responses also frequently occur following exposure to traumatic experiences in civilian life, such as natural disasters (hurricanes, floods, tornados), terrorism, or interpersonal violence (abuse, violence, rape).

Most troops will successfully manage the readjustment process with no need for outside help. It may take a few months, but life will return to normal following demobilization with few major problems. Almost all troops, however, will have some behaviors, reactions, or symptoms that are clearly a result of war zone experience, especially during the first few weeks at home. These behaviors are a normal part of the readjustment process. They are common reactions that should not come as a surprise and do *not* automatically mean you have posttraumatic stress disorder or any other major psychiatric problem. (See Chapters 11 and 12 for more on these problems.)

Often times, "**war zone stress reactions**" (also called **combat stress reactions** or **acute stress reactions**) only become obvious after you return home. While you're still in a dangerous war zone environment, the adrenaline rush and automatic reactions that you experience are not only adaptive and normal, but they might actually save your life given the circumstances. These include being hyperalert, ever watchful, ready to react within a split-second of any provocative activity, and shutting down your emotions so that they don't interfere with your performance. However, once you return home, these same responses draw attention to themselves because they don't belong in a family or community setting. After you've returned home, you may continue to think about events that occurred while you were deployed, sometimes even acting as if you're back in a combat situation. You may walk around feeling upset, "keyed up," numb, or detached. These war zone stress reactions can last for days or weeks and are a *normal* reaction to war zone experiences.

COMMON REACTIONS TO
SPENDING TIME IN A WAR ZONE

Below is an at-a-glance list of reactions that commonly occur after spending time in a war zone. As you read through the list, you'll see that Alex, Kathleen, and Tony have demonstrated many of these reactions.

REACTIONS THAT AFFECT DAILY ACTIVITIES
OR YOUR PHYSICAL BODY:

- Trouble sleeping, overly tired
- Stomach upset, trouble eating
- Headaches and sweating when thinking of the war
- Bad dreams, nightmares
- Lack of exercise, poor diet or health care
- Rapid heartbeat or breathing
- Existing health problems become worse

REACTIONS THAT AFFECT YOUR BEHAVIOR:

- Trouble concentrating
- Jumpy and easily startled
- Being on guard, always alert
- Too much drinking, smoking, or drug use
- Flashbacks or frequent unwanted memories
- Avoiding people or places related to the trauma
- Problems doing regular tasks at work or school

EMOTIONAL REACTIONS:

- Irritable or angry
- Experiencing shock, being numb, unable to feel happy
- Feeling nervous, helpless, or fearful
- Feeling sad, guilty, rejected, or abandoned
- Edginess, easily upset or annoyed
- Feeling hopeless about the future

REACTIONS THAT AFFECT YOUR RELATIONSHIPS:

- Feeling withdrawn, detached, and disconnected
- Emotional shutdown resulting in loss of intimacy
- Mistrust of others
- Being overcontrolling or overprotective
- Having lots of conflicts

It's important to understand that different service members will respond to their experiences in a war zone in different ways. Some of these war-related behaviors and feelings will apply to you, while others will not. That said, everyone will be changed by their deployment experiences in some way. Most troops who experience common war zone stress reactions like those listed above will successfully readjust to civilian life over time. Still, it can be helpful to discuss these reactions with a professional. You don't have to be an emotional mess to benefit from learning some coping tips from a counselor, therapist, or chaplain, especially if reactions are creating trouble in your life.

Some troops will have a rockier course and will continue to struggle with reactions and difficult war-related memories of their experiences. We don't really know why some people struggle while others do not. What we do know is that these invisible injuries of war can make returning home very difficult.

A small but significant group of returning troops may have to deal with more than these common post-deployment reactions. They may develop PTSD or other mental health problems that require professional attention. We address these issues in Chapters 11 and 12.

We can't emphasize strongly enough that a need for professional help does *not* indicate a personal weakness or character flaw. Sometimes the protective behaviors that kept you alive during deployment get on the wrong track or can't shut down after you've returned home safely. It's also important to recognize that even serious post-deployment psychological problems can be treated successfully and cured. If your reactions or symptoms are causing trouble in your daily life, we urge you to seek professional assistance before they cause serious disruption. Our main reason for writing this book is to provide you with important information that will help you readjust to daily life more successfully. If you need help, the sooner you get it, the sooner and better you'll be able to handle things on your own.

PHYSICAL REACTIONS

Our bodies are affected by severe stress or trauma in a variety of ways. Below we have listed the most common physical reactions troops have when they return home from deployment.

SLEEP PROBLEMS

One of the most common problems that returning troops suffer from is trouble sleeping. Reestablishing normal sleep habits after a deployment often takes time because of switching time zones and changes in your overall physical exertion and mental vigilance. Insomnia can occur, and when you do sleep you may have nightmares. Or you may have no trouble sleeping, but wake up feeling overly tired and spent rather than well-rested in the morning.

In order to minimize sleep problems, try to reestablish a normal sleep routine as quickly as possible by going to bed and getting up at the same time every day. Don't do other activities in bed besides sleep and sex. If you're awake for more than twenty minutes after going to bed, get up and do something relaxing until you feel sleepy again. Do not drink to help yourself sleep. You might try learning some relaxation techniques, such as deep breathing, yoga, or meditation.

EATING AND RESPIRATION PROBLEMS

Eating patterns can be disturbed, appetite may be reduced, and some may experience stomach upset. Your body may feel like it's been kicked into high gear, experiencing increased heart rate, sweating, rapid breathing, and hypervigilance, or being always on the alert for danger. Your general health may become worse as a result of not taking care of yourself. Strive for healthy lifestyle habits, such as a balanced diet and proper exercise.

Kathleen had symptoms of anxiety and panic as soon as she returned home, as evidenced by her need to leave the busy, noisy restaurant on her first day back. Her heart began to race and she felt like the room had suddenly become small and she was trapped inside. Shortly after demobilization, she also began to experience headaches every day. Both Kathleen and Tony are having difficulty sleeping at night. Their insomnia is often intensified by vivid and sometimes frightening nightmares.

Tony has started to play video games late at night because he can't sleep. He's actually avoiding sleep. The nightmares and constant images that play over and over in his head make him seek distraction and the video games seem to help with that. The games have become his major activity since he's become a couch potato who no longer exercises during the day. Anything else he does just doesn't have the same thrill and excitement as the video games.

Tony and his wife Laura awoke one morning to find that the furniture had been moved to barricade the door to their bedroom. They both know that Tony must have moved it in his sleep because it is far too heavy for Laura to move; however, Tony had no memory of having done this.

REACTIONS THAT AFFECT YOUR BEHAVIOR

Many service members experience reactions after homecoming that interfere with their normal daily activities.

UNPLEASANT RECURRING MEMORIES FROM THE WAR

In addition to nightmares, repeated memories of war zone events may appear to you during waking hours. You may find that you're having unwanted memories of combat experiences that you'd rather forget. **Flashbacks**, or memories that are so realistic you feel like you're back in the war, can occur following exposure to a situation that reminds you of something that happened during deployment. This may cause you to avoid certain people and places because you don't want to be reminded again. These thoughts and memories can make you feel like you need to be constantly on the alert or on guard and can also make you feel jumpy and easy to startle.

Alex is still operating in high gear even though he's been home for almost two months. He recently started taking a class again at his college. He finds that he's having a terrible time concentrating on his coursework. He's still constantly checking his back and unable to focus. The other day, while sitting in a classroom, someone suddenly shut the door with a very loud slam. Next thing Alex knew, he was hitting the deck. He went face down on the classroom floor, taking a classmate down with him. Needless to say, he was quite embarrassed by this incident, especially because his behavior was dictated by automatic reflexes. Even though in his head he knew that he was safe from attack, Alex couldn't stop such automatic jumpy reactions to sudden noises such as slamming doors or people banging their books down on their desks. His combat training just took charge and his reflexes made him react as if it were another blast.

Alex has also changed from a laid-back, easygoing person to someone who gets upset easily and overreacts to minor situations. His brother Sam noticed that Alex yells at his niece and nephew when they get a little rowdy or, sometimes, even when they exhibit normal childish behavior. Alex seems to blow everything out of proportion and acts irrationally. Finding the gun in Alex's bedroom at their mother's house was the last straw. Sam won't let his children spend as much time as they had with their uncle. Alex says nothing, but he's deeply hurt by this since he had been like a second father with unlimited access to the children before his deployment.

DIFFICULTY CONCENTRATING

You may find it difficult to concentrate or remember important information. This can really interfere with your ability to function intellectually at work or school. Simple things may draw your attention and sometimes even feel overwhelming, such as having too many choices in the grocery store. If you're returning to your civilian job, you may be bored by the lack of stimulation your old job now provides you. Handling regular daily activities may seem pointless after what you have been through. Be sure to add responsibilities, activities, and so forth back into your life slowly.

Tony is having a terrible time getting back into his regular job selling cars. He's bored by the prospect of standing around all day, bartering with people in order to try to sell automobiles. He doesn't feel like talking to these people and listening to their minor problems; it all seems so mundane and unimportant. He misses the adrenaline rush and sense of importance that he felt every day while he was deployed.

SUBSTANCE ABUSE

It can be easy to allow the overuse or misuse of alcohol, tobacco, street drugs, or prescribed medications to become your strategy for dealing with some of these common post-deployment responses to war zone stress. You may find that you're drinking more or drinking to stop thinking or feeling. Or you may use alcohol to slow down or to sleep. It's tricky because at first the alcohol will seem to reduce some of these common reactions to trauma, especially by blotting out disturbing feelings. But, as you know, in the long run, alcohol use can easily get out of hand and be extremely harmful. Drinking reduces your ability to maintain close relationships and makes others feel you don't care. At first it may seem to relax you, but it will begin to increase your anxiety, feelings of depression, and mood swings. Drinking impairs your ability to think straight and perform tasks such as driving. Excessive drinking can also cause other health problems, such as damage to the liver, heart, and even the brain. It's associated with obesity, sexual problems, and muscle disease. We discuss substance abuse further in Chapter 12.

Like Alex, Kathleen too is constantly on alert and finds that she scans the roofs of buildings as she walks through the streets. Her heart is constantly pounding and she only seems to calm down when she has a glass of wine, or is hiding off by herself. She doesn't want to see people at work. She's getting headaches all of the time, especially when her thoughts turn to her tour of duty. When she has a drink, the thoughts subside, but the headaches continue. She hates that she can't stop her mind from returning to many of the horrible scenes she witnessed; scenes of death and destruction. She just wants to forget it all.

EMOTIONAL REACTIONS

You will likely experience a range of emotions following your time in the war zone, such as anger, sadness, grief, and guilt, among others.

GRIEF

Grief is a normal part of losing someone you care about or even losing someone you don't personally know. It can be very painful to learn that one of your brothers- or sisters-in-arms, a member of your large military family, was killed. With the number of deaths among U.S. service members reaching well over 3,800, most units have suffered casualties and many troops have lost someone with whom they had bonded. However, losing a buddy to a bullet, IED, or suicide bomb may result in **traumatic grief,** which differs considerably from "normal" grief. When you experience traumatic grief you may be preoccupied with thoughts of the person who died, may feel anger, resentment, or bitterness related to the death, or may experience a state of shock, walking around emotionally numb or dazed. For an in-depth discussion of the nature of grief and how to handle it, turn to Chapter 8.

SADNESS AND GUILT

Sadness is also common. The loss of a buddy, missing family at home, empathy for victims of horrible living conditions—all of these things can lead to deep feelings of sadness. However, feeling down or sad more days than not and being unable to enjoy any of the things you normally like to do may be a sign of depression, which we discuss in more detail in Chapter 12. Many returning service members also feel (often irrationally) guilty that some of the things they did or didn't do during their deployment may have led to deaths or harm to others. We address guilt in more depth in Chapter 7.

FEELINGS OF ABANDONMENT

Once you return home, you may find you feel abandoned, or even rejected and unaccepted, and believe that no one understands what you've been through. This can happen because you feel out of place because your experiences have changed how you perceive things. You may feel that you can't relate to anyone at home and that they are not relating to you. It may seem like everyone you know is just going on with their lives without you. This may make you doubt yourself or mistrust others. It may lead you to avoid social situations. Having support from your family and friends is the best thing you can do to prevent problems from becoming worse, so it's extremely important that you try to continue to keep yourself connected to others. We discuss helping you reconnect with loved ones in Chapter 9.

FEELING FEARFUL OR HOPELESS ABOUT THE FUTURE

After you return from the war zone, you may find yourself acting nervous or feeling fearful, helpless, or hopeless about the future. Being overly cautious can feed this nervousness and fear. You may find you're overly cautious at home because you were used to being on guard all of the time while you were deployed, watching for any potential sign of danger.

It's normal to feel somewhat discouraged about life following your return. These feelings should pass with time, as you grow accustomed to being home again. However, if these feelings or thoughts become intolerable or so severe that you wonder whether life is worth living, please seek assistance. A suicide hotline is available twenty-four hours a day: 800-273-TALK (8255). Press 1 to access veteran-specific information.

FEELING ANGRY OR AGGRESSIVE

Anger is very common following deployment to war. Feelings of helplessness or lack of control can lead to anger. Such feelings may also make you edgy and irritable around other people. You may find that you've become short-tempered, easily annoyed or upset, and withdrawn. We cover anger and aggression and offer coping advice in Chapter 6.

FEELING NUMB

You may find that you feel numb inside instead of angry, sad, or disconnected—too numb to experience any emotions. Such emotional numbing is usually a psychological reaction our minds use to block out intense and unbearable negative feelings of anxiety, grief, or despair. The problem with this reaction is that you can't block out negative feelings without also becoming numb to love, joy, and compassion. Many people describe this state of numbness as feeling dead inside.

In order to deal with this numbness, try to schedule fun activities to ensure that you participate in pleasurable and enjoyable experiences. Remind your loved ones that you love them. Try to keep active instead of hiding away from all emotions.

> Tony's emotions are a wild roller coaster. He firmly believes that no one at home has any idea how to relate to him after all he's been through. He's decided to avoid all social gatherings, but now finds that this just adds to his feelings of rejection and isolation. He often feels sad and alone but also angry at the entire world, occasionally flying into a rage and destroying things in his path. At other times, he feels nothing. He does not blame anyone for not wanting to be around him, since he believes that they wouldn't want to spend any time with someone who is responsible for his own friend's death and who frightens his own children. Laura and the boys watch helplessly as this unfolds. Despite their concern, Tony's rejection of their attempts to provide emotional support has caused frustration on their parts and widened the distance between him and the rest of the family.

REACTIONS THAT AFFECT RELATIONSHIPS

Post-deployment emotional stress reactions can create serious problems within your relationships as well. They can affect how you relate to and interact with your partner, children, parents, and friends. They can cause trouble and conflict on the job and can interfere with your ability to handle money and deal with finances. Strong emotional reactions such as anger, irritability, and avoidance as well as more subtle reactions like withdrawal, detachment, and feelings of disconnectedness can make you hard to be around. Here are some other common reactions that can have an affect on your relationships.

MISTRUST AND COMMUNICATION PROBLEMS

Some service members find that once they return home, they develop a lack of trust in others. During your deployment you became accustomed to trusting only those closest to you, in your unit. It can be difficult to switch gears and begin to confide in your family and friends again. Naturally, this lack of trust in those at home can sometimes trigger interpersonal conflicts. You may have a tendency to continue to be secretive and provide information to your family and friends only on a "need to know" basis. Even if you do trust your partner, parents, or friends, you still may fail to communicate and share enough with them because of these habits. Being at war and away from people you love may create some distance between you that can be hard to understand and overcome. Your relationships may suffer as a result. In a marriage, especially a young marriage, such a loss of intimacy can be very damaging and difficult to restore later on.

Make reconnecting with your loved ones a top priority—we suggest scheduling individual time with each of your family members (and friends). As we said earlier, remind those you love that you care. Talk to buddies if that seems to help, but at the same time don't let your war buddies come between you and your family and other friends. You must maintain good communication with your loved ones in order to reinforce your bond and successfully get through reintegration.

Communicating about your experiences at war can be a tricky thing. Some troops want to talk about everything that happened during their deployment, while many don't want to talk at all because they feel that no one can understand what it was like unless they've been there. If you do want to talk, keep in mind that your family and friends may find it difficult to listen to some of the graphic details of your deployment experiences. This doesn't mean that they have no interest in what you've been through; war and the carnage it involves is simply upsetting for some people to hear about, and it can be even harder when they envision you, someone they love, in harm's way. Try not to take it personally if someone in your family or a friend reacts this way. Don't clam up and decide to keep everything to yourself. This will only make you feel more isolated and misunderstood. Try sitting down with each of your loved ones and setting some ground rules about what can be discussed and under what circumstances. This way, you don't have to worry about upsetting anyone and can avoid misinterpreting silences as a lack of love, interest, or support. Such ground rules can be reassuring for everyone.

Ever since he returned to his neighborhood, Tony could tell no one under-stands what he's been through, especially those at work. His coworkers be-come silent whenever he enters the room. He's had almost no successful sales since his return and has had two blowouts with his boss, who doesn't appear to be cutting him any slack. Tony hasn't gone back to church and refuses to go to the boys' baseball games because he constantly gets into arguments with their coaches or the umpires. He avoids his friends, never returning their calls. Tony is devastated about the growing distance that continues to develop between him and Laura. While he was deployed they communicated frequently by cell phone or through email, but now that he is home they seem to have nothing to say. Tony senses that his boys are frustrated with him and Laura tells him that they sometimes find him to be frightening. Mary, their new baby girl, cries every time he holds her. Tony has started to think about requesting another deployment. At least life was simple and straightforward when he was over there . . .

Being Overcontrolling

Some service members can be overcontrolling when they get home and insist that everything be done their way. The time you've spent in the hierarchical structure of the military has accustomed you to a world without ambiguity, where the aims are clear and everyone knows what needs to be done. At home you may feel that no one else knows how to do the job properly or want people to leave "your stuff" alone. This need for control can make you overbearing with your family and overprotective of your children. In the war zone, you may have lived with constant fear about your inability to control your environment, which can make you feel like you need to protect those for whom you are responsible at home. This may be expressed in a number of ways, such as a persistent and unreasonable concern about your family's safety, or constantly telling the kids to be careful, or even frightening them by being overly cautious and overly alert for dangers that are not there. Needless to say, your partner and children have become accus-tomed to operating quite independently during your absence, and they may become very irritated or even rebellious about your unwanted and misguided protective attention.

Keep reminding yourself that you're not under the circumstances you were while at war and that every decision is not one of life or death. Also remember that your children are still learning and will not be perfect. We mentioned previously that learning some relaxation techniques can be helpful for sleeping problems—these same techniques can also help you become less controlling.

Isaac is finding that Kathleen seems less and less like the woman he fell in love with and wants to marry. She's often anxious and moody. She seems constantly depressed and avoidant, and they have experienced a loss of intimacy, both emotionally and physically. No matter what he tries to do to appease her, she reacts negatively, often with angry outbursts with no warning. When she first returned, despite their ups and downs, there were precious moments when it seemed like old times. They would have a quiet dinner, some nice wine, and recapture their pre-deployment closeness. Now Kathleen is drinking too much, which has made things very difficult, and precious moments are a thing of the past.

Her relationship with her mother has also deteriorated. Instead of being the one to reach out to her mom after an argument, as was the usual pattern before deployment, Kathleen withdraws, grabs a drink, and completely shuts her mother out. Even though he doesn't like her very much, Isaac has even begun to feel sorry for his future mother-in-law. For Isaac, these changes have become very worrisome. It's unlike Kathleen to distance herself so much from him and her family. He's beginning to worry that things may turn out badly.

GENERAL TIPS FOR COPING
WITH COMMON STRESS REACTIONS

Below we offer some general advice on how you can best cope with the typical reactions and symptoms you may experience after you return. Even if you're not having trouble with the return home, these suggestions can still be useful as you ease back into your civilian life.

Suggestions to help you cope:

- Remember that readjusting to civilian life takes time—don't be hard on yourself for experiencing some problems along the way.

- Take your time adding responsibilities and activities back into your life.

A NOTE OF CAUTION

Almost all service members returning from the war zone, as well as other individuals who have gone through a traumatic experience, will experience some of these behaviors and reactions. It's vital that you remember that having these reactions does *not* automatically mean you have PTSD. (You should also be aware that only a mental health care provider can diagnose PTSD.) **In other words, it would be abnormal if you *didn't* experience some of these feelings and behaviors following what you have been through in the war zone.**

- Try not to drive your car for a few weeks when you first arrive home. Give yourself time to readjust to the civilian world and how people drive in the United States again.
- Don't drink when feeling depressed or to avoid disturbing memories.
- Reconnect with your social supports. This may be the last thing you feel like doing, but do it anyway. Social support is critical to successful reintegration.
- Talk about your deployment experiences at a time and pace that feels right to you.
- Review Battlemind (see Chapter 4) to understand where some of these automatic behaviors come from.
- Remind your loved ones that you love them.
- You need to talk about the experiences you had during deployment—if you can't talk to family or friends, be sure to talk to a chaplain or counselor.

How Family Members Can Help

Family members can help by learning how to identify common stress reactions: the normal emotional and behavioral responses that can occur following your loved one's return from deployment. Remember that reintegration takes time and patience. However, when your time and patience have been exhausted, you may need to consider some type of intervention with your loved one. (See Red Flags on page 81 for more information.) Taking appropriate action can help you deal with current conflicts and can also prevent more severe problems in the future. Below is a list of things family members can do to help your returning service members ease back into civilian life, as well as some things you should avoid doing.

What you can do:

- Provide opportunities for your returning service member to talk about war experiences.
- Don't be afraid to ask about the war or how your loved one is doing.
- Show that you are on his or her side by offering attention, interest, and care.
- Accept your own limitations—understand what you can and cannot do.
- Educate yourself about common reactions and issues that typically follow deployment.
- Find out about available resources and services that you or your service member can use if necessary.
- Be supportive with the expectation that your loved one will fully readjust to civilian life eventually.
- Be patient.
- Take time during this transition—make adjustments slowly.
- Involve your service member in daily family activities, but do so at a pace that he or she can accept.

What you shouldn't do:

- Do not force or pressure your loved one to talk.
- Do not stop him or her from talking.
- Try not to make judgmental statements (e.g., don't say things like "what you had to do is so awful!").
- Avoid telling your service member what he or she "should" do.
- Do not tell your service member that he or she will be okay or is lucky it was not worse.
- Watch for clichés or easy answers (e.g., try not to say things like "war is hell").
- Avoid giving your loved one advice without listening thoroughly.
- Don't rush things. It takes time to become reacquainted and comfortable with one another again.

RED FLAGS

If you continue to experience the reactions described in this chapter more often than not for longer than six to eight weeks after you return home, or if they begin to interfere with your personal life or work to the extent that you can't function effectively, we recommend that you seek outside assistance. Persistent reactions, if left untreated, can turn into more serious conditions such as posttraumatic stress disorder, depression, or other mental health problems. Resolving problems early can help fix or prevent relationship issues and other more persistent and chronic problems from wreaking havoc on your life. The key is to recognize when you need help. We go into further detail about these more serious behavioral and mental health problems in Chapters 11 and 12.

In addition to persistent reactions or symptoms that don't begin to resolve within six to eight weeks, you should seek help from a qualified mental health care professional if any of the following are present (see the Resources on Counseling/Therapy for information on where to turn for help):

- Substance abuse (alcohol, nicotine, illegal drugs, or prescribed medications)
- Significant changes in mood or behavior
- Suicidal thoughts, gestures, or comments
- Threats of harm to self or others
- Arrest/incarceration
- Assaults/domestic violence

The rest of this book focuses on specific issues that you may encounter after deployment, such as anger and aggression, trouble reconnecting with loved ones, guilt, the mental and emotional impact of dealing with severe injury, and PTSD. Each chapter describes how and why these reactions might express themselves and provides some specific examples. We then show how such behaviors may affect you and your family. Finally, we offer suggestions for coping with these issues and discuss when you should seek professional help.

Remember that the post-deployment stage of the emotional cycle of deployment can take up to a year or more to work through. Knowing what to expect and for how long will be a big help as you work to successfully reintegrate into your civilian life.

6

ANGER AND THE
ADRENALINE TRAIN

Anger is one of the most common problems that troops encounter after a military deployment to a war zone. In fact, many officials in the Vermont Army National Guard have told us that anger was the most frequent reaction that they saw among troops returning home from war in Iraq, Afghanistan, and the surrounding countries. This emotion, which stems from the high level of arousal and aggression you need for survival during war, can make reestablishing your connection with your family and friends a difficult challenge. If you find that you're getting into arguments and fights with family members and others, often for little or no reason, then post-deployment anger is likely the culprit.

WHY DO I FEEL THIS WAY?

As the Battlemind program points out (see Chapter 4 for a refresher), mindsets that are necessary for survival in the war zone can cause problems in your civilian life if you continue to use them once you've returned home. Anger, or aggression, is one of those mindsets. In preparation for war, service members are taught that it's necessary to be aggressive. Anger is a motivating and adaptive emotion in many circumstances—particularly in a war zone situation—and helps troops survive. It mobilizes you and can help you to persist and overcome obstacles. It also acts as an emotional release; it can be a relief to blow off steam and express anger. Following are some of the reasons why you may be feeling anger.

ANGER IS EASY

There are lots of reasons you may feel angry after you've returned home. First, anger is usually easy to tap into (and therefore accessible at a moment's notice) and is often used to mask underlying feelings that are much more difficult to deal with, such as sadness, depression, or guilt. Post-deployment anger can also stem from discouragement or frustration you may have felt during your deployment and now during reintegration.

ANGER AT OTHERS WHO DON'T DO WHAT THEY'RE SUPPOSED TO DO

Following the rules is critical on the front, and you may become angry if others around you aren't "following the rules" or doing what they're supposed to do at home. This may even start during your deployment. While at war, problems become amplified. This means that any faults you may find in your fellow comrades or superiors prior to deployment become more obvious during critical situations; just at the moments when you believe the person needs to perform better. You may believe that others are not carrying out their jobs the way that they should. This same anger about others not following the rules or meeting expectations can manifest itself with your family or with people in the community; for example, you may get very angry over illegal traffic maneuvers or getting cut in front of in line. Because you're feeling that others aren't doing what they're supposed to be doing, you may try to take over and wind up becoming overcontrolling. Overcontrolling behavior can create problems in your relationships. For example, you might find you're constantly telling your partner that he or she can't do anything right. Or you might get irritated over the slightest mistake someone innocently makes. This behavior, obviously, can cause serious problems with your children. We discuss this in more detail in Chapter 9.

Another reason you might easily become angry with others is because anger can easily be displaced onto the wrong person or into the wrong situation. Make sure to understand where your anger is coming from and that you're not taking it out on the wrong person. Also be careful to not overgeneralize. When people get angry, their anger often spreads to other situations and people without their awareness.

Anger Stemming from Trust Issues or Feelings of Betrayal

The anger you're feeling may be related to issues of trust and betrayal. When service members come home from war, they often realize that they're exasperated with the way life works, with government and military systems, furious about being dragged into a war when war was unexpected, or angry with God. Thinking about what happened in the war zone, such as lapses in leadership, promised support never turning up, needless combatant or civilian casualties, or preventable deaths can also lead to anger. You might find yourself thinking things like "I can't trust anyone" or "after all I have been through, I deserve better than this." Some of these angry feelings are justifiable and understandable. You should acknowledge your anger, but you also need to keep it in check. Many ways of expressing anger will *not* get you what you want, and they may in fact hurt your relationships. Try to deal with the situation or circumstances that anger you by doing something constructive, like voting or other types of community action.

Anger in Response to Being Victimized

Anger is a normal response to being victimized and also can be directed toward a perpetrator of violence. It goes almost without saying that service members feel rage and anger toward the enemy who's trying to kill them. In addition to IEDs, landmines, gunfire, and other explosions, during war some troops may find themselves the victim of other types of violence, such as being kidnapped or tortured. This can lead to more direct anger toward an individual or particular group. **Military sexual trauma (MST)** also occurs for both men and women in the military and commonly leads to anger. (See box on military sexual trauma in this chapter for further information.) Often times, victims of violent interpersonal assaults such as this are not even aware that they're angry. Anger stemming from interpersonal violence can last for long periods of time after the offense takes place. Victims often mistakenly blame themselves for such violence, which can also be expressed as anger.

> *Tony feels like everything is his fault; the lack of communication in his family, his comrade's death, his frightened children, his declining relationship with his wife, Laura. He is constantly numb and depressed, or frustrated and furious. He's irritated with his friends and neighbors who no longer come to visit. But at the same time, he thinks, "Who can blame them for not wanting to be around when I am such a 'joy' to be with right now." Tony is angry and bitter at his own behavior and his inability to control his destructive outbursts.*

ANGER OVER FEELINGS OF FEAR OR LOSS OF CONTROL

Your anger and irritability may be associated with the fear or loss of control you felt at times during your deployment. In times of extreme stress, terror, or life threat, such fear may be expressed as fight, flight, or freeze responses. Anger can motivate you, protect your feelings of self-esteem, or make you feel in control. You may feel angry from discouragement or frustration over leaving a job unfinished, such as leaving when the war is not finished, or at the injustices of the world that you can do little or nothing about. Watch to make sure that your anger matches the situation that made you angry. Think of alternative actions that you can take before getting angry. Even simple strategies, such as counting to twenty, can help you avoid an angry outburst. Simple things such as this can help you to avoid acting impulsively. You may also be angry that you're unable to control your anger now that you're home. This is often a sign that you need to get some outside assistance from a counselor or therapist.

ANGER CAUSED BY PHYSICAL TENSENESS

Someone who is physically tense tends to be angry as well. The hypervigilance and constant states of alertness required during deployment can add to this tension and make you more likely to be short-tempered and easily upset or annoyed by small things. Lack of sleep can add to this mix, magnifying the emotional states that already exist, and reducing your mental capacity to handle things in a more appropriate manner. This physical tension, which may begin during deployment, often carries over when you return home. This is one of the reasons that some down time is needed after you spend time in the harsh and taxing environment of the war zone.

WAYS IN WHICH ANGER AND AGGRESSION ARE EXPRESSED

Although anger is a natural emotion, it can be expressed in both healthy and unhealthy ways. When anger and aggression follow you home from the war, they can manifest themselves unexpectedly in various situations. You may find that you're impatient and easily frustrated. A typical example is overreacting with anger to a slight provocation that you previously would have shrugged off without difficulty.

> *Kathleen is completely pissed off at the entire military system. She hates that so many have suffered, hates that her unit could not do more and was not properly trained in some of the normal customs of the culture that would have made life so much easier, and hates the headaches she is always having and how she feels every day now that she's home. To complicate things even further, right before Kathleen returned home, MAJ McNamara, a good friend of hers, confided that she had been sexually assaulted by someone in her unit. Hearing this reactivated all of Kathleen's previously suppressed rage and shame regarding her own sexual harassment during her previous deployment, feelings that she's worked so hard to put behind her.*

Kathleen realizes she's been short with Isaac, but doesn't really appreciate how difficult it's been for him to deal with her daily bursts of anger and testy overreactions to the slightest annoyance. This has created a widening emotional gulf between them because he constantly worries that anything he does will set her off. Her anger has also affected her relationship with her mother. In fact, her mother now finds Kathleen so intimidating that she's stopped trying to control her daughter's life. On the one hand, this is a positive benefit since Kathleen now enjoys an independence from her parents that she never had before. On the other hand, her intense irritability has really poisoned the atmosphere as far as her family relationships are concerned.

Angry reactions can be empowering. They can give you a feeling of control because others will give in to your demands rather than risk a fight. Kathleen's changed relationship with her mother illustrates this point. Although your anger may be energizing, feel justified, and make others yield to your demands, there's a price to pay for these apparent benefits. Your anger will create distance between you and your loved ones. In addition, it often masks deeper problems, such as Kathleen's unresolved rage and shame about her sexual harassment.

THE ADRENALINE TRAIN

Alex feels a constant need for action. Although his missing limb limits his freedom of movement to a certain degree, he feels wired all the time. He remains up late every night, continually playing fast-paced video games. He also has trouble sitting still during class. Alex keeps all of this to himself, hardly speaking to his mother, brother, or other family members about his constant state of high arousal. This silence is in sharp contrast to his behavior before deployment, when he was outgoing, fun loving, and talked a mile a minute. He misses the high-speed pace of the days he spent overseas.

You may return from deployment and find yourself riding on the "adrenaline train"—talking 100 miles per minute, hyperactive, and wholeheartedly wired. The high levels of intensity in combat can produce this effect. Arousal levels are elevated and expressed through fast-paced behaviors. It's common for service members who experience war zone trauma to seek out situations that are high paced, perhaps dangerous, and that make them

Military Sexual Trauma

Military sexual trauma is unfortunately a common occurrence and happens during times of peace as well as during war. MST includes sexual harassment (pressure for sexual favors, being put down because of your gender, sexual overtures when you've made clear this is not welcome, or sexual comments or gestures about your body or lifestyle) and sexual assault (grabbing or touching, intercourse, or other penetration).

The VA defines military sexual trauma as sexual harassment that is threatening or physical assault of a sexual nature. MST happens to men as well as to women. In fact, half of veterans with MST are men. This is because although MST affects women much more frequently than men, there are so many more men in uniform than women that the number of individuals affected is about the same. MST is a very private affair in which you may feel completely isolated, full of shame, and utterly powerless to expose or punish the perpetrator. You may feel that no one can help. MST is further complicated because the perpetrator works or lives close to you, may be a member of your unit, or may be a commanding officer who has power over your career, promotion, or needs. The strong bonds that form in military units can make matters worse by making you feel that you need to keep quiet so that you don't jeopardize your unit coheison. Many victims of MST report that they had to choose between giving up their military career and accepting the daily shame and humiliation of continuing to work side-by-side with the person who assaulted him or her. Many choose to "suck it up," to keep the MST a secret, and try to continue to perform their duties as if nothing had happened.

Although there's no set reaction to this type of trauma, many victims struggle with anger after the incident or assault. You may experience feelings of fear, shame, distrust, embarrassment, guilt, or sadness. Some service members have no reaction for months or years while others react right away. MST can also cause other problems to occur, such as sexual dysfunction, troubles with intimate relationships, and difficulties with trust. Although anger is a natural reaction to trauma, remaining intensely angry over a long period of time can interfere with recovery. MST can lead to PTSD, depression, and alcohol or drug abuse. (See Chapters 11 and 12.)

If you've experienced a military sexual trauma, it's important that you get help to deal with it. If you are an Active Duty and believe you have been sexually assaulted, contact the Sexual Assault Response Coordinator (SARC) in your unit to make a confidential report (or an unrestricted report). You can also call Military OneSource at 1-800-342-9647, and every VA hospital and Vet Center has trained MST counselors. Counseling can help you learn effective coping skills and enable you to address the fear, anger, and self blame that may be hindering your recovery. For help totally outside the military system contact the Rape, Abuse & Incest National Network at 1-800-656-HOPE.

stay alert to match their aroused state, such as buying a new motorcycle, playing violent video games, or skydiving. Though Alex is not talking much, his hyperactivity clearly means he's on the adrenaline train and may be covering up some of his feelings of sadness about the loss of his leg.

> *Tony's wife, Laura, cringes as she hears him crashing around in the garage, wildly throwing things around in a fit of rage. Laura is relieved that the car isn't in the garage so he will not smash the windshield again. Although uncharacteristically withdrawn and quiet around the family or others, his personality sometimes completely changes when he's alone. He gives in easily to minor frustrations, often exploding with rage and becoming violently destructive. Laura has tried to take it all in stride. After all, Tony hasn't taken out his aggression on her or the children. Of course, it's a different story when he's behind the wheel of the car.*

AGGRESSIVE DRIVING

Aggressive driving is another common expression of anger often experienced by returning troops. Defensive driving went out the window once you entered the battlefield. It was replaced with all-out aggressive driving, full speed ahead where everyone else is supposed to move out of the way and let you pass. This is necessary on the battleground, but back at home, it's dangerous.

Tony now floors the accelerator and takes off straight out of the driveway without looking right or left to see whether another vehicle is coming. On the road he's always tailgating and speeding. It's gotten to the point that Laura tries to avoid driving with him. They've had several fights about how he drives when picking the boys up from school.

For the first few weeks after you return from deployment, it would be wise to allow someone else to take the wheel when you need to drive somewhere. Once you begin to feel more at home with the pace of life back in the United States, then you can start driving again. This is particularly true if you're feeling edgy or upset. It's a good idea to discuss the issue of driving before you leave for deployment. We suggest you make an agreement that for at least one month following your return, a family member will be responsible for the driving.

ANGER AT NORMAL CHILD BEHAVIOR

Tony has become both angry and impatient with the boys. He seems to always be irritated with them and no longer joins them in rough-housing games. The boys miss the fun-loving father they once knew. They have also started to resent their dad's strong objections to playful activities that they all previously and frequently enjoyed. During his deployment, the boys had been allowed to play rambunctiously. Tony now objects to these games because he's worried that they're not safe. His overriding emotional preoccupation about his children's safety has made him unaware that he has become overprotective to a fault. Needless to say, the boys are very unhappy with this turn of events. When they complain about his meddlesome intrusion into their activities, Tony becomes enraged and punitive. As a result, they have started to play in secret and avoid him whenever possible. The boys are aware of their father's violent outbursts that usually occur in the garage, and now they're frightened of him.

Some service members have angry reactions to normal child behaviors. These types of reactions may represent both post-deployment anger management problems as well as exaggerated fears about possible dangers to which your children might be exposed. During war you experienced constant threat, but now you're home where this threat no longer exists. Of course, it's always important to be concerned about the safety of your kids, but such worries need to fit the realities of the situation at home. It's important to realize that the habits that helped you survive in war have no place in your civilian life where the environment is completely different. (See Chapter 9 on reconnecting for more information on understanding children's reactions to help you deal with them.)

EFFECTS OF ANGER
ON FAMILY AND YOUR LIFE

Intense feelings of anger and aggressive behavior can cause marital, relationship, and family problems and jeopardize friendships. We've provided a number of examples to show how relationships can suffer because of angry and aggressive feelings, behaviors, and beliefs. Isaac finds that he's distancing himself from Kathleen. Tony's kids are becoming afraid of him, and he and his wife are constantly fighting about one thing or another. And Alex and his mother never talk.

Angry feelings keep people away. They also prevent you from having positive connections with loved ones and others. This is neither what you want nor what you need right now. Because social supports are so crucial to successful reintegration, you must work to foster your relationships, not destroy them. At the same time, stifling your anger and aggression can actually make things worse over time. The key is to recognize your anger and deal with it appropriately.

You're not the only one who may be dealing with angry feelings— your family may also be angry with you. They may be angry because you were deployed in the first place, especially if you signed up or volunteered for an additional tour of duty against their wishes. They may be angry with you for leaving them alone with their worries about your safety or angry at the government for going to war in the first place. They may resent the fact that they had to shoulder all of the responsibilities at home while you were off on a military adventure with your buddies.

Aggressive behaviors can also affect your relationships at work by impairing your ability to resolve even minor conflicts. As we mentioned previously, even the most minor mistake may set you off. Anger can also cause problems with concentration and can lower your frustration level, which in turn makes you short-tempered with coworkers, family, and friends. These things can also make you less effective and impair your job performance and relationships.

Uncontrolled anger reduces your ability to think clearly and to make good decisions. It allows minor conflicts to be magnified into large problems. It affects the relationships you have and prevents you from starting new relationships. Unfortunately, anger can be a stubborn issue to overcome. There may be a part of you that doesn't want to give up this anger because, sometimes, it helps you get the results you want. Being angry can keep people away whom you don't want to deal with. It can make you feel in control by getting others to do or not do things, and help you get your own way. In fact, you may resist getting a grip on your anger because you recognize that your intimidation of others, more often than not, has kept you in control. Once you appreciate how damaging your uncontrolled anger has become, however, you will recognize that appropriate anger management will make you more—not less—powerful and effective.

COPING WITH ANGRY
AND AGGRESSIVE FEELINGS

Instead of trying to handle your anger after it has already occurred, it's better to learn coping skills and problem-solving techniques that will prevent you from lashing out with uncontrollable anger. It's also helpful to remind yourself to roll with the punches and keep from getting frustrated too easily. People with a low tolerance for frustration tend to be more likely to lose their tempers. They quickly give up trying to control their responses when things don't instantly go their way. Here are some general strategies for coping with situations that can lead to angry and aggressive feelings:

- Recognize when you are angry. Since returning service members don't always realize how angry they are, learning to recognize when you are angry can go a long way toward alleviating it.

- Sometimes it's hard to know that you're angry. You may only recognize that this is happening when someone close to you finally points it out to you. Listen to others when they try to tell you that you're having issues with anger.
- Learn how to avoid getting angry in the first place. Learn ways to deal with irritation and frustration and how to keep someone from provoking you into aggressive behavior. Count to ten or twenty before reacting, walk away, and remember to think about the ultimate consequences of your responses.
- Pay attention and learn what cues or situations trigger your anger.
- Be aware of anniversary dates that might remind you of events that trigger your anger. For example, anticipate feeling angry on the anniversary of the day that your unit was bombed, or that you sustained a serious injury.
- Avoid drugs, alcohol, and other substances that make anger worse and impair both judgment and control.
- Try to prevent physical states that may make you more susceptible to aggression, such as hunger, fatigue, lack of sleep, or pain.
- Limit your exposure to unsafe or overarousing places or situations that may trigger your anger, such as noisy, crowded places or busy airports.
- Try to reduce the magnitude of your anger when it occurs by being honest with yourself about its actual intensity. This will allow you to take steps to reduce your level of arousal and anger.
- Learn about alternative ways to deal with anger, such as better communication skills to help you discuss angry feelings, or writing things down when you're angry.
- Discover some methods that will help you reduce your arousal level, such as relaxation methods, physical exercise, yoga, taking time-outs, or breathing exercises.
- Remind yourself of Battlemind principles (see Chapter 4 for a refresher on this topic) and how some of your angry or aggressive behaviors, while adaptive in the war zone, are not helpful now that you're home.

KNOWING WHEN YOU NEED MORE HELP

If your anger or aggressive behavior has escalated to the point where threatened or actual violence against your family or others has occurred, it's crucial that you seek professional help for your problem. Professional counselors, such as chaplains, or those who work in behavioral health, primary care, nursing, Vet Centers, or family assistance programs can help you address your anger and combat stress reactions. Anger or aggressive behavior that's out of control needs immediate attention. We urge that you not wait until things get completely out of control and something occurs that can't be fixed. See the Resources on page 241 for more information on where you can turn for help with your anger.

SUICIDE RISK

The risk of suicide is higher for veterans who are faced with feelings of aggression, anxiety, or agitation. These threats or behaviors need to be taken seriously and addressed. Call the Suicide Hotline at 800-273-TALK (8255) or go to your nearest emergency room if you feel you may hurt yourself. Also see section in Chapter 12 on violence and abuse.

7

GUILT AND MORAL DILEMMAS

As a service member, the act of war requires you to participate in situations and take actions that you never would under normal circumstances. Killing and destroying the enemy is an essential part of warfare; but to do so is contrary to many of the moral lessons we are taught throughout our lives. This dilemma can lead to feelings of guilt and regret that, if left unchecked, can interfere with your reintegration into civilian life.

WHY DO I FEEL THIS WAY?

Many troops who serve in a war zone will experience some form of remorse. You may feel guilt over things you did while at war, or over actions you didn't take. Almost all service members feel guilty about experiencing fear while in the war zone. It's important to remember that any strong emotional reactions you have during your time in the war zone, such as guilt or fear, are outside of your control. No veteran chooses to be afraid. It's not a matter of just controlling your emotions or rationalizing your way through a fearful situation. If it were, we could all avoid feeling guilt or fear in any situation.

Guilt results when people act against their moral values, doing things that are contrary to their beliefs. As a warrior, you're trained to follow commands. You must carry out orders even in situations in which negative consequences may occur. After the heat of battle has cooled down, you have time to reflect on split-second decisions you had to make about whether to attack a target or refrain from doing so. If things went wrong in some way, you may blame yourself for what did or did not happen. While this is a normal human tendency, this type of guilt isn't really based on the facts—it's usually biased in some way. Thus believing things like "I could have done this," or "I should have done that," is frequently based on erroneous memories of what actually took place. Guilty thoughts may convince you that you're responsible for a bad outcome that you really never could have prevented in the first place. You may think that some actions that you took were not reasonable or justifiable. You may think that you should have known what was going to happen before it actually did, also known as **hindsight bias**. People sometimes blame themselves for not being able to predict the future, especially when bad things happen. For example, a commander might blame himself when Soldiers in his unit are wounded, or a medic may feel guilty that he was unable to save his friend's life. While there's usually no logical basis for such guilt, it can be intense, relentless, and the cause of profound despair both during and after deployment.

Sometimes service members, in trying to make sense of their war experiences, take too much responsibility for bad things that happened, for what they did or didn't do, or for surviving when others didn't. This is also known as **survivor guilt**. Guilt and self blame are common for those who have been through difficult combat situations, as you try to assign meaning to what happened.

MORAL DILEMMAS

War can make people question their religious beliefs and practices. Since killing is contrary to all religious and moral beliefs, wartime experiences place many service members in a moral dilemma. Although troops may feel less conflicted about killing enemy combatants who fight for a cause that threatens our national security or way of life, witnessing the gruesome death and destruction of innocent bystanders, especially women and children, can raise agonizing spiritual and moral dilemmas. If you're in a critical situation and all options available to you are not good, the most moral and righteous thing you can do might still lead to a negative outcome, such as someone getting killed or having to leave a wounded civilian behind. However, just because the outcome was bad doesn't mean that your decision was bad. Your intentions were in the right place and you did the best you could.

Despite their good intentions, some troops feel that they've sinned or committed a moral or religious wrongdoing, even if they were following orders. This is why psychological, emotional, and spiritual reactions to combat are often mixed together and must be addressed thoroughly when it's safe to do so—not during the heat of battle, but soon thereafter, before your thoughts and imagination have had time to run away with themselves and make things worse. It's also one of the main reasons why military chaplains are embedded in each combat unit. They're uniquely qualified to confront such issues and help you through them. (See box on page 102 for more on military chaplains.)

HOW GUILT IS EXPRESSED

Tony is burdened with guilt over the death of his close comrade. He has become consumed by memories of his friend's death as well as thoughts about "what if. . .". Although he carried out his combat assignment flawlessly, he still has the nagging belief that he should have acted differently and feels completely to blame for his buddy's death. He constantly has nightmares about the situation and wishes he could live it all over again so things could turn out differently.

Many troops mistakenly believe that they could have prevented a death or injury to others, either because of what they did do or what they didn't do. As we mentioned earlier, such thoughts usually reflect unrealistic hindsight bias, but the resulting guilt can be overpowering, inescapable, and sometimes incapacitating.

Alex recalls a story about what happened to a Marine who was guarding a roadblock outside their base. A car approached and the guard signaled for the car to stop. When the car continued to move forward, the young Marine shot his firearm into the ground as a second warning. The car still kept on coming. Protecting his post against VBIEDs and following protocol, the guard then shot directly into the vehicle and was soon able to stop its approach. As he and his fellow Marines inspected the now-halted vehicle, he discovered, to his dismay, that he had shot a woman in the passenger seat. Her husband, the driver, was hysterical, sobbing, and unarmed. Not only had the Marine killed an innocent woman, but one who was in labor and on her way to the hospital to give birth. This discovery was so devastating and his guilt was so enormous that the young Marine had to be hospitalized and put on suicide watch.

At the actual time that a war trauma occurs, you're usually in a crisis situation with little time to think things through thoroughly in order to make decisions. The moment is also often emotionally overwhelming. It's only after the trauma has occurred that you have time to consider what happened, to think about all possible outcomes and to rehash the series of decisions and events that took place. It's true that decisions you made under duress and pressure might have been different had you had enough time to carefully consider all options, but this is a luxury you didn't have.

Sometimes you're more upset about what you *did* do, rather than what you didn't. Even good decisions can—and sometimes do—turn out badly. You may also tend to think of the good things that might have happened had you acted differently, thereby forgetting about the bad things that were also possible had you made that choice. If you don't act quickly in a crisis situation, you may face even more risks. Conversely, it's human nature to focus primarily on the one negative outcome that did occur and overlook all the good outcomes that happened most of the time.

Your guilt may cause you to believe that you're responsible for what happened. You may put yourself down because you feel you should be or want to be punished. At home, this type of guilt can lead you to avoid social interactions. It can cause you to withdraw from your family and friends and even become depressed. Some troops turn to drugs or alcohol in an effort to avoid their guilty feelings. They may obsess over what happened or have nightmares about the incident. Guilt can be debilitating. It can paralyze you and make you unable to take action for fear that you'll "screw up" again.

IMPACT ON FAMILY AND RELATIONSHIPS

Your family will want to help you relieve your guilt. They want you to understand that you're not responsible and help you work through things or to forgive yourself for things that happened that are hard to live with. However, guilt is very hard for family and nonmilitary friends to help you overcome. You may not want to talk about things that you experienced during your deployment because you don't want to have to remember them yourself. Or perhaps you don't want your family to know about some of the things you had to do, or the atrocities you have seen. You may think that your family and friends can never fully understand what happened during combat because they weren't there. Whatever the reasons, many troops avoid talking to family and friends about the guilt they feel. In turn, these feelings of guilt can be very damaging to your important relationships. Not only do you feel guilty and want to isolate yourself as a form of self-punishment, your inability to discuss these feelings with your loved ones makes them feel shut out. Their reaction to being shut out often leads to less communication on their part as well. It's a vicious cycle that only creates further withdrawal and isolation. Sometimes those whom we're closest to can't help us to understand and make sense of things we've done in our lives. If you feel this is the case for you, you will likely benefit greatly from an outsider's perspective. It may be best for you to talk things through with a chaplain, counselor, therapist, or comrade you can rely on. It's very important that you work through your guilt over what has happened and try to make sense of it.

RELIGIOUS IMPLICATIONS

It's often said that "faith is found or lost in a foxhole." In times of war, some troops turn to religion for strength, while others begin to feel doubts and question how a loving God can allow the terrors and atrocities that they are witnessing to happen. Spirituality is examined, and beliefs are questioned about purpose and meaning in life. Whereas this focus on spirituality that occurs during and after war can lead to deeper spiritual faith, it can also foster rage, disbelief, and alienation. Since people turn to religion for explanations about why things occur, when things happen that can't be explained by your beliefs or religion, it can lead to feelings of turmoil and a profound sense of disillusionment. In other words, war is often experienced as a challenge to your beliefs, which may either drive you away from your religion or strengthen your faith.

The anger, disillusionment, and questioning can be consuming and detrimental to your performance during war. If your feelings cause you to turn away from your religious beliefs, you may lose the comfort and sense of belonging you've relied on in the past. These thoughts and feelings of doubt may continue to affect you after you return home. If you're struggling with questions about your faith, we advise you to seek help from a military chaplain. Chaplains are extremely experienced in dealing with the issues we mentioned above and know firsthand how time in the war zone can affect you.

Those who have strong beliefs and those whose religious beliefs are strengthened during war usually find that faith helps them through their hardest times and provides them with the strength to make it back home safely. It offers a way to cope with stress, and provides many with a way to bridge gaps in their understanding of the world. Participating in worship services can provide social support, which is clearly beneficial. This is true while you are deployed as well as after you return home.

Military chaplains are one of the best resources available to you and your family in times of need. They're available both during deployment and after you've returned home. Chaplains are extremely well trained and quite familiar with the kind of guilt you may experience. Most military chaplains have been through deployments side by side with the troops. They understand the issues you're facing. They're also well-informed about other sources of support that you may find beneficial, such as peer support meetings, family programs, marital enrichment classes, counselors, psychologists, and so forth. Furthermore, chaplains are uniquely positioned within the military because everything you tell them is completely confidential. The only other place where you can seek assistance that offers complete confidentiality is the local Vet Center (with the exception of the responsibility to report abuse). There are over 230 Vet Centers, which are located in every state in the country (www1 .va.gov/directory/guide/vetcenter.asp?isFlash=0).

MILITARY CHAPLAINS NEED SUPPORT, TOO

The job of a military chaplain is very demanding. Chaplains are trained in a wide variety of religious practices. Because discussions with chaplains are confidential, they are often the first to hear about issues service members are struggling with, no matter if it's a religious struggle, moral issue, interpersonal conflict, or emotional problem.

Chaplains are unarmed, yet they go with the troops into every imaginable situation in the field. They usually have an armed support that accompanies them wherever they go. There are too few chaplains available, often only one for every thousand troops in the field. They are committed and resourceful service members who know the importance of their role.

Because they hear so many problems and difficulties, chaplains need to ensure that they too are getting the emotional support that they themselves need to remain strong. A recent 2006 military study reports that 27 percent of chaplains surveyed said that they were experiencing high or very high levels of burnout. In other words, they are human too and need to attend to their own emotional needs, seek social support, and not let themselves be overwhelmed by their workload. Effective chaplains know that they must take good care of themselves if they're going to be able to help others.

COPING WITH AND OVERCOMING GUILT

We all experience errors in thinking. Understanding this can help you work through your guilt. The key is to talk your feelings through with someone. Your partner, parents, or close friends are not always the best ones to help with this. You may not be able to get an objective perspective from them because they're so close to you. If this is the case, you may need to explain this to them; when you do so, try to be gentle and mindful that they just want to help you.

Forgiving yourself is an essential step toward overcoming your guilt. In order to do so, you'll likely need to change your understanding of what caused the bad outcome to happen. This does not mean that you're condoning, excusing, or denying that something bad happened. Instead, you're shifting from negative or resentful recollections to a more understanding perspective about your limitations as a human being and unpredictable outcomes and random events that no one can control. Before you can forgive yourself, it's necessary to first reexamine what actually occurred and look for inaccurate or unreasonable thoughts and feelings that have caused you to feel so much guilt. Then you must challenge these thoughts and feelings. It's only after you've reached this point that you will find a way to move toward self forgiveness.

Here are a few ways to help you reframe the way you think about things that happened in the war zone that you feel guilty about:

- Recognize all the possible reasons why this event might have occurred. This should help you to realize that even if you had an impact on the outcome, it's likely that the actions of others, bad luck, and other factors also played a role.
- Ask yourself, what was my intention? You may have overlooked how you actually wanted things to happen because of the negative result that occurred.
- Place yourself in someone else's shoes. Seeing the same situation from another's perspective can help you see things more clearly, and help reframe the way you think.
- Carefully examine thoughts that include "I should have . . ." or "yes, but . . . ," and be honest with yourself about the reality of the situation, as you saw it, during this pivotal event. Examining your thoughts can help you see what truly occurred.
- Acknowledge that even if you could have prevented something from happening, it doesn't mean you caused it.
- Don't judge yourself based on the bad outcome, but on what you tried to accomplish, even if it wasn't possible for you to succeed.

Tony believes that it was completely his fault that his buddy died. However, his friend wouldn't have died had there been no war, if there was no bomb, if there was no enemy launching the bomb. Therefore, Tony's belief that he could have saved his friend is really just wishful thinking. Given what Tony knew at the time and what he actually could have done, there's no way he could have prevented this death. Unfortunately, Tony is feeling too guilty and grief stricken to consider what happened from a realistic perspective. He'll need to reach such a point and be able to reframe things before he can forgive himself and address his guilt.

Here are some questions that you can ask yourself to challenge the way you are feeling or thinking about situations that make you feel guilty:

- What evidence is there to support this thought/feeling?
- What is the evidence against this thought?
- Are my thoughts based on feelings rather than facts?
- Am I using words that show extremes in my thinking, such as "must" or "always"?
- Am I overgeneralizing from a single event, thinking I'm always to blame when I made one small, minor mistake?
- What positive statement could I say to myself instead of the negative things I usually think of?
- What are other possible outcomes that could have happened?

Having guilty feelings doesn't mean that you're responsible for what happened. It's important to be sure that your guilt isn't caused by biases in the way you're looking at things. How you feel is neither proof that you actually bear responsibility nor that because of this guilt you should stay away from others or beat yourself up. When all is said and done, there's no way to know for sure whether things might have turned out differently.

Sometimes things happen in the line of duty that could not be avoided. When examined closely, it become clear that they are an integral part of what happens in warfare. As part of your duty, you may have done things for which you cannot forgive yourself. Women, children, and bystanders are often killed, as well as enemy combatants. How these actions make you feel later on is something you may have to learn to handle.

Sometimes mistakes are made that shouldn't have happened. Sometimes these mistakes led to bad outcomes, outcomes for which a service member may share some responsibility. In other words, sometimes guilt is based in fact. This is not unusual. People do make mistakes, sometimes at the worst possible moments. You may need to learn to live with some of your guilty feelings. We strongly advise you to seek help from a chaplain, counselor, or therapist to deal with guilt. Of course no one can change what happened, but with help from the right people we can change how to accept what happened and move on with our lives.

As we mentioned earlier, talking to others can be very helpful. Talk to a military chaplain, other service members who have been through similar experiences, or visit your local Vet Center. Veterans who have been in combat or other war zone situations staff Vet Centers, so they can relate to what you're going through and may be able to provide new perspectives or help you cope. When talking with others about your guilt, try to be open to their perspectives, which may be much more objective and forgiving than your own.

WHEN TO SEEK PROFESSIONAL HELP

Although everyone feels guilty about something from time to time, it's important to recognize when guilty feelings get out of hand. Watch out for guilt that begins to impair your daily functioning or lasts for months and months with no end in sight. If you are religiously inclined, persistent negative thoughts such as "God has abandoned me" or "God is punishing me" can be a warning sign that indicates a problem. Continual guilt can have a profound negative impact on your life and on your relationships with others.

> *Tony is a prime candidate for seeking further assistance. His intense and persistent survivor guilt has taken over much of his daily life, and it has now lasted a full six months since his return from theater. He's unable to listen to anyone else's speculations about what might have really happened. He doesn't even want to consider viewing things differently.*

If you can't stop feeling intense guilt about what you did or didn't do during a traumatic event, it's time to seek professional help. Sometimes all you need is for someone to help you distinguish what you actually "knew" during the event versus what you "know" now. On the other hand, sometimes you need to accept your guilt and move on with life. These are extremely complicated and painful challenges that are best to work through with the understanding and compassion of a professional such as a chaplain, counselor, or therapist.

8

HANDLING
GRIEF

Death is a major life stressor no matter where or when it happens, but the sudden death that occurs in war zone situations can have an even greater impact on your ability to move forward and reintegrate into civilian life. Many veterans report that the closest relationships they form in their lives are with comrades with whom they served during the war. You may feel the same way. High levels of trust and strong bonds form between individuals within the same military unit. These bonds and mutual respect are further strengthened by shared experiences during deployment. That's why the death of a comrade is such an intense loss.

Although this chapter focuses on dealing with the loss of someone you were close with, you may experience grief over others you only knew casually or even over the loss of military members you didn't know. This is normal, as these service members were still a part of your military family. All of the same symptoms and coping mechanisms you'll read about here apply.

GRIEF IS A NORMAL RESPONSE TO DEATH

Bereavement is a common and universal experience. In the first weeks following the death of someone close, you'll experience waves of different emotions and feelings, such as:

- Intense loss and sadness
- Extreme distress
- Crying
- Longing for things to be different or for the person who is gone
- Feeling dazed or shocked
- Missing your deceased buddy
- Feeling unable to accept the death
- Feeling that your friend's death was unfair
- Feeling empty
- Feeling responsible in some way
- Constantly thinking about the person who died
- Not enjoying things you normally enjoy doing
- Being unable to feel positive feelings
- Staying away from family and friends, withdrawing
- Trouble concentrating
- Wanting to talk about or think about the deceased
- Seeking to be close to reminders of the person
- Having thoughts and/or concerns about your own mortality

You may also experience some physical symptoms, such as tightness in your throat, shortness of breath, stomach problems, feeling overly tired, and feeling light-headed, as though you might faint. These emotional and physical symptoms should slowly but steadily decrease over time. The worst of these feelings should be essentially resolved within six months of the death, although the pain of loss can last for years. If after one year you're still having intense feelings, you should seek help from a mental health professional or a chaplain. Your primary care physician is also a good resource for finding a professional who can help you move past your grief.

The level of grief experienced following the death of someone you're close to will vary by individual. Your level of grief will be directly affected by the number of losses you've had to endure and especially by

UNDERSTANDING ANTICIPATORY GRIEF

Anticipatory grief involves beginning to try to accept a loved one's death while he or she is still alive. This is more common among family members who are dealing with the absence of their service member than in service members themselves. For example, a mother whose youngest son is deployed to Ramadi may be so distraught with fear that he'll be killed that she might begin to feel anticipatory grief. Anticipatory grief can lead to the first stages of mourning and includes depression, extreme concern for the person, and preparing for a future life without that person.

how close you were to the person (or people) who passed away. As we mentioned earlier, the frequency and intensity of your grief will decrease with time, but you can expect these feelings of grief to intensify during anniversaries and at other times that bring the deceased person strongly to mind.

TRAUMATIC GRIEF

Some troops experience a different and more severe form of grief called traumatic grief. Traumatic grief usually occurs when you've lost someone close under violent and sudden circumstances. It's often characterized by searching or yearning for the person who has died, disbelief or a lack of acceptance that death has occurred, and can also include anger and/or guilt. Traumatic grief can lead to low energy, low social functioning, and withdrawal.

Traumatic grief happens more if you witnessed the death or if you feel that you were powerless to keep your comrade alive or if you blame yourself for making an error that resulted in his or her death. Traumatic grief is also more likely if you've already experienced multiple deaths, are angry at certain people (perhaps commanding officers) whom you hold responsible for this death, or if you're too busy in the field to acknowledge or mourn your comrade's death at the time it happened. If you had a difficult relationship with your parents during childhood or a very close, and possibly dependent, relationship with the person who died, you're also at greater risk for having such problems.

Traumatic grief is different from normal grief. Traumatic grief continues over a longer period of time than the normal grieving process and can persist indefinitely. This is partly because it sometimes seems impossible to make sense of a sudden violent death. Another reason why it lasts longer is because the grieving person needs time to process the trauma as well as the death itself.

You may have traumatic recollections about your friend's death as opposed to the comforting type of memories that usually accompany non-traumatic grief. To properly cope with traumatic grief, you'll need to deal with your memories and feelings about the violent circumstances of the death before you can begin the normal grieving process. In order to put your traumatic grief in its proper context, make sure you're familiar with the common stress reactions that can affect anyone deployed to a war zone, which we cover in Chapter 5, and how to cope with them. Also see Chapter 11 on posttraumatic stress disorder.

Traumatic grief involves a traumatic experience and feelings of depression, but it differs from both PTSD and depression. (See Chapter 11 for more information on PTSD and how it's related to trauma.) In the case of traumatic grief, the bereaved individual will usually seek out reminders of the deceased, as opposed to the kind of avoidance characterized by PTSD. If you're experiencing traumatic grief you might experience intrusive thoughts, like those involved in PTSD, but these thoughts will be memories about the person, not the violence of the life-ending traumatic event. Although the sadness following traumatic death shares much in common with depression, traumatic grief doesn't usually involve the feelings of worthlessness and the slowing down of thoughts and actions characteristic of depression. (See Chapter 12 for more information on depression.)

HOW GRIEF IS EXPRESSED

Many troops have trouble expressing their grief because they're trained not to show their emotions. Rather than expressing your grief, you may try to distract yourself by drinking too much, making yourself so busy that you don't have to think about your friend's absence, or displace your

DIFFERENTIATING TRAUMATIC GRIEF

Tony is unable to stop thinking about his friend who was killed by a VBIED in the convoy that Tony himself was leading that day. Tony was shocked by the death and is now experiencing survivor guilt. Ever since his buddy's sudden death Tony has been withdrawn and unable to enjoy the things he used to love to do, like play ball with the boys. He feels guilty and angry, and he longs to be able to see his friend again. Tony's been home for months now and still has nightmares about that day, seeing the Humvee blow up over and over again. When he actually does talk to his wife about anything to do with his deployment, it's always because something reminded Tony about this incident and the loss of his buddy.

grief with feelings of anger (especially since anger is one emotion that is not taboo to display in the military). You may also withdraw so that others won't see you're upset. However, mourning is the way all of us express our reactions to death—bottling it up will usually only lead to bigger problems.

There are five stages of grief that people usually go through—denial, anger, bargaining, depression, and acceptance. These stages generally occur in all grief, and they may be expressed in a different order than we've listed above. In addition, the process of mourning may differ from one culture to the next. At first you may deny that the loss has really happened. It just can't be true. You're full of shock and disbelief. You may be angry with the person who died simply because he or she died and left you. You may also become angry and blame anyone or anything you hold responsible. You might find yourself trying to come up with ways that could have made things different, offering to bargain your life for the one that's been taken; anything that will replace the loss. You may become depressed, feeling sad and numb after your comrade dies, feeling the pain and loss of grief. You may be distressed and disorganized or feel a sense of despair and hopelessness. As mourning progresses, the turmoil of your feelings tapers off and you can accept the reality of your loss.

Grief doesn't just happen in response to death; it can also occur following the loss of a limb through injury, or loss of a relationship through divorce. Another loss, mentioned later in Chapters 11 and 12, is the loss of the person you used to be before going to war. These kinds of losses are life changing, and the same stages of grief we mentioned above will occur. However, since these losses don't involve death, you may not initially recognize the symptoms. If you find yourself going through a major life change like the ones we mention here, consider where you might be in the grieving process. Also keep in mind that the coping mechanisms for grief are the same, no matter why you're grieving.

When family members are trying to deal with the death of a service member, mourning can involve adjusting to new realities. New responsibilities must be taken on and new skills must be developed to fill the role previously occupied by the deceased person. When you are dealing with the death of a comrade in the war zone, there is a void left in your daily life, a void that may persist when you get home. In both cases, you've lost someone close with whom you can no longer share new experiences or rehash old memories. You may have difficulty adjusting to this loss or even feel resentful about this void in your life. In time, however, most people will recover. Although your loss will remain, and you'll always wish your deceased loved one was still with you, you'll have to find a way to move forward in your life.

EFFECTS ON FAMILY

Your family may have trouble understanding what you're going through when you have an unrelenting focus on the death of a comrade. If you let it go on too long, your unresolved grief, anger, and irritability may push your family away and make it increasingly difficult for them to support you. Hopefully, you will become aware of these danger signs, and seek assistance—perhaps from a chaplain or counselor—so that you will be able to go through a healthy process of mourning. It can be especially difficult for your family if you're showing signs of traumatic grief, such as high-risk behaviors like drug use or dangerous activities like motorcycle racing and skydiving, talking about suicide, or intense outbursts of anger and agitation. If you or anyone in your family notices any

DON'T AVOID YOUR GRIEF

People normally try to avoid painful feelings. Since grief is extremely painful, people sometimes try to avoid going through the necessary grieving process. Although this may seem like a good strategy in the short run, it's been shown that some form of mourning is best for most of us. Failure to acknowledge and deal with grief can be unhealthy and may lead to angry outbursts, alcohol or drug use, irritability, and even physical problems such as high blood pressure. It's important to recognize that grieving takes time. Until you've dealt with it, your life may be on hold because of your inability to focus and concentrate on anything else.

All of this can be complicated by the military mindset ingrained in troops to help them effectively function in a war zone. You've been hardened emotionally, taught to create a protective absence of feeling within yourself, and it can be difficult to let go of this mindset and grieve properly. (See Chapter 4 on understanding Battlemind for more information on how to leave war zone mindsets behind when you're at home again.) Remembering that grief is a normal and necessary process can be helpful. The purpose of funerals, memorials, and other ceremonies is to have a publicly acceptable place to express these feelings, so we encourage you to participate in them. It may also be helpful to allot yourself a private time each day to express your grief and let it out, such as in the shower.

of these symptoms, particularly if they've lasted longer than six months, we urge you to seek professional help.

Family can help their service member cope with grief by not forcing their own method of coping on him or her. Each person has their own time and method of coping. Avoid minimizing the loss and telling him or her to "get over it." Be aware of your own feelings and be a good listener. Know that you cannot solve the problem; you just need to make yourself available to the mourning person. Try offering practical help with daily activities and continue to invite the bereaved person to do enjoyable activities. Even if he

---

Finding Meaning in Death

When someone close to you is killed or dies, it causes you to question life: What does this death mean? Why do we have to die? What is life really all about? Making meaning out of a death is a very personal challenge. It's often helpful to seek religious or spiritual support. Each culture has developed specific explanations and rituals for dealing with death. You may find that such approaches help you come to terms with unexpected death.

Other ways that may help you find meaning in death include celebrating the life of the person who died, contemplating the circle of life, the belief that love never dies, or the belief in something beyond death. Sometimes it seems impossible to find meaning in death. However, the search for meaning may bring you close to others, who offer support during this time of pain. You may also find it helpful to talk with others who are grieving over similar losses but have found their own ways of dealing with it. You should also consider reaching out to family, friends, clergy, or others for their support and assistance.

---

or she refuses these invitations, keep asking. And, be on the lookout for the danger signs mentioned previously.

COPING WITH GRIEF

Human beings form strong bonds of affection and attachment with certain others. When these bonds are broken, as happens with death, strong emotional reactions can occur. As we discussed earlier, letting go is best accomplished through the grieving process. That is usually the best way to deal with the loss of someone whom you care about deeply.

At the same time, not everyone experiences emotional distress when moving on from a loss. You may work out your grief in other ways. Although our military culture tends to encourage you to keep your emotions in check, with expressions such as "you're holding it together well," expressing your grief verbally or in some other manner seems to be the best way to deal with it. Holding back your feelings or avoiding them by drinking or overworking may appear to be for the best in the short run, but that only means you're not dealing with them and that you will pay the price later on. If you can't mourn, as described previously, try some constructive ways to work out your grief, such as exercising, connecting with nature, volunteering for church or community projects to help others in need, or dedicating some meaningful project to the person who died.

When grief runs its natural course, the symptoms we've discussed should decline within six months. You can try to prevent the problems and extended distress associated with chronic, long-term grief by seeking out social support. Grieving works best when it's carried out with a loving family, friend, or supportive community. Here are some general tips to help you cope with grief:

- Make sure you have enough space and time for normal healing.
- Avoid social isolation.
- Get support to help you deal with the life changes caused by your buddy's death.
- Let people who care about you take care of you.
- Share your loss with others.
- Don't let others tell you how to feel.
- Don't tell yourself how to feel. Be patient.
- If you're religious, turn to your faith community for social support and/or rituals that are healing.
- Permit kids to discuss the deceased. Remember that they will likely need to reconsider the death through each stage of their development.
- Plan ahead for emotional surges at anniversaries, holidays, and milestones in life, and know that it's completely normal.

KNOWING WHEN TO SEEK PROFESSIONAL HELP

Regardless of the source of your grief, it's very important that you find a way to work through your feelings so you can move forward with your life.

Military Assistance with Death

It's important for families of military members who have perished in wartime to know that the death was for a worthy and noble cause, that there's some meaning to the loss. Casualty Affairs in the Army and similar organizations in the other military branches create a context for healing. Their programs, which promote a positive meaning for the loss, can help with recovery. The person who notifies the family is not the person who will offer future support. This support lasts for an extended period of time, anywhere from one week to one year.

Funerals, eulogies, and other ceremonies that are common forms of mourning in the United States can also help with adjustment. Military leadership knows this and helps organize eulogies and other ceremonies to help in any way they can with this incredibly difficult time.

Unresolved grief can continue to cause symptoms years after the death takes place and put serious strain on your well-being and important relationships.

The two main indications that you need professional assistance to handle grief are: (1) if you are experiencing considerable difficulty in your social and work life, and (2) if the reaction is prolonged (although this is sometimes hard to gauge). Crying excessively two or five days after a death is normal, but crying this much a year later would indicate you probably need some help. However, there is no set standard, and everyone is different. Culture also plays a role. Usually family members will recognize if things have gone on for too long and bring the issue to your attention. At first you may use avoidance as a primary coping mechanism, but the longer avoidance continues, the poorer your adjustment to the death will be. If you feel so hopeless that you've begun to consider harming yourself or others, it's definitely time to seek advice from a professional.

Though traumatic grief is markedly different than depression and PTSD, it can be accompanied by one or both of these conditions. See Chapters 11 and 12 for further details about these specific mental health issues.

9

RECONNECTING WITH YOUR PARTNER, CHILDREN, FAMILY, AND FRIENDS

It's common to feel disconnected or detached from others when you return home from the war zone. These feelings of isolation can happen for many reasons. You may simply feel incapable of telling people about what happened during your time in the war zone. Maybe you feel you'd be intruding on your partner, family, and friends by speaking about the war, or think that it's not worth talking about because people who have not been there might not be able to understand. You may feel an excessive desire to be alone or to avoid family gatherings, or perhaps you have difficulty feeling or showing positive feelings, which can create problems in your relationships as well as isolate you from family and friends. Finally, some family problems are caused by unresolved tensions from before your deployment or that developed while you were away. These unsettled feelings need to be addressed now that you're home. Regardless of the reason for your feelings of disconnect, rest assured that there are measures you and your loved ones can take to reduce the distance and reconnect with one another.

NORMAL REACTIONS TO SEPARATION

Separation is tough on relationships, tough on marriages, tough on kids. The separation that occurs while you're deployed to a war zone will undoubtedly affect your family relationships. When you're apart from your family, you can't share common experiences. You miss one another. Your mere absence can create insecurity, misunderstanding, and distance within your family. This tension needs to be resolved once you return home. Relationships always involve at least two people, and it's important to remember that each person has an influence on the relationship. If one of you is having a hard time, all of you will be affected.

As we discussed in Chapter 1, some normal distancing occurs prior to deployment as you and your family prepare to handle your impending separation. During deployment, you're pulled away from your normal life into a completely different world. The bond you'll form with your comrades will be intense; it's unlike any of the relationships you have at home. In many ways, the members of your unit will become your family while you're deployed. Back at home, the emotional separation experienced by your family is compounded by worries about your safe return from deployment. When the reality of the separation sets in, those at home often begin to realize that things will be more difficult than they expected. Parents with deployed partners often find the separation particularly hard; they tend to experience more depression and higher levels of stress than others.

Again, all of these separation reactions are normal given your situation, but they can still create a disturbing sense of disconnection between you and your family and friends once you're back home.

CHILDREN AND SEPARATION

The impact of separation on your children is difficult to gauge, as it can influence children differently at various developmental stages, but it's safe to say that separation has a detrimental effect on most children of any age, even babies and toddlers. Fortunately, most kids don't require professional help to get through their separation from a deployed parent. Still, there are steps that troops and their partners can take that will help children of all ages cope better with separation and reintegration:

- Make sure infants get very consistent care during deployment.
- Provide constant reassurance to all kids—but especially young children—who often wonder "what's going to happen to me?"
- Keep normal schedules and routines as much as possible.
- Give your children some kind of security object to keep with them while you're gone—a favorite sweatshirt or a special stuffed animal—something that they can tangibly hold on to in order to help them maintain a connection with you during deployment.
- Work on keeping your marriage stable, because children do best in this type of environment.
- The partner at home should try to express as positive a reaction to the deployment as possible.
- The partner at home should be sure to get the support he or she needs from friends, family, and the community. (Good family support is especially helpful in making things easier for adolescents.)

It's important to point out that, in general, separation has more impact on boys, who often have behavioral adjustment issues, disciplinary problems, and troubles at school. If you have a son (or sons), we suggest you and your partner keep a close eye on him so you can deal with any problematic reactions to your deployment sooner rather than later.

HANDLING THE EFFECTS OF COMMON STRESS REACTIONS

The symptoms that often occur following experience in a war zone change how you feel and act. As a result, the impact of traumatic experiences that occurred during deployment can affect everyone else in your family when you get home. Your family will react to the fact that you have gone through a trauma. They may tiptoe around the issue at first or question you to see if you have changed. At the same time, posttraumatic symptoms may make you difficult to get along with, or may cause you to withdraw. Common stress reactions such as anger, avoidance, or constantly being on alert and overly watchful can create or exacerbate relationship problems. Irritability, aggression, and anger can lead to conflict with your loved ones or cause them to avoid you. It can be very hurtful and confusing for everyone in your family when these changes occur. Unless you've been talking with them honestly and openly about your experiences during deployment and your feelings now that you're home, they probably won't understand why you're behaving this way. They'll also find it hard to be around you if you're constantly edgy or easily annoyed.

HYPERVIGILANCE AND OVERPROTECTIVENESS

You may continue to feel guarded after you return home—always on alert, watching every corner and every rooftop. You may jump and startle easily at sudden noises, such as a truck tailgate slamming shut, or you may hit the deck when you hear the screeching thud of a heavy object being dropped. This hyper state of alertness, which during deployment was associated with dangerous situations, can make you overprotective of your family and friends. This overprotective and overcontrolling behavior can become irritating to them and may also frighten them.

Alex keeps a gun under his bed so he's prepared for anything that might happen. His need for protection is particularly strong because he's felt incredibly vulnerable since his amputation and loss of mobility. This same sense of hypervigilance makes Alex overprotective of his niece and nephew to the point that his brother, Sam, does not want them to spend so much time with him. Sam worries about the negative effect this overly cautious attention is having on their growth and psychological development.

Alex is allowing his Battlemind to take control even though he is no longer in the war zone. He has no real need for a firearm in his bedroom. It is unsafe. Because Sam would not allow his niece and nephew to visit, Alex finally gave in to his brother and locked his weapon up where it belongs.

Knowing that hypervigilance is a common reaction following time in a war zone can sometimes help you get a handle on it at home. This need for control, however, is often hard to notice on your own. Usually it takes someone to point it out to you; so if someone does, try not to brush it off. At the same time, your family and friends need to realize that you can't just flip an "off switch" and make it go away. Hopefully you all can take comfort in the fact that these feelings normally decrease with time.

> *Tony has also been overprotective of his boys. He always wants to know where they are at every second. In order to make sure that they're safe and to suppress his own aggressive feelings, he's stopped roughhousing with them (something which everyone used to enjoy). This has also widened the emotional distance between him and his boys.*

Overprotectiveness usually comes from a need for control and safety. Some service members become extremely overprotective of their children following deployment to a war zone. You might find that you're strictly enforcing rules, constantly saying "Don't do that!" or "Be careful, it's not safe!" When doing activities with friends, you may try to run everything exactly the way you see fit. You may need to know your partner's whereabouts all the time. It's important to recognize that families usually don't function well under this type of control and order. You need to remind yourself that you're now home where it's safe, especially in comparison to the dangerous war zone environment where you spent many months. Here's a good example of a situation in which shared decision-making and good communication minimized such problems.

> *Following her return, Kathleen was upset with Isaac about the way he handled the bill paying while she was deployed. She had always taken care of the finances, both when she lived alone before her first deployment and later, after they began living together. Before her longer second deployment, they'd jointly agreed that Isaac would take over this responsibility. He had continued to do so after her return. Despite her criticism, Isaac had not "messed up." He merely had a different style of doing things. In reply to her adamant concerns, Isaac reminded Kathleen that they'd decided this together and that they could rediscuss the issue now that she was home. When prompted to talk about the particulars of her irritation, Kathleen realized that she had been blowing things out of proportion. In the end they decided to continue with Isaac handling the bills, at least until the war was over and there was less probability that Kathleen would be redeployed again.*

As we mentioned above, Kathleen and Isaac made it through this challenge because of good communication, but also because Kathleen realized that she was still using her battlemindset. Her need for control and order in this situation comes from her need to maintain order in war zone situations where decisions could mean life or death. Now that she's home with Isaac, this is no longer the case. She has to work at it, but she realizes that everything doesn't need to be perfect.

Anger and Fear

Anger and aggression are common combat stress reactions, but these reactions may frighten the people around you—as well as yourself. Fear, or lacking a sense of control, is often masked by anger. You may find yourself getting into arguments with others, often for minor reasons. As we discussed in Chapter 6, continued angry outbursts or overreacting to everyday situations will have a negative impact on your relationships and might mean that you should get professional help. Otherwise, the people who care about you most won't know how to behave when they're with you. They'll begin to feel that they're constantly walking on thin ice and that nothing they say or do will be okay with you.

> Tony has managed to contain his angry outbursts so that he only releases his rage when he's alone in the garage or someplace else out of sight (though not necessarily out of hearing range). However, his family knows this is going on and it's causing them distress.

You may also experience fear and anger because you're concerned that there are things in your home environment that you can't control. To avoid feeling helpless, you may overcompensate and try to stay in complete control over all members of your family. If you are irritated with others because they're not "following the rules," your feelings probably have much more to do with your own need to follow the rules during deployment than with the behaviors of others at home. Your inflexibility, because of your need for control, may make others become hostile toward you. This can become a self-fulfilling prophecy because once you have generated hostility in others, you now actually have a reason to be angry with them. Chapter 6 discusses how your angry and aggressive feelings have a negative impact on your relationships with children and family. It also suggests some ways to cope with such a situation.

AVOIDANCE

Avoidance is the symptom or reaction that is most problematic in relationships. As we've discussed, avoidance is a common reaction after experiencing a traumatic event of any kind. However, avoiding anything that reminds you of your war zone experiences can create some major difficulties when you get home. For instance, you may begin to avoid all public places because you feel unsafe. Or you may avoid seeing other people for fear they might ask you about your time at war. This creates isolation and withdrawal, which pull you away from relationships. This makes it impossible for your family and friends to provide the social support you need to readjust to life back home.

Because memories and thoughts about traumatic experiences are disturbing, a natural reaction that many troops have is to try to not feel that way. One strategy to avoid such distress is emotional shut down. However, when you shut out negative feelings, you may not be able to feel or express positive emotions either. In other words, you may wind up blocking out your love for your family and your enjoyment of activities that used to bring you pleasure. This lack of positive emotional expression can have a devastating effect on all of your close relationships. If your loved ones feel unimportant or believe you no longer love them, they'll inevitably feel neglected and hurt.

Wanting to be alone or avoiding family gatherings eventually creates isolation. You need the support of your family and friends for a healthy readjustment. Even though you might feel like you want to withdraw, it's worthwhile to fight these urges and try to reconnect with family and friends. Other things that can help include:

- Scheduling small activities with a few people at a time.
- Spending individual time with each family member.
- Planning enjoyable activities—doing things will help you get back to your old self.
- Working to restore well-being and positive emotions instead of giving in to isolation, even if it's hard at first.

Some service members turn to alcohol or drugs to avoid thinking or feeling anything about their combat or other war experiences. We discuss substance abuse issues in detail in Chapter 12, but be aware that even periodic excessive drinking or use of drugs can harm your relationships and can cause similar problems to what we've just described.

WHAT YOUR FAMILY MAY BE FEELING

Knowing that something terrible can happen to you at any moment while you're deployed can make your family very fearful. Deployment creates many reactions in your family that can influence your relationships. Even after you return, your family may be angry with you for leaving, or feel frustrated or depressed and sad because things are different now. Below we describe some of the ways that your family can be affected by deployment and its aftermath.

FEAR

Very often, once you're back home, you may feel "on edge" and become focused on trying to stay safe. You may want to get a guard dog, or put up security lights, or have weapons in the house in order to protect family members, like Alex did. If you're very worried about safety, it can make everyone else feel unsafe too. Additionally, sometimes what helps you to feel safe—like keeping a loaded weapon under the bed, for example—can actually make others in your family feel very fearful and unsafe.

Your family may also experience fear if you're angry or aggressive when you get home. Many service members who were deployed to a dangerous war zone become angry and aggressive suddenly and automatically if they feel they're in danger. They also may become angry and aggressive when they're unable to reach their goals. Family or social problems caused by explosive and uncontrollable surges of war-related anger and aggression often become a vicious cycle that only makes things worse. You get angry and aggressive. Then your family member reacts with anger and frustration. Now you feel justified for your anger even though you recognize your initial anger was displaced . . . and around it goes.

No matter why you're acting angry or aggressive, it naturally makes your family fearful and can make them want to distance themselves from you. If you're sensing this reaction in your family members, consider whether aggressive and angry behavior on your part may be to blame. Chapter 6 has advice to help you work to curb your anger and help prevent these fearful reactions.

ANGER

After the honeymoon period wears off, family members are often angry with their service member. On the one hand, this could be in response to angry and aggressive behavior on your part. But it could also be in response to other common stress reactions that may have disrupted your family life after you got home. Your family may feel angry and frustrated at having been forced to handle so much responsibility during your deployment. They may be angry because you haven't assumed some or all of your old responsibilities now that you're home. They may even be angry if you want your old responsibilities back without discussion, because they've now grown used to and may even enjoy doing some of the things you used to do. Some family members get angry at their service member for withdrawing, or for feeling sad when they don't understand why. New roles, rules, and behavior can easily trigger angry reactions.

Your partner may experience anger if he or she believes that you would prefer to be with your friends rather than your family, especially after everything your family has sacrificed. Remember that it takes time to reconnect and patience to get through the first months of readjustment. Honest and open communication between you and your family about your feelings and about renegotiating roles now that you're home is the best way to diffuse anger.

SADNESS AND DEPRESSION

After the initial elation caused by your return has passed, some of your family members, particularly your partner, may find him or herself feeling sad or even depressed. This often has to do with unrealized expectations. While separated, you and/or your partner may have started to romanticize your relationship. Communication between you will change once you're back together. For instance, perhaps your partner's writing was intimate and personal during deployment, but now that he or she is home, he or she hardly says a word, and of course no longer writes. When reality sets in and a fantasy is destroyed, it can lead to feelings of loss and sadness or avoidance and withdrawal. Because of personal changes in one or both partners, loss can occasionally become permanent, with relationships ending in separation or divorce.

WORRY

Many of the common post-deployment reactions that you may experience can cause your family to worry about you. A wife might worry that her husband, who often reacts with anger and violent behavior to the least provocation since he returned from Iraq, will be injured in a fight or get in trouble with the police. A daughter may worry that her mother will make herself ill by drinking too much as a way of coping with her unwanted memories of things she experienced while deployed. A service member's inability to keep a job following deployment may cause his or her family to worry constantly about money and the future.

One young woman whose husband was home on leave told us the following story:

> *My husband was home on leave and we found a babysitter and went to a karaoke bar one evening while he was home. We had done this many times before and had lots of fun. Across the room there was a young man who had Arab features. My husband couldn't stop staring at the man. I pointed out to him, "Hon, you are staring at that guy. Come on, we're supposed to be having fun! Listen to the song." He continued to stare and seemed unable to control himself. This was a different side of my husband—one I had not seen before. I felt frightened and worried and just wanted to be able to help him.*

WHO IS THIS PERSON?

One challenge every returning service member must face is adjusting to changes in the family that occurred while they were gone. No one is the same as they were before deployment.

Many of the changes that you may have undergone and that are illustrated by our examples are normal consequences of intensive training and war zone experiences. You could say that Battlemind was in full effect. Behaviors that are reasonable and necessary in the war zone will take some time to dissipate once you return home. This is why it's vital for you and your family to know what to expect following war.

Your family at home has also changed. Your children have grown and developed new behaviors, skills in school, or ways of thinking about themselves and the world around them. Partners and other family members may have taken on more responsibilities and new roles in the family. Your entire family needs to acknowledge these changes, and you must work together to establish a new family pattern that works for everyone. Be aware that if problems in relationships were already present before deployment, they're likely to return after you are reunited. For some, these problems will be worse than they were before.

> Tony and his family are a mess. The boys hardly recognize the father whom they love. Because Laura and Tony cannot seem to connect, they spend less and less time together. Although their relationship was strong prior to his tour, Laura feels that Tony is not the same man he was before deployment. Tony has trouble understanding why things can't just be like they were.

ADVICE FOR RECONNECTING WITH YOUR LOVED ONES

Men and women often have different ways of integrating back into the family after deployment. To cope with stress, men tend to isolate themselves and seek support outside the home from old friends or military buddies. Women tend to try to talk about their feelings and experiences with their partners, but can become easily frustrated, irritable, or dissatisfied with what they regard as inadequate support. Both men and women often feel that no one understands what they've been through. Male partners of female troops may come to resent or misunderstand those negative feelings and thereby find it difficult to provide the support their partner really needs.

Both women and men often miss the camaraderie with their buddies that sustained them in the war zone. They often want to spend a substantial amount of time with their comrades. Their efforts to recreate this closeness in civilian life are usually not successful and may be very disruptive to their family life. Spending too much time with your buddies and forgoing family time makes your family feel unimportant. You need to find a balance between friends and family that allows for good, quality family time. This is the best way to foster family closeness.

Overcoming any control or overprotective behaviors that are having a negative impact on your relationships with others can be challenging. Keep in mind that the problem may not be that others can't meet your expectations, but your expectations themselves. Others don't need to be perfect in order for you to survive or exist in peace. You may need to continually remind yourself that you're back home where it's safe in order to overcome your overwhelming belief that your loved ones need more safety and protection. (Reviewing the Battlemindset again in Chapter 4 may be helpful here.)

Partners

Reconnecting with your partner is easier if your relationship was strong prior to your deployment. Problems you had before your deployment will not magically be gone upon your return. Partners who look at deployment as a threat to their marital relationship—rather than a challenge—tend to have more problems readjusting and reconnecting after deployment is over. Let one another know you're committed to making your relationship work. Because of the experiences you both have been through, it'll take time to reestablish your previous level of intimacy. Give one another space, but also make sure to set aside private time to get reacquainted. Do little things (buy her flowers, make him his favorite dinner, plan a weekend getaway) to let each other know you care and are there for them.

Children

Reconnecting with your children presents a unique set of challenges. The most valuable thing you can do is to spend some quality time alone with each of them in order to reestablish your bond. Children often feel resentment, sorrow, or anger when a parent is deployed. Depending on their age, they may also feel a sense of abandonment. Homecoming may actually bring back your child's normal fears of separation. During deployment, your child may have learned to rely more on the parent who remained at home. It's important for you to understand these things and not take a cool or angry reaction from your child as a personal criticism. Instead, try to reassure your child and be patient. A child needs at least one consistent person to talk to, be with, and rely on. You shouldn't lie to your child, but you shouldn't tell him or her more than they can handle. Children have wild imaginations, school-age kids in particular. It's easy for them to take something you say about your experiences during deployment and blow it way out of proportion.

Remember that children don't have the same perspective as adults. They're not throwing tantrums or acting out just to frustrate you. They're trying to communicate feelings that may be too complicated for them to understand or express. Don't be surprised if your children go back to exhibiting behaviors that they had previously outgrown, such as thumb sucking or bed-wetting, both during the time you're gone and for a while after you return home. These problems usually resolve themselves over time.

These frustrating behaviors often stem from children's need for security and constant reassurance. Families should make an effort to surround themselves with warm and loving people who can help provide the social support that will help children cope with the stresses of deployment and reintegration. If problems persist and communication can't be restored, consider trying family counseling. It can be very useful in helping all of you successfully reunite. The military provides many resources to help military kids cope with the challenges that come up during and after deployment. Your Family Assistance Centers can help, as can Military OneSource. See the Resources section for contacts and more information and services for kids.

FRIENDS

Friends need to be prepared for the changes in their returning military friends. Returning troops may have little patience with common civilian complaints after everything they've been through and witnessed. Do your best to be understanding about the bonds your returning friend has formed with his or her comrades while deployed. Acknowledge that you can't completely understand what he or she has been through, and try not to be offended if at first he or she confides more or spends more time with military friends. It's not that your friend no longer needs or appreciates your friendship; rather, he or she just needs to be with people who understand what deployment is like, especially right after returning home. Don't pressure your friend to talk before he or she is ready. When your friend does want to talk, show sincere interest in hearing about deployment experiences, but know your limits. We also encourage you to learn about Battlemind and the common normal stress reactions that emerge following time spent in a war zone, so you can offer your returning friend the best support possible. Educate yourself on the resources and services available to assist veterans and their families in case they need some extra help.

PARENTS, SIBLINGS, AND EXTENDED FAMILY

Parents and other extended family members must make many of the same readjustments as partners. You too will have to realize that you've all grown and changed, and this will lead to differences in your relationship with your returning family member. You too need to take time to get reacquainted. However, you also need to be aware of boundaries. It's easy for parents and others who have played a caregiving role for a service member in the past to fall into old patterns and want to protect and take care of him or her again, as is the case with Alex's mother. It's hard to let those feelings go. If your service member is now married or in a relationship, remember that the nuclear family has to come first. Honor the importance of those reconnections, and do your best not to interfere or become overbearing.

As parents or part of the extended family of a returning service member, you are important social supports. In turn, you also need your own supports to cope with separation, worry, and reintegration challenges. Often parents and extended family feel they have few resources available to them. However, the Family Program of the National Guard (found in every state) provides assistance to all military family members, no matter what your relationship or what branch of service. It doesn't matter if your child is deployed from California and you live in Minnesota, or if your nephew lives in Hawaii and you live in New York. Your local Family Assistance Center will talk with you and help you get the information and resources you need. Check out their Web site at www.guardfamily.org.

AVOIDING THE CYCLE OF WITHDRAWAL AND ISOLATION

It's important to understand that trying to help a service member overcome the isolation and withdrawal that's so often part of normal reintegration can create a vicious cycle that's difficult to break. You may feel a need to withdraw and avoid everyone when you return from the war zone. At the same time—or even in response to this avoidance—your family and friends may try even harder to reach out and keep you connected and involved. You may resist these attempts, and redouble your efforts to isolate yourself. And so it goes. Perhaps eventually you will give in and begin to come out of your shell. If not, the people who care about you will finally give up and stop inviting you to join them. Then, by the time you're finally ready to talk, your partner or friends may be too angry, frustrated, or resentful to be receptive or supportive. Both troops and their families and friends need to be aware of this vicious cycle and be willing to work through the difficult and raw feelings that usually develop. If you can't do this, either with or without professional assistance, your relationships are at risk of being destroyed.

In order to avoid the vicious cycle of isolation and withdrawal, both you and your family and friends need to interact on a constant give-and-take basis. The focus should not just be on how your family can help you. Rather, it should be on how you all can help each other to reintegrate and reconnect successfully.

REESTABLISHING TRUST AND INTIMACY

When you return from the front, you need to relearn how to feel safe, comfortable, and trusting again with your family. This means that you must get reacquainted and communicate with your partner, children, parents, friends, coworkers, and others. It can take some time. Try to be patient and not rush things. Also try to remember that your family needs your understanding as well. While you were deployed, they almost certainly had extra responsibilities, felt lonely, and had to deal with overwhelming problems without your help. If you have children, it will make things easier for everyone if you and your partner show your trust in each other's roles as parents and support joint decisions. Try to remember to acknowledge when you agree with one another's decisions and always present a united front when making family decisions.

To reestablish trust and intimacy, you must be able to share things with one another. If you're having trouble talking about your time at war, here's some advice on how to talk about your experiences:

- Do it when you're ready, but recognize that you may need to do some work to become ready. At some point, you should be able to share at least some of your difficult war experiences with those who love you.
- Try not to become angry when others ask about your deployment. Try to recognize that they want to know because they care and want to understand, even if they won't be able to understand completely.
- Remember you are no longer on a classified secret mission. It's okay to talk when the time is right.
- Know that nobody is to blame. Work at both being able to come together without judging each other as well as letting go of anger and frustration. ·

TALKING THROUGH YOUR ANGER

You and your family may feel angry about many things during your mutual readjustment period. As we've said, although anger and conflict are normal reactions following exposure to war, they can hurt your relationships. Anger can make it hard for you to think clearly. It's also hard to talk to someone who is angry. Here are some strategies you can use to take a break from a conversation that is becoming heated:

- Agree that either of you can call a time-out at any point.
- Agree that if someone calls a time-out, the discussion must stop right then.

- Decide on a signal you'll use to call a time-out, such as a word you say or a hand signal.
- Agree to tell each other where you'll be and what you'll be doing during the time-out—and stick with this.
- Tell each other what time you'll be back to continue the conversation.

While you're on a time-out, instead of stewing over your anger, cool down a little and try to redirect your thoughts. Think calmly about how you will talk things over and solve the problem. After you come back:

- Take turns talking about solutions to the problem.
- Practice listening without interrupting.
- Be open to the other's ideas. You will both have good ideas.
- Don't criticize each other.
- Focus on things you both think will work.
- Agree which solutions you will use and implement them together.

IMPROVING GENERAL COMMUNICATION

In addition to difficulties talking about your war zone experiences, you and your family may have trouble talking about feelings, worries, and everyday problems. Here are some tips for improving your communication with one another:

- Practice being a good listener: establish eye contact or even hold hands, listen carefully and repeat things back to make sure you understand, ask questions for clarification, and don't allow your own issues to prevent you from hearing the other person.
- Be clear and to the point.
- Don't interrupt.
- Repeat what you hear to make sure you understand, and ask questions if you need to know more.
- Don't give advice unless you're asked. Ask how you can help.
- Be positive. Blaming the other person or being negative won't help the situation.

Facing Violent Behavior

Anger can be frightening, and if it leads to violent behavior or abuse, it's dangerous. If violent behavior occurs, family members should get to a safe place and call for help right away. Make sure children are in a safe place as well. You can call the National Domestic Abuse Hotline, twenty-four hours a day, at 800-799-SAFE (7233) or 800-787-3224 (TTY).

- Put your feelings into words. Your loved one may not know you're sad or irritated unless you're clear about your feelings.
- Help your family put feelings into words. Ask, "Are you feeling mad? Sad? Worried?"

THINGS FAMILY AND FRIENDS CAN DO

Family and friends of a returning service member should not try to force him or her to talk about his or her war experiences. Instead, give your loved one opportunities to talk about the war and his or her reactions and feelings whenever he or she feels comfortable doing so. Above all, be careful not to be judgmental or negative during these conversations. Family members should be aware that service members may be more comfortable talking with their buddies about their time at war and should try not to take this personally. It's their way of protecting you from knowing what they saw and did as well as protecting themselves from any judgment (real or imagined) on your part. If you feel your service member is having trouble talking about his or her deployment experience, encourage him or her to speak with a chaplain or counselor about it. You can also urge your service member to talk with you or a professional instead about concerns he or she may have about the prospect of sharing the details of war experiences. Again, try not to take signs of withdrawal personally and do your best to be patient. Readjustment takes time. The best thing you can do is to provide opportunities for open and accepting communication whenever possible. Your goal is to help your returning service member understand that although he or she may feel that no one wants to hear his or her stories, that's not true.

WHAT FAMILY MEMBERS
CAN DO TO HELP WITH DISCONNECTEDNESS

As the family of a returning service member, your most important role is to be genuine, loving, and supportive. Adult family members can help by learning and understanding some of the readjustment stressors and emotions a service member may experience after he or she has served in a war zone. Because reconnecting can be a challenge, here are some other things you can do:

- Be ready to get used to sharing control of the family and important tasks and goals again.
- Keep up with family traditions and celebrations.
- Make sure there's a plan in place to help your returning loved one reconnect with daily schedules and responsibilities. For example, when he or she is first back, make them responsible again for a few things, and increase the number and amount of responsibilities over time.
- Encourage your kids to express their feelings with you.
- All children do better if they hear about bad news rather than have the truth hidden from them. That said, you should make sure to communicate with children fittingly for their age group.
- Remember that every person in your family counts.
- Take care of yourself so that you can be there for your children.
- Be honest about your own needs and expectations rather than hiding them in an effort to protect your service member.
- Be supportive and respectful of your service member's need for time to adjust.
- Be ready to learn and use new skills or tools for coping with the difficulties that reintegration can cause.
- Be open to seeking professional help with readjustment, since it can go a long way toward making homecoming an easier transition.

- Learn some ways to improve your relationship by taking a couples or communication class.
- Do whatever you need to do to relieve your own stress. This can include turning to others outside your intimate relationship for emotional and social support as well as physical stress-relieving activities, such as exercise, yoga, or meditation.

As with any important experience, the more you can learn and develop appropriate coping skills, the better your chances of a successful reintegration.

WHEN TO SEEK PROFESSIONAL HELP

When the usual measures don't work, it's time to acknowledge that you're having problems connecting with your family and friends. If these difficulties are not addressed, they can worsen and might lead to marital separation and divorce, family violence, and other serious problems. Communication is key to working through such problems, so when communication isn't working—or can't be established—talking to a counselor or therapist for support and assistance is crucial. Your partner should also be prepared to seek counseling for him or herself as well as your children, if needed. Oftentimes, couples counseling can help identify the problems in communication and readjustment. Counseling can also help to clarify the specific needs of individual family members.

In some cases, it's critical to get help right away. This is true if weapons are involved in altercations or in instances of domestic violence of any kind. If you feel you're in crisis or you know someone else who is in crisis, call the National Suicide Prevention Lifeline at 800-273-TALK (8255), your local VA Medical Center, or Vet Center. Here are some other useful numbers for those in crisis:

- The National Domestic Violence Hotline is 800-799-SAFE (7233).
- Call the National Center for Victims of Crime can be reached Monday through Friday, 8:30 a.m.–8:30 p.m. EST at 800-FYI-CALL (394-2255).
- The National Center for Violence Against Women provides online resources at www.nvaw.org.

10

OVERCOMING
BARRIERS TO CARE

Almost all service members and their families will experience some difficulties with reintegration, but fortunately most will make it through this
time of readjustment just fine and will return to normal life within ten to
twelve to eighteen months. However, there are some individuals and
families who will experience more trouble readjusting than others, and
may need professional help to get them through this difficult time. In this
chapter we discuss what resources are available to make your transition
easier and offer advice for overcoming some of the barriers you may
encounter. We also discuss issues of confidentiality regarding your health
information and provide information about various interventions and
treatments for difficult problems that can develop.

We recognize that the military mentality emphasizes strength, and
many troops may have a problem with the idea of seeking outside help for
their reintegration problems. But asking for help when you need it is *not* a
sign of weakness. In fact, knowing when and how to get help is actually
part of military training. For example, if a "wall" cannot be scaled without

a foothold from a buddy, you're not going to get over the "wall" on your own. Getting assistance from others is sometimes not only the best but actually the *only* way to improve your life and the lives of your loved ones.

The mental and emotional problems that can occur following time in a war zone can happen to anyone. No one knows exactly who will be affected. Take the following example:

> Several Soldiers are patrolling silently behind a broken down partial wall of a destroyed building. They are all alert, guns up and ready, cautiously advancing, stalking toward the direction from which enemy fire has just showered their unit. Suddenly, they are surprised by an ambush from behind. Bullets zing past each Soldier's helmet and they are all suddenly thrown against the wall as a bomb explodes amidst them.
>
> One member is killed. One has half of his leg blown away. The others are strewn about the demolished scene with various injuries. The bomb had no particular individual target. It was pure luck whether you were injured by the blast, or not. There was nothing more that anyone could have done to be better prepared or protected.

Just as the explosion randomly injured members of this reconnaissance unit, luck often determines whether your war experiences will produce *invisible* psychological injuries that can prove incapacitating. Since the bravest troops are more likely to place themselves in harm's way, the bravest may actually be more likely to sustain both the visible and invisible injuries of war.

THE STIGMA SURROUNDING
MENTAL HEALTH PROBLEMS

Feeling pain is a normal physical reaction, a signal to your brain that your body is having a problem that requires attention. Mental pain does the same thing: it tells you that you need to take action to overcome a serious problem. Unfortunately, our American, and especially our military, culture can make it difficult to admit that you have psychological pain and even more difficult to seek mental health treatment if you do need help. This is because of fear and stigma. People fear that they will be labeled as weak or "mental," or that others will think less of them because they have sought professional assistance. They also fear that psychological problems can't be fixed or believe that they should be able to just get over it on their own. These fears have created an unnecessary stigma about having a mental health problem.

It's really a double whammy. On the one hand, you may be suffering from feelings or thoughts that are overwhelming, or that seriously interfere with your life in important ways. Yet, such psychological problems can be helped, as we discuss throughout this book. On the other hand, you may fear that if you admit to needing mental health assistance, you'll be ridiculed by your peers, seen as weak or cowardly, and considered unsuitable for military service because you weren't tough enough to "suck it up" or didn't have the right stuff. You may be afraid that seeking treatment will label you negatively and even damage your career. In other words, the stigma surrounding mental health issues pushes service members in precisely the *wrong* direction because it pushes them to avoid seeking help at the most important time, when they recognize that a serious problem exists that they can't solve on their own. Unfortunately, avoiding your problems will only prevent you from receiving early intervention or treatment. It is important to focus on the fact that learning skills to deal with things or getting early treatment could solve your problems before they cause real damage to your life.

OTHER BARRIERS
TO SEEKING ASSISTANCE

This resistance to seeking outside help for mental health problems is just one of the barriers that can stand in the way of getting the help and resources available. Other difficult barriers include your physical distance to available services, transportation issues, and other beliefs. Your work schedule might make it hard to take time off for appointments or to even make calls to get appointments. In some places certain services may be unavailable or the facility may be too busy, so it may take a long time to see someone after you've made an appointment. If childcare is hard to find or too expensive, this may also prevent you from keeping appointments. You may worry that you can't afford professional treatment or that treatment won't work. You may be afraid that working your way through the benefits or insurance systems will be confusing and discouraging. Fortunately, there are people and advocates who can help you navigate these challenges. Organizations such as Tricare and Military OneSource as well as the Department of Veteran Affairs, VA Medical Centers, Vet Centers, chaplains, family programs, and many others offer free advice, counseling, and therapy for six months to five years following a deployment.

Avoiding your problems is one of the most common reactions to invisible psychological injuries of war and is a major barrier to getting the help you need. Because you really don't want to revisit the traumatic memories and overwhelming feelings associated with your war zone experiences, you may delay or completely avoid seeking help even though you know you need it. In other words, if you don't want to think about the problem, it's hard to look for a solution. Social support is a very important factor that can help you through hard times, yet you may find it hard to accept if reactions such as avoidance, alienation, and detachment are causing you to reject available support from your partner, other family members, friends, and from the community.

You might not know what kinds of problems can benefit from professional help. Or you might not be fully aware of the services and resources that are currently available to you. If you're thinking that it might be good to get more information or talk to someone who can offer more advice, you may not know where to go. It's important to learn about what resources and services are available, so that you can both access these services if you need them as well as point others in need to places so they can receive help. There are lists of resources and services that are available for a variety of concerns in the Resources section of this book. (See page 241.)

OVERCOMING BARRIERS

Be a problem solver. You learned how to do this successfully in the military and now you need to apply it to helping yourself and your loved ones. It takes a lot of guts to acknowledge you may have a problem. You have the guts. Remember it's a sign of health to admit you have a problem and take action. Ignoring what's happening or pretending there is no problem is not a solution. There are many resources and effective solutions out there—you just need to take that first step.

KNOWLEDGE IS POWER

Acknowledging your problems and being prepared to face them are crucial first steps to overcoming the problems themselves. The next steps are: understanding what's happening to you, getting information on how to cope, finding out where to get help, and learning about the type of services and treatments that work. This chapter is about preparing to take the most important step: asking for assistance. It's also about how you can overcome some of the barriers that might otherwise get in your way.

Learn about the services and resources that are out there already. The VA, Vet Centers, your State Department of Veterans Affairs, and your local Agency of Human Services can all help you. See the Resources section for some ideas to get you started. For example, most VA hospitals offer transportation assistance to veterans in the form of transport or travel reimbursement. The more you know about the problems you may face and how to solve them, the better equipped you'll be to improve your life and that of your family.

To help you work through the "red tape" that often surrounds medical and mental health resources, there are a variety of advocates, or people who provide support, guidance, and advice, who can assist you. They have experience dealing with the confusing benefits and bureaucratic systems that seem like they are set up to make things harder—not easier. Veteran's Service Organizations (VSOs) have staff who are more than willing to help you in many ways—free of charge—including helping you navigate through the maze of paperwork. State and legislative offices and many other organizations also offer free advocacy services. (See the Resources section for contact information.)

FAMILY INVOLVEMENT

Family members are often among the first to notice problems in a service member's readjustment following deployment. While your service member needs a reasonable amount of time to readjust, problems that persist for months, if unattended, can permanently affect his or her marriage, relationships, work, and other daily functioning. If your loved one is using harmful strategies to cope with stress, such as drinking, drugs, withdrawal, and isolation, or has sudden emotional outbursts that seriously disrupt family life, it's probably time to encourage him or her to seek professional help. It's also important to watch for any negative impact these behaviors may have on children and teens. If you have concerns, you should discuss them openly with your loved one in a spirit of understanding and not blame.

Although many service members do seek assistance at the urging of their families, it's not always easy to get your loved one to go for help. A study of troops returning from Iraq found that only 40 percent of those who acknowledged having mental health problems reported that they were interested in receiving help. Many of them admitted that their reluctance to seek mental health treatment was caused by the fear and stigma we discussed earlier. They also stated their concern that seeking mental health treatment would hurt their image or even ruin their military careers. In order to help counter this stigma, try emphasizing to your service member that he or she needs to seek counseling and treatment for the sake of the entire family. Explain that effective treatments exist and early treatment can prevent their problems from worsening.

Community Involvement

Who would you turn to if you had a problem? Who are the first people you think of calling for support and advice? It's probably someone you feel close to. When we're in trouble, we tend to turn to those who know us best, those we can trust, like our family and friends, or even our coworkers or neighbors. This means that every member of every community should be prepared to offer a hand, if asked, to a returning service member or his or her family. We all need to share the responsibility of understanding the roadblocks to reintegration faced by service members and their families. It's our responsibility to educate ourselves on the local services and resources available to help with reintegration so we can help troops and their families get back on track if necessary. It's the least we can do, considering the sacrifices they've made.

HOW CONFIDENTIAL IS A
SERVICE MEMBER'S MEDICAL INFORMATION?

Let's face it. Your military medical records are less confidential than medical records of regular civilians. Information that passes between a doctor (including a counselor or therapist) and a service member is protected under privacy laws, but there are exceptions to this rule in the military. (See below for further explanation about this.) The only truly protected confidential communication in the military is that between service member and chaplain or a Vet Center counselor. (The one exception to this is if the communication contains information about child or domestic abuse. When that occurs, a counselor is legally responsible to report this to the proper authorities.)

If you're no longer on Active Duty and seek medical attention at the VA, your medical information will not be offered to the Department of Defense and will not be given to military personnel without your explicit signature. Only under certain circumstances, following a specific request, would this information have to be made available to commanding officers. Our understanding is this is a rare occurrence and must be accompanied by specific justification. However, if you're an Active Duty service member and you're seen at the VA through a military health agreement where the Department of Defense is paying for the health care, this information becomes part of your military medical record. As with health information collected by military doctors, this information will be available to Command. If you see a private medical practitioner, those records are not accessible to the military and are private.

At the same time, all troops are required to report to their unit any change in health status, and this includes mental as well as physical health. Once a year, and every five years when service members go through a periodic full physical exam, you are requested to disclose medical information. You're required to give written consent to disclosure of your health records if you want to remain in drills or be reassigned to Active Duty. This raises questions about how honest you may be willing to be in answering any mandatory questions about your mental health or other private matters during these routine exams. You may feel your health information should remain private. You may also be less willing to seek help for personal problems because you're afraid that this information will become available to your unit. While it's understandable that you value your privacy and don't want such information to be shared, your first priority must be to protect your well-being and ability to function properly.

BE OPEN ABOUT
YOUR HEALTH ISSUES

Although it's understandable that you want your health records to remain private, being in the military makes complete confidentiality impossible. Commanders need to make informed decisions about each of their service members' fitness for duty so they can achieve their military objectives while keeping their troops as safe as possible. There is certain information that commanders need to know in order to make assignments that are in line with what each service member is capable of doing. This optimizes effectiveness and safety for the unit as a whole. For instance, a Marine with a broken arm should not be shooting a gun in the forward lines, nor can a Soldier suffering from a serious traumatic brain injury be expected to make the best decisions while under fire. We all can agree that there are good reasons why the medical status of a seriously impaired service member should not be kept secret.

For these same reasons, it's only important for commanders to know the mental health status of a service member *if* it will impact the safety and effective functioning of the unit. Most commanders understand this and only request such medical information when they feel it's absolutely necessary. Yet many service members fear that if they acknowledge and seek help for the slightest mental or emotional difficulties, it will hurt— or even end—their military careers. You are far better off dealing with your problems early, before they become incapacitating or extremely disruptive. If you delay seeking help because of avoidance or stigma, it will increase the likelihood that your problems may actually cause you to lose your job, your relationships, and your happiness. Mental and emotional problems can be managed or treated, and early detection is essential.

We acknowledge that not all military authorities understand that seeking help for mental health issues is the proper choice for troops, although it's best for them to encourage such help-seeking behavior because most problems can be successfully addressed. We also know that the military wants to maintain its forces at maximum strength and is working hard to end the stigma surrounding mental health issues in order to take care of its own and maintain operational readiness.

TALK TO YOUR REGULAR DOCTOR

Rather than beginning your search for help by looking for a mental health care provider, it's sometimes best to start by speaking with your primary care physician (PCP) about any symptoms you're experiencing. If you think you have PTSD, or just some of the reactions or symptoms, such as nightmares or racing thoughts, associated with it, it's important for you to let your regular doctor know. This information can help your doctor plan regular medical treatment or refer you to other services that may help, such as a psychologist, a social worker, or Vet Center services. Sometimes your primary care physician's office can even help you set up another appointment with those that offer these other mental health services.

Below you will find the Primary Care PTSD Screen (PC-PTSD) that's been designed by the VA's National Center for PTSD for use in VA and in primary care and other medical settings. The PC-PTSD is brief and problem focused. A positive response to the screen does not necessarily mean that you have posttraumatic stress disorder. However, a positive response does indicate that you may have adjustment issues or war-related problems and should receive further assessment and, possibly, assistance from a mental health professional.

Current research suggests that the results of this screen should be considered "positive" if you answer "yes" to any three items. However, we repeat that a positive screen does not mean that you have the disorder. It simply means that more assessment is highly recommended.

COMMON TREATMENTS
FOR MENTAL HEALTH ISSUES

Many people don't really understand what's involved in behavioral or mental health treatments. Usually treatment involves talk therapy, medications, or a combination of both. Talk therapy is not the Freudian

---

Primary Care PTSD Screen

In your life, have you ever had any experience that was so frightening, horrible, or upsetting that, in the past month, you:

1. Have had nightmares about it or thought about it when you did not want to?
2. Tried hard not to think about it or went out of your way to avoid situations that reminded you of it?
3. Were constantly on guard, watchful, or easily startled?
4. Felt numb or detached from others, activities, or your surroundings?

---

chat on the leather couch we see in the movies. Many people are still under the mistaken impression that therapists want to "analyze your brain," or just sit there and nod their heads after everything you say. Therapy, actually, is quite practical and involves using your common sense. It usually involves the following steps:

- Assessment: an evaluation that might include a paper and pencil measurement tool, an interview, or other series of questions to diagnose the nature of your condition
- Education about the problem and how it affects you and others
- Goal setting about ways to improve your life
- Learning new coping skills
- Learning to look at yourself and understand and accept your thoughts and feelings, what triggers your symptoms, and how you interact with other people

There are a lot of skills that can help with your reintegration or recovery, including skills for lowering bodily tension, skills for communicating better with your family and friends, and skills for handling anger and conflict. Treatment involves learning new ways to deal with the things that make you frightened, depressed, angry, or sad. It can involve learning to look at things in a different way. More detailed information about a variety of therapies and medications used for treating psychological and

OVERCOMING NEGATIVE ATTITUDES
ABOUT MENTAL HEALTH STIGMA

Although we're slowly beginning to overcome our American cultural stigma regarding mental health issues, we've got a long way to go. In addition to public social stigma, people often have a private stigma, or they *feel fearful of others' negative reactions* to the fact that they have psychological problems, even though most people are very understanding. Therefore, it's probably best to accept that some stigma about mental health problems still remains, whether it's social stigma or self stigma. Unfortunately, stigma is a fact of life. We need to work around it to get needed treatment and to educate everyone so that this stigma will, eventually, disappear. Here are three strategies that have been used to try to combat the stigma about mental health problems:

PROTEST

Protest is a strategy that some have used to try to overcome stigma. It involves groups protesting inaccurate portrayals of mental health issues. These protests send two messages: they tell the media to stop reporting inaccurate information, and they tell the public to stop believing negative views. This requires that people reject the stigmatizing feelings they might have and, hopefully, change their beliefs about mental illness. Unfortunately, sometimes when we try to suppress thoughts and feelings they only become stronger. However, this strategy does seem to help in pushing the media to stop reporting stigmatizing messages and images of mental illness.

EDUCATION

Education helps to replace incorrect ideas that people have about mental illness and treatment with accurate information. A more accurate understanding can help reduce uncertainty and fear of the unknown and correct mistaken beliefs about things such as severity, causes, and treatment effectiveness. Mental health problems, like any medical difficulty, vary from mild to severe. Most problems are mild and will improve if you take action early enough to prevent them from getting worse. Counseling or therapy is very practical and involves commonsense steps. You have regular conversations with a trained counselor who will help you think about your situation and figure out how you want to change it. You learn more about what your problem is and how it's affecting you. You can work with counselors and other veterans to get support while you make gradual changes to improve your situation. If counseling isn't enough, psychological issues can be treated with medications and therapies that have been shown to be effective. Educating yourself and others on all the different types of effective help that are available is an important strategy to overcoming negative attitudes and stigma.

Contact

A final strategy that can be helpful in overcoming stigma is making direct contact with people who have actually suffered from various mental health problems and who have benefited from counseling or treatment. For instance, if your mother suffered from depression for years and is now on medication that allows her to be herself again, this type of direct contact is likely to help you overcome some of your own doubts and fears. Contact allows you to see that people just like you have had psychological problems and are happy that they sought treatment to make their lives better.

behavioral problems that most commonly develop in service members after deployment is covered in Chapters 11 and 12.

CHOOSING A THERAPIST

Selecting a therapist is an important and personal decision. A therapist who works well with one person will not necessarily work as well with another for a variety of reasons. The connection between individuals differs. People usually want to feel the therapist understands them and is emotionally available. We encourage you to meet with several therapists before deciding on which one to go with. You should ask each therapist questions about his or her education and experience in dealing with the problem or problems that you face. Ask about his or her area of expertise. Find out what kinds of treatment each therapist offers and what the treatment entails. Learn about the types of treatments that are available for conditions like PTSD and other post-traumatic reactions so you can ask informed questions and understand the answers about what treatment will be provided. Ask what each therapist expects of you during treatment and also what you can expect from him or her.

To locate some therapists near you, ask friends and family members for referrals, or seek recommendations from your primary care physician. You can also call your local VA Medical Center or Vet Center, your state psychological association, or university or college department of psychology for leads. Look in the government section of your phone book under "Department of Human or Health Services" for listings under "mental health." Check your local Yellow Pages under "psychologists," "psychotherapists," "counseling," "social workers," or "mental health services." There's also a wealth of information available online. The Center for Mental Health Services Locator at www.mentalhealth.samhsa.gov/databases is a good place to start.

If you're not quite ready to seek treatment but feel you're having real difficulty readjusting, you may choose "watchful waiting" or take a wait-and-see approach. This should be an active process over a set period of time. During this time, you should learn more about coping or educate yourself about your potential problems and treatments. If you get better on your own, you obviously won't need treatment. However, if your reactions and symptoms do not get better after three months and they are either causing you distress or getting in the way of your work or home life, talk to someone. Talk to a chaplain, to someone at your local Vet Center, your regular doctor, or another health professional. Sometimes it's useful to take medication to make therapy even more effective or to help you get started in treatment. Remember that learning about what treatments work, where to look for help, what happens during such treatments, and what kind of questions to ask can make it easier to get help if you need it.

YOU ARE NOT ALONE

The most recent national study of adults found that 46 percent of people in the United States have had a psychological disorder during their lifetime. Military members were included in this survey. If almost half the people in the United States have had some type of psychological disorder, you probably know many people to whom this applies. However, they may not have talked about it because of the stigma we mentioned earlier. In addition, many more people suffer from mild rather than severe psychological problems, conditions that benefit from counseling, therapy, or medications.

In the next two chapters, we offer information on posttraumatic stress disorder (PTSD) and other mental health problems that often occur following deployment to a war zone. In the study of U.S. adults mentioned above, PTSD was experienced by 7 percent of Americans surveyed at some point in their lives. In addition, lifetime depression was found among almost 17 percent of Americans.

Although military folks are tough, toughness has nothing to do with mental health problems. Anyone can develop psychological and emotional difficulties. There are many risk factors that can contribute to the likelihood of developing mental health problems. Although the risk factors vary from problem to problem, service members deployed to war are certainly at risk because of the nature of their job. So we need to recognize that military personnel are not immune to mental health issues. We need to do a better job educating you about this and making it easier for service members like you to find and receive the help you need. Finally, we need to continue to wage war against the stigma associated with mental health issues so that we can achieve this goal.

11

POSTTRAUMATIC
STRESS DISORDER

As we've emphasized throughout this book, even if you experience some of the common reactions that occur following your return from deployment, you'll likely be back to normal given a little time. However, no matter how many preventative measures are taken, some troops will go on to develop a mental health problem after deployment to a war zone. The most common problem to occur is called posttraumatic stress disorder (PTSD). Though only a small proportion of service members will develop PTSD, it's important for you to be aware of the signs and symptoms so you can better assess your own situation.

WHAT IS PTSD?

Posttraumatic stress disorder is a medically recognized anxiety disorder that can develop in anyone after they've been exposed to extremely stressful conditions. The condition can be diagnosed one month or more after experiencing the traumatic event.* As we mentioned in the last chapter, 7 percent of the general population has had PTSD. The likelihood of service members developing PTSD is even higher because they're more likely to experience traumatic events if they've seen action in a war zone.

People with PTSD often relive the traumatic event through a variety of symptoms, such as nightmares and being bombarded by unwanted and uncontrollable memories about the traumatic experience, and often feel detached from others. PTSD is associated with biological changes as well, such as increased sensitivity in the brain's system for dealing with threat and fear. It causes significant distress and can be severe enough to cause problems with daily functioning. Most importantly, PTSD is a treatable condition.

To be considered for the PTSD diagnosis, a mental health practitioner or other qualified medical professional must first determine that you've been exposed to a traumatic situation that meets the diagnostic criteria for "trauma." *The Diagnostic and Statistical Manual of Mental Disorders,* or DSM IV (the guide medical professionals use to categorize different mental health problems), defines trauma as: "An actual threat to the integrity of self and to the life of self or witnessing someone close to you . . . and experiencing the event must cause fear, helplessness or horror."

Obviously, many of the stressful experiences that occur during war qualify as traumatic. Being shot at, bombed, subjected to sexual harassment or assault, or engaging in actions that are very difficult, such as attacking or killing the enemy, witnessing atrocities, or helplessly watching the death or injury of innocent bystanders, all qualify as traumatic. Other trauma also can cause PTSD, such as serious accidents or injury, natural disasters, terrorism, and child abuse.

DIAGNOSING PTSD

Only a qualified mental health practitioner, such as a psychiatrist, psychologist, psychiatric nurse, or clinical social worker, can diagnose you

---

*During the first month following a trauma, individuals may experience Acute Stress Disorder (ASD). This may have happened in theater. We do not go into the details of ASD here, but it's important to know that most people who have ASD do go on to develop PTSD. Alternatively, many people who never experience ASD can develop PTSD.

with posttraumatic stress disorder. When assessing your condition, the mental health practitioner will look for a combination of specific symptoms to help make a proper diagnosis. These symptoms fall in three categories: re-experiencing symptoms, avoidance and numbing symptoms, and hypervigilance or increased arousal.

Re-experiencing Symptoms

Bad memories of a traumatic event can come back at any time. You may feel the same fear and horror you did when the event took place. There's often a trigger—a sound, sight, or smell that causes you to relive the event. Here are some examples of re-experiencing symptoms:

- Having bad dreams, nightmares, or night terrors
- Unwanted thoughts or memories
- Feeling like you're actually going through the event again, which is called a flashback
- Becoming emotionally upset after a trigger (such as hearing a car backfire) that brings back memories of gunfire and war
- Becoming physically aroused (such as a racing heart, rapid breathing, sweating, etc.) after seeing a news report of a rape bringing back memories of assault if you were harassed or sexually assaulted

Avoidance and Numbing

People with PTSD often go to great lengths to avoid things that might remind them of the traumatic event they endured. They also may shut themselves off emotionally in order to protect themselves from feeling pain and fear. Here are some examples of avoidance and numbing symptoms:

- You may try to avoid situations or people that trigger memories of the traumatic event. You may even avoid talking or thinking about the event.
- You may avoid any reminders of war such as movies, articles, or TV coverage of war.
- You may keep very busy or refuse to seek help in order to avoid having to think or talk about the event.

- You may feel dead or hollow inside, unable to have any feelings at all.
- Emotional numbness may cause you to be unable to have positive or loving feelings toward other people; this will seriously affect your relationships with your partner, family, and friends.
- You may avoid contact with family, friends, and others whenever possible.
- You may not be interested in activities you used to enjoy.
- You may be unable to remember parts of the traumatic event.
- You may feel that your future and life span have been cut short.

HYPERVIGILANCE OR INCREASED AROUSAL

Those suffering from PTSD may operate on "high alert" at all times and often have very short fuses. The following are some examples of hypervigilance symptoms:

- You may feel that you're always in hyperdrive or having a continual adrenaline rush.
- You may always be alert and on the lookout for danger.
- You may suddenly become angry or irritable.
- You may be easily startled by unexpected noises or when someone surprises you.
- You may feel on guard all of the time.
- You may have a hard time falling asleep or staying asleep.
- You may have trouble concentrating when trying to focus on something.
- You may fear unnecessarily for your safety or the safety of others.

Notice that these are all symptoms we've been discussing as common, normal reactions to a traumatic event. Therefore having these symptoms doesn't, in and of itself, mean that you have PTSD. In order to be diagnosed with PTSD, you have to exhibit a particular set of symptoms: one of the re-experiencing symptoms, three avoidant or numbing symptoms, and two of the hyperarousal symptoms. Your symptoms must persist for at least one month after the event, meet the traumatic definition on page 66, and must cause significant distress or problems with your daily functioning.

WHAT'S IT LIKE TO HAVE PTSD?

As you will see below, many of the symptoms of PTSD are common reactions that occur following experience in a war zone. The difference is
that in PTSD, they're much more intense, much more disruptive, and
they don't go away. If these symptoms don't decrease over a few months,
or if they cause significant problems in your daily life at work or at home,
it's time to seek treatment from a professional. Remember, there are
very effective treatments for PTSD, but you need to ask for help in order
to receive them.

If you have PTSD, your life revolves around the unbearable emotions
unleashed by your memories of the traumatic event. It's hard to concentrate while you're awake because the memories intrude on your thoughts
while you're trying to think about something else. At night, you may
wake up in a sweat, your heart pounding and your mind full of rage, fear,
or panic because of intense nightmares about things that happened in the
war zone. You are constantly on the lookout for reminders that might
trigger such memories; it might be a movie, a televised newscast, or the
smell of certain foods, or certain sounds like gunshots, helicopters, or
screams. When you encounter such reminders, you may become very
emotional or your body might react with a pounding heart, profuse
sweating, or a headache. Sometimes such reminders can trigger a PTSD
flashback, which is like being in a horrible time machine where you actually believe you're back in the war zone surrounded by the enemy, witnessing death all around you, or watching helplessly as innocent children
are caught in a crossfire.

Memories associated with PTSD are so unbearable that you'll do almost anything to avoid them. This often means avoiding any situations
that are likely to retrigger such memories, such as movies or social gatherings where you fear that someone will ask you to tell them what happened during the war. As a result, you may not want to leave your house
for fear that you will see, hear, or smell something that will reactivate the
traumatic memories. This can obviously be a problem for your family,
who will want to interact with friends and neighbors as usual.

Perhaps the worse part of having PTSD is the emotional shutdown or
"psychic numbing" that often takes hold. By "numbing out," you can't feel
a thing. This is a psychological strategy to protect you from the unbearable

feelings unleashed by the traumatic memories. The problem is that when you shut out the fear, guilt, sadness, or shame, you also shut down your capacity to feel love, happiness, or enjoyment. This has two devastating consequences. On the one hand, you feel dead inside. On the other, your inability to express and receive love from your family can cause major family disruption, sometimes ending in divorce and social isolation. People with PTSD are very lonely because they reject offers of friendship and avoid social contact.

When you have PTSD, you're on high alert all the time. The adrenaline is pumping and you're constantly on the lookout for dangerous situations. With such a constant state of arousal, you can't sleep, can't concentrate, are very short-tempered, and very jumpy. As they say in the military, "your head is on swivel" as you constantly scan your environment for dangerous situations even though you know on some level that things are really pretty safe. This preoccupation with danger is usually out of your control and may be expressed as overly suspicious or overprotective behavior. Needless to say, this can also cause a great disruption in your family life.

People with PTSD don't feel they can tell other family members about what happened. This is partly because they don't want to have to remember what happened, partly because they don't want to subject others to the realities of the war zone, and partly because they believe that a civilian can't possibly understand what they've been through. Service members with PTSD often state that they have lost the person they used to be. They feel that they have been changed so much by the traumatic experience that they have become unrecognizable to themselves and others. What is worse, they don't like the person they have become. People with PTSD often feel that they are unlovable or don't deserve the love of partners and family. Because of this, they often experience depression as well. When considering the losses that may lead to depression (see Chapter 12), the PTSD-related loss of self may be the most unbearable loss of all.

Tony continues to blame himself for being unable to prevent the death of his comrade. Since returning home, he has been anxious, irritable, and on edge most of the time. He has become preoccupied with concerns about the personal safety of his family and often erupts into bouts of rage. Sleep has been difficult, and when it does occur, it's often interrupted by vivid nightmares during which he thrashes about, kicks his wife, or moves furniture in his sleep. His boys complain that he's become so overprotective that he will not let them out of his sight. His wife, Laura, reports that he's been emotionally distant since his return. His friends have grown tired of inviting him to social gatherings because he consistently turns down all invitations. Tony acknowledges that he has changed since returning from deployment. He reports that he sometimes experiences strong surges of fear, panic, guilt, and anger, and that at other times he feels emotionally dead, unable to return the love and warmth of family and friends. Life has become a terrible burden.

Adjustment at work has also been difficult for Tony. His employer, who has patiently supported him (although he does not realize this!), reports that his work has suffered dramatically, that he seems preoccupied with his own thoughts, irritable and impatient with customers, that he often makes mistakes, and that he has not functioned effectively at the automobile dealership where he was previously a top salesman. The intense cohesion of the military unit was far different from the lack of camaraderie he now feels with his coworkers at his civilian job. Furthermore, he finds it difficult to feel challenged, fulfilled, or stimulated by selling cars because he's aware that only a few months earlier in Iraq, "on-the-job" decisions could affect whether he and his comrades lived or died. He also has difficulty concentrating on work because his mind is so often preoccupied with vivid re-experiencing of combat scenarios.

It is very likely that Tony is suffering from PTSD. The pattern of symptoms of re-experiencing, avoidance, and arousal, combined with the impact they have on Tony and his family's everyday lives are a sign that Tony should be evaluated by a professional. Steps can then be taken to improve his life and the life of his family.

CO-OCCURRING PROBLEMS

PTSD is only one problem that can develop following traumatic events that occur in a war zone. We discussed traumatic grief in Chapter 8. Depression, substance abuse, excessive smoking and/or drinking, panic attacks, severe anxiety, and physical health issues also commonly occur, which we discuss further in Chapter 12. However, it's important to understand that these other problems often co-occur with PTSD. In fact, there's an 80-percent chance that a person with PTSD will meet diagnostic criteria for at least one other psychiatric disorder. Such individuals are also at a higher risk for medical problems and illnesses. Because these problems can co-occur, it can make living with someone with PTSD even more difficult.

Sometimes physical problems can be a blessing in disguise, since there's no stigma attached to going for medical help when there seems to be a "good" reason to do so. There are currently major initiatives within both the military and VA medical systems to train primary care physicians to screen all patients for PTSD and to provide treatment for those who meet diagnostic criteria. One reason why many more troops and veterans are receiving treatment for their PTSD is because such care is being provided within the primary care setting. This approach is called "integrated primary-behavioral health care," and it consists of a treatment model in which primary care physicians and mental health professionals work together within the primary care setting. Going to see a primary care physician can be the first step to getting a referral for the help you need.

WHY DO SOME PEOPLE DEVELOP PTSD?

Mental health professionals don't know why some traumatized people develop this condition while others don't. We do know that it's *not* a sign of weakness. Many people who are brave or strong end up with PTSD or its symptoms after going through a traumatic experience.

As we said earlier, most people who go through a traumatic event don't get PTSD. How likely you are to get PTSD depends on many factors, such as:

- How severe the trauma was
- The intensity of your reaction to the trauma
- Whether you were injured
- Whether someone you were close to died or was injured
- How much your own life was in danger
- How much you felt you could not control things
- How much help and support you got following the event

HOW MANY SERVICE MEMBERS DEVELOP PTSD IN THEIR LIFETIME?

Adults, children, women, and men can all develop PTSD. It's estimated that 30 percent of Vietnam veterans developed PTSD at some point since military service, half of whom have recovered. Troops who had the heaviest exposure to traumatic events are more likely to develop PTSD than others. Within the U.S. civilian population, about 60 percent of men and 50 percent of women experience at least one traumatic event during their lifetime (such as disasters, sexual assault, and severe accidents). At the same time, about 7 to 8 percent develop PTSD. In other words, most people who experience trauma never develop PTSD. For those who do, however, because of the advances in early treatment that have been made, the sooner service members get help, the sooner they will recover. Additionally, many of those who do develop PTSD will recover completely.

HOW PTSD IMPACTS FAMILY

The symptoms of PTSD and other post-traumatic reactions change how a trauma survivor feels and acts, so traumatic experiences that happen to a service member can affect everyone else in his or her family. PTSD can make your loved one hard to get along with because he or she is irritable, uncommunicative, or has isolated him or herself from the rest of your family. When PTSD persists without treatment, it can cause major problems in a family. It's important to understand how families can be affected.

Family members coping with a loved one who has PTSD may find themselves reacting in many ways. Some families may experience most of the following reactions, while others may experience only a few. All of the reactions described are common in families who've had to deal with a family member suffering from PTSD.

SYMPATHY

People feel bad when someone they care about has had to endure the traumatic and sometimes horrifying experiences of war. One of the first reactions many family members have is sympathy for their loved one. You may feel sorry when your loved one continues to suffer from symptoms of PTSD and other posttraumatic reactions, like the common ones we discussed in Chapter 4. It may be helpful for your service member to know that you sympathize with him or her, even if you can't completely share or understand exactly what he or she is going through.

Although it might be surprising to some, too much sympathy from family members can actually backfire and have a negative effect. You need to be careful that your sympathy doesn't lead you to baby your loved one with PTSD or treat him or her like an invalid. This can send a message of low expectations, a message that you don't believe your loved one is strong enough to overcome his or her problems. For example, if a partner has so much sympathy for his wife that he doesn't expect her to work after she returns from deployment, the wife may think that he doesn't have any confidence in her ability to recover from her PTSD. Oversympathizing can become patronizing and cause a sense of hopelessness and defeat in your service member. It can make things worse by provoking excessive arousal and anger or creating deeper withdrawal and avoidance.

NEGATIVE FEELINGS

Sometimes family members may find themselves having very negative feelings about their traumatized service member, believing that he or she no longer possesses the qualities that they loved and admired. A person like Tony, who was outgoing before the war, may become withdrawn. A person who was fun and easygoing before deployment may become ill-tempered or now has a drinking problem. It can be hard to feel good about someone who seems to have changed in so many ways.

You may also react negatively to behaviors your loved one develops following a trauma. For instance, if he or she is drinking excessively, it may disgust you. Aggressive behaviors and angry outbursts may drive you away. You may also react negatively to your service member because you have trouble making sense of the traumatic event that he or she experienced. Sometimes family and friends have negative feelings even when they know that the way they're viewing the traumatic event is unfair; it just makes them feel that way. The best way to avoid these negative reactions is to educate yourself on PTSD. This book is only one of many resources that can help you recognize the typical signs of this condition. You should also consider encouraging your loved one to take action to overcome PTSD, which almost always involves professional treatment and ideally includes the entire family. Even if he or she refuses treatment, you and the rest of the family would likely benefit from some type of support. Such support can be found through family support programs, such as Family Assistance Centers for both Active and Reserve Component families, as well as community resources such as grass roots organizations, churches, and employee assistance programs. (See the Resources section on page 241 for more ideas.)

Returning veterans who are experiencing PTSD symptoms may gradually realize they're behaving "out of line." They may recognize that their shutdown is driving their family members and loved ones away. Or they may realize that their self-imposed isolation is destroying marital, family, and social relationships. This is because, lacking information about PTSD, they may not understand how their PTSD-related behavior is creating a difficult—if not impossible—situation for their families. If this isn't addressed soon enough, their families may start to drift away because they perceive their loved one as cold, distant, and unwilling to do anything to improve the situation.

AVOIDANCE

Just as returning service members are often afraid to talk about what happened to them, family members are frequently fearful of hearing about the graphic details of war zone encounters. If your loved one is having trouble with guilt, you may hesitate to discuss the war because you fear it will cause him or her more guilt, pain, or shame. Sometimes, if the traumatic event your service member endured is associated with shame (such as with rape), you may avoid talking about it because it's so difficult to discuss or because you feel it's inappropriate to talk about such things.

You may start to avoid the same things your loved one avoids because you want to help keep him or her from experiencing further pain, or because you're afraid of his or her reaction. For example, the wife of a veteran who doesn't want to interact with other people may stop making plans for social events or outings because she's afraid of upsetting her husband. Though she's aware that this isn't fixing the problem, she at least feels some sense of control. She knows that if the family goes to a public event, the veteran will be grim, anxious, irritable, and hypervigilant the entire time they're there. If they don't go, she can control things and not let this happen. These are difficult choices for any family to make. In this example, although the wife doesn't want to upset her husband, she also doesn't want to deprive herself or her children of the normal social life that every family has every reason to expect. It's always best if you can discuss this kind of dilemma openly with your service member. In this example, an acceptable solution might be for the husband to stay home while the wife and children go out, so long as everyone can agree to this compromise. Sometimes, however, the hypervigilance associated with PTSD can be a big problem. The veteran might be so fearful that his wife and children will be in danger without his protection that he will forbid them to go out on their own. If things get to this point, professional assistance is necessary.

DEPRESSION

Depression is common among family members when their loved one with PTSD acts in ways that cause feelings of pain or loss. There may be serious changes in your family life when your loved one has PTSD or posttraumatic symptoms. He or she may feel too anxious to go out on family outings as you did in the past or may not be able to work because of PTSD symptoms. As a result, your family income may decrease and you may be unable to buy things and do things the way you did before. You may feel unloved or abandoned if your partner withdraws and avoids being emotionally or sexually intimate. Your children may feel hurt that their parent won't come to see them in school activities or sports if he or she can't be in crowds because of PTSD-related hypervigilance. When PTSD lasts for a long time, you may begin to lose hope that your service member or your family will ever get "back to normal." All of these factors and more can cause depression. We discuss this topic further in the next chapter.

ANGER AND GUILT

In addition to problems that may occur because of a returning service member's irritability and anger, family members may also feel anger or guilt when their loved one has PTSD. You may feel guilty if you feel responsible for his or her happiness or general well-being but can't make a difference no matter how hard you try to help. You may also feel guilty if you can't convince your service member to get professional treatment. You may feel guilty for not providing enough support, even if your loved one rejects your best efforts. For some traumatic events, a family member may feel responsible for the incident. For instance, a husband whose wife experienced military sexual trauma may feel guilty because he was unable to protect her from the attack.

Sometimes family members feel anger toward the person with PTSD and wish the service member would just "forget about it" or "get over it" and get on with life. You may be angry when your loved one continues to think over and over about his or her traumatic war experiences. This anger may come from frustration. You may be angry if your partner can't keep a job or drinks too much; won't go out with you or avoids being intimate; or won't take care of things around the house or help with the kids. Family members may also feel angry and irritable in response to the PTSD-related anger and irritability your service member may be expressing. It's important to recognize that anger on all sides is in reaction to PTSD and that both you and your loved one must get past this anger in order to deal with the underlying reasons for it. A good way to manage such anger is to understand its source. At the risk of being repetitious, this is where education about PTSD can make a difference. Understanding that these feelings of anger and guilt are no one's fault, but rather a manifestation of the PTSD, can free up everyone to try to solve these problems without blaming one another.

HEALTH PROBLEMS

Bad habits that family members may have, such as drinking, smoking, and not exercising may worsen as a result of trying to cope with a loved one's PTSD symptoms. Parents or partners can become depressed or begin to abuse drugs and alcohol. Sleep can become a problem for some members of your family, especially if sleep is a problem for your service member. You may be unable to sleep well because you're depressed and/or worried. When you constantly feel worried, angry, on edge, or depressed, you're more likely to develop stomach or intestinal problems, headaches, muscle pain, and other health problems. If these physical problems persist, you should visit your primary care physician for an evaluation.

RECOVERING FROM PTSD

The severity of posttraumatic stress disorder varies from mild to severe. As with other medical or psychiatric disorders, some people with PTSD are able to lead full and rewarding lives despite the constant problems caused by their symptoms. Others will recover from their PTSD on their own, without professional assistance. But for the minority of service members with PTSD who develop a persistent chronic and debilitating mental illness, they are not likely to improve without mental health and community services to help them function properly. After treatment, some make a full recovery, some experience partial improvement, and others may never improve. Sixty percent of those who develop PTSD will recover, whether or not they've ever received treatment. There are three general classes of PTSD:

Chronic PTSD: PTSD in those who don't recover is often called chronic PTSD. Some, however, may show improvement in how well they function at work or at home, or in how severe or disabling their symptoms are, but their PTSD nonetheless remains chronic.

PTSD in Remission with Occasional Relapses: Some service members with PTSD will have periods of time with few or no symptoms (remission) followed by periods of time when they experience the full pattern of PTSD symptoms (relapse). This is usually due to being exposed to a situation that reminds them of the original traumatic war experience in a significant way. This exposure brings up long dormant memories and feelings.

Delayed Onset PTSD: There's a delayed version of PTSD in which service members don't exhibit PTSD until months or years after their time in the war zone. Sometimes these people had a few but not all PTSD symptoms and developed the full disorder when something pushed them over the edge. Sometimes, people have coped very success-fully with their war zone trauma for many years until a situation occurs that retriggers intense memories of the original trauma. For example, a war zone veteran who is once again in a life-threatening situation, such as an armed robbery or sexual assault, may develop a full-blown case of PTSD. Sometimes the trigger isn't as obvious. An example of this would be if a Vietnam veteran, who's son or daughter is deployed to Iraq, begins to experience traumatic memories and PTSD again, triggered by his firsthand knowledge of the dangers of war.

EFFECTIVE TREATMENTS

There are several treatments for PTSD that may work for you, including talk therapies and medications, that have been shown to be effective in treating some of the symptoms of PTSD. Typical PTSD treatment usually involves as-sessment, **psychoeducation**, and, depending on the severity and the par-ticular set of symptoms, therapy, medication, or both. There are a number of factors that influence what kind of treatment you will receive. Patient pref-erence is a major factor. If you want to talk about your trauma and don't want to take medications, you'd be a candidate for psychotherapy. On the other hand, if you don't want to discuss your traumatic experiences, you'd likely be a candidate for medication. Sometimes there aren't enough trained psychotherapists available, so medication becomes the only immediately available option. And sometimes a combination of psychotherapy and med-ication is necessary to achieve the best results.

Psychoeducation

Psychoeducation is a form of **therapy** that involves learning about what PTSD is and how the symptoms influence your life. Usually the therapist helps you to understand that you're not losing your mind and that many others have suffered in a similar way after exposure to various traumas, including the extreme stress of warfare. Any therapist should be able to provide you with this information.

Sometimes this education can be provided through **peer counseling** from other service members who've experienced PTSD. VA's nationwide

Vet Center program is a major resource for peer counseling. Many VA Medical Centers have vet-to-vet peer support groups that provide this kind of counseling. Your local Veterans Service Organization can tell you how to contact these peer support groups. The groups often meet at a Vet Center. They may also meet at a neutral location such as the VA, family support program locations, or local churches. See the Resources section on page 241 for mqre information.

Individual Therapy

Cognitive Behavioral Therapy (CBT) has been shown to be the most effective treatment for PTSD. In fact, CBT has been designated the treatment of choice in all **evidence-based clinical practice guidelines** for the treatment of PTSD published to date. Troops suffering from PTSD often mistakenly perceive the world as dangerous, see themselves as powerless or inadequate, or feel guilty for outcomes that could not have been prevented. CBT involves working with your cognitions, or thoughts, to change your emotions, thoughts, and behaviors. There are several types of CBT: Exposure Therapy, Cognitive Processing Therapy (CPT), Eye Movement and Desensitization Therapy (EMDR). Most of these treatments require up to ten to twelve sessions.

Exposure Therapy, sometimes called prolonged exposure, uses careful, repeated, detailed imagining of the trauma (exposure) in a safe, controlled environment in order to help you face and gain control of the overwhelming fear and distress that both occurred during the trauma and is also triggered by traumatic memories. The goal of treatment is to disconnect the memory from the intolerable sense of fear and distress with which it has been associated.

Cognitive Processing Therapy (CPT) focuses on trauma-related thought patterns as well as the intense emotions that occur following a trauma. In CPT, the therapist will ask you to produce a written narrative about your war zone trauma. He or she will then use **cognitive restructuring**, a technique that enables you to first identify and examine upsetting (and often inaccurate) trauma-related thoughts and then teaches you to challenge those erroneous thoughts and replace them with more balanced and accurate ones.

Typical mistaken thoughts include perceiving the world as dangerous, seeing oneself as powerless or inadequate, or feeling guilty for
outcomes that couldn't have been prevented. Cognitive restructuring has proven effective in helping service members with PTSD
overcome unbearable trauma-related feelings such as guilt and
shame.

Eye Movement Desensitization and Reprocessing also includes elements from both exposure and cognitive therapy. It involves
thinking about the traumatic event while simultaneously moving your
eyes back and forth. It's based on the theory that these rapid eye movements reprogram the brain so that traumatic memories will no longer be
upsetting. Although research suggests that the eye movements are really
not necessary, it also shows that EMDR is an effective treatment.

OTHER THERAPIES

Some other therapies you might hear about are **brief psychodynamic
therapy** and **stress inoculation training**. Whereas exposure therapy
focuses on trauma-related fear reactions and CPT focuses on the maladaptive thought patterns resulting from traumatic experiences, brief
psychodynamic therapy focuses on unconscious processes believed to be
expressed as PTSD symptoms. According to psychodynamic theory, traumatic thoughts and feelings are understood to be so intolerable that
they're forced out of conscious thought through a process called **repression**. The therapist attempts to restore psychic balance by exploring and
confronting this unconscious material. When you become aware of this
unconscious material, you're able to exercise more control over repressed thoughts and feelings and thereby reduce your symptoms. This
approach usually requires ten to twelve sessions.

Stress inoculation training is an approach that teaches techniques for reducing anxiety, developing better coping skills, and correcting inaccurate
thoughts related to a trauma. This is another form of cognitive behavioral
therapy that's usually conducted by a clinical psychologist. Unlike exposure
or CPT therapy, however, the focus isn't on traumatic material but rather
on how to manage the anxiety and other symptoms produced by PTSD.
For example, one technique is called "thought stopping," in which you

learn how to stop trauma-related thoughts when you start to experience them. Like the other treatments described, stress inoculation therapy usually requires ten to twelve sessions.

GROUP THERAPY

Group therapy is another popular approach to treating PTSD. Usually, groups consist of individuals who've all survived the same type of trauma, such as war zone veterans, rape victims, or disaster survivors. Sharing experiences helps each group member recognize their common emotional, behavioral, and psychological difficulties. The group also provides mutual social support as well as an opportunity to learn more effective coping skills. Therapy groups are usually led by one or two mental health professionals. Such treatment is available in military, VA Medical Center, Vet Center, and other settings. Group therapy may vary in length; you may go for anywhere from ten to twelve weeks to many months.

MEDICATIONS

There are some medications that are being used successfully in the treatment of PTSD. Medications can reduce PTSD symptoms as well as the anxiety, depression, and sleeplessness associated with the disorder. They can also make it easier for you to participate in **counseling** or therapy. **Selective serotonin reuptake inhibitors (SSRIs)**, which enhance the activity at those nerve cells that release the neurotransmitter **serotonin**, have emerged as the treatment of choice. Two SSRIs— sertaline (Zoloft) and paroxetine (Paxil)—have been approved by the U.S. Food and Drug Administration as indicated treatments for PTSD. Other SSRIs also seem to be effective. Treatment results with SSRIs are especially exciting because they appear to help lessen all three symptom clusters of PTSD (see page 153 for the list of symptom clusters). Three other non-SSRI medications—venlafaxine (Effexor), prazosin (Minipress), and risperidine (Risperidol)—have also shown promise in clinical trials. As we've learned more about the biological changes that occur in the brains of people with PTSD, a number of new medications have been developed that are currently being tested.

TELLING YOUR TRAUMA STORY

Discussing traumatic war zone experiences and sharing painful feelings can be very difficult. It's understandable that you might be worried or afraid that therapy might cause you to be overwhelmed by sadness, pain, grief, or anger. But talking about traumatic experiences can be a key to recovery if you can talk to someone whom you trust. It enables you to take a fresh look at your experiences and your beliefs about them. This kind of therapeutic talking may require many meetings, but over time you will discover that your memories have become more controllable and less painful or frightening.

COPING WITH PTSD

Even after you begin to recover from PTSD, you may continue to remember and react to the traumatic memories every now and then. The difference is that such memories will no longer dominate your life and create difficulties for you and your family. It's important to keep in mind that recovery is an ongoing, daily, slow but sure process. You will not suddenly be cured. But as healing progresses, you'll have fewer PTSD symptoms, your symptoms will become less disruptive to your life, you'll gain more confidence in your ability to cope with your traumatic memories, and you'll be better able to manage your emotions.

As you travel through the healing process, we urge you *not* to use drugs or alcohol to deal with your problem. Don't isolate yourself from other people or stop doing pleasurable activities. Avoiding thoughts about the war, avoiding places that remind you of negative things, or avoiding getting treatment will not keep away distress. Instead, avoidance prevents you from learning how to effectively cope with your stress reactions.

Below are some suggestions that you can use to deal with the symptoms of PTSD (re-experiencing, increased arousal, avoidance, and numbing) that will work in conjunction with professional treatment:

- If you have flashbacks, remind yourself where you really are and that you're safe.
- Remind yourself that memories of times at war are normal and are just memories.
- Know that although reminders of the war can feel overwhelming, they will lessen over time.
- Remember that rapid breathing, feeling light-headed, and heart pounding are not dangerous.
- Remember that bodily sensations such as a racing heart and rapid breathing are only temporary and will soon go away.
- Learn ways to relax and to slow down rapid breathing, such as relaxation breathing, yoga, or meditation.
- Remember that thoughts like "I'm going to die" or "I will lose control" are part of PTSD and not related to reality; in fact, they only make panicky feelings more distressing.
- Talk to someone you trust about what you're feeling, such as a trusted friend or a religious figure.
- Walk away from irritable situations; take time to cool off.
- Take an anger management class.
- Exercise daily: this can help reduce tension.
- Do not exercise vigorously within two hours before bed because it will interfere with sleep.
- Stick to a regular bedtime.
- For trouble concentrating, write things down, use lists, and give yourself extra time to do or learn things.
- Plan on doing only a realistic number of things each day and break tasks down into small chunks to get each done.
- Try to regularly do the activities that you enjoy (or used to enjoy) even if you don't get much pleasure out of them at first.
- Do little things to remind loved ones that they're important to you. For example, leave small gifts, write short notes, or make brief phone calls to touch base.
- Remember that common reactions to war zone stress happen to most service members and will likely decrease over time.

Ways you can help family, friends, and others understand PTSD:

- Let them know that PTSD is a medical condition that can be treated.
- Talk about your recovery. This will help them understand the challenges you overcame.
- Show them your strengths and talents. Don't let PTSD keep you from going after things you want to do.
- Show people how you want to be treated by the way you act yourself. Treat others, and most of all yourself, with respect and set an example for everyone.
- Explain that you may need breaks during activities. Your symptoms may make it harder to focus on things for a long time.
- Work with your family and doctor to set manageable goals. Let them know what changes you want to make in your life.

Ways family can help someone with PTSD:

- Tell your loved one you want to listen and that you also understand if he or she doesn't feel like talking.
- Learn as much as you can about PTSD.
- Go with your loved one to visit the doctors and participate in his or her treatment.

Keep encouraging your loved one to have contact with family and friends and to do fun things. Your service member's withdrawal symptoms may make him or her hesitant to be around other people, but, because social support is vital, keep trying. Give your loved one space, but keep offering.

12

RECOGNIZING OTHER
MENTAL HEALTH ISSUES

In addition to PTSD, there are several other mental health issues that can develop if you experience major stressors during deployment to a war zone. They include depression, alcohol or substance abuse, violent and abusive behaviors, anxiety disorders, and suicidal thoughts or suicide. These conditions often occur simultaneously with PTSD (when two conditions occur at the same time, they are said to be **comorbid**), but they can also develop on their own. In this chapter you will learn about the nature of these problems, how to recognize their warning signs or symptoms, and various ways you can cope with them.

DEPRESSION

Depression can vary from person to person, but it's generally characterized as feeling down or sad more days than not, unable to experience pleasure, and losing interest in hobbies or activities that you used to find enjoyable or fun. Depression can cause you to feel excessively low in energy and be overly tired. You may also feel a sense of hopelessness or despair, or feel that things are never going to get better. We all experience sadness or feel down from time to time—that's a normal part of being human. Depression, however, is different. It lasts longer and is more serious than normal sadness or grief. As with PTSD, there are specific criteria you need to meet in order to be diagnosed with depression. A proper diagnosis can only be made by a mental health professional.

Depression is more likely to occur if you've experienced a personal loss during deployment, such as the death of one or more close friends. A loss that is particularly painful among people with PTSD is the sense that you've lost the person you used to be (see Chapter 11). Because depression can cause you to become suicidal, it's important to get professional help as soon as possible.

> *Tony no longer enjoys playing with the boys or hanging out with his friends. He never wants to go to church or barbeque with neighbors like he used to. He feels tired all of the time and he has no motivation to do anything. He not only has trouble sleeping, but his appetite is down and he has lost sexual desire.*

As you learned in Chapter 11, Tony is having an extremely difficult time readjusting to civilian life and feeling like his old self. He may have PTSD, and so he needs to be assessed. His relationships are in jeopardy, his job performance is poor, and he can't seem to get back on track. Based on the additional symptoms above, Tony is also likely suffering from depression.

WARNING SIGNS

If you notice that you (or someone you know) seem to be feeling down most of the time or are less interested in things you used to enjoy, this may be a warning sign of depression. Also be on the lookout for the following symptoms:

- Crying with no explanation
- Inability to derive pleasure from things that used to be enjoyable
- Low energy, constantly tired
- Sleep problems

- Guilt
- Decreased intellectual ability or capacity to remember things
- Weight loss or weight gain
- Slow thoughts and/or actions

Depression, like PTSD, is treatable with medications or therapy, though research shows that a combination of both usually works best. Therapy for depression involves some of the same elements we discussed in Chapter 11 on PTSD. Sometimes doctors need to try a variety of medications before finding one that works. If you're on a medication, it's important to be patient and not suddenly stop taking it. If you do, you'll quickly become depressed again. These medications take time to build up in your system, so you need to give them time to see if they are effective, and consult your doctor before making changes.

Coping with Depressive Symptoms

In addition to therapy and/or medication, here are some additional strategies for coping with the symptoms of depression:

- Talk to a close friend or family member about how you're feeling.
- Plan something fun or enjoyable each day, even just a little something.
- Keep active and exercise.
- Break tasks into small pieces and do what you can when you can do it.
- Allow yourself to feel your feelings. If this seems hard to do, try letting yourself feel them for a few minutes at a time at first.
- Give yourself time to feel better: change doesn't happen overnight and you will have highs and lows.
- Eat balanced regular meals.
- Listen to relaxing music.

SUICIDAL THOUGHTS AND SUICIDE

War experiences and combat stress reactions, especially those caused by personal loss, can lead a depressed person to think about hurting or killing him or herself. If you suspect someone you care about is feeling this way, don't be afraid to ask if they are thinking about killing themselves. If a comrade or family member talks about suicide, you must take it seriously.

Although Tony was not thinking about ending his own life, he knew of a young Soldier in another unit who had started to feel so guilty about the death of an Iraqi mother he accidentally shot that he became suicidal . . .

CPL Jameson could not stop thinking about what had happened. Several weeks ago, while standing at his post, he observed in the distance a car speeding toward the gate. As it came closer, he and the other guard held up their weapons to warn the car to stop its approach. The car did not slow down. Then they waved their weapons to make sure that the driver saw them and understood their warning. But the car continued on at the same speed. CPL Jameson then shot into the ground as a final warning. Although this made the car swerve, it speeded up again and kept coming. At this point the young corporal was afraid his post was under attack and that he only had a few seconds in which to react. As trained, he fired into the vehicle to bring it to a halt. The windshield shattered and the automobile finally came to a stop. The next thing he remembered was the shrill scream of despair that rose into the air from inside the vehicle. This was a sound that the young corporal could not get out of his mind. It echoed and has continued to reecho, haunting him day and night.

When he looked inside the car he discovered that the driver had not been shot. Instead a passenger lay drooped in the front seat, blood spattered and not moving. She had died instantly from the bullet. The car had not been a VBIED as he had feared. Instead of an explosive device, the car was carrying a young married couple who were rushing to the deathbed of a family member in the next town. The surviving husband, the driver, was inconsolable with grief and CPL Jameson was overwhelmed with guilt because he could not justify what he had just done, despite all the logical explanations.

Two months later, CPL Jameson was hospitalized and on a twenty-four hour suicide watch.

If you or someone you know is experiencing guilt about something that happened in the war zone, it's crucial to be on the lookout for suicidal thoughts or impulses. Such episodes increase the chances of suicide more than anything else. Other things that can increase suicide risk include: being male, abusing alcohol, being sixty-five years or older, unmarried or homeless, and having a family history of suicide.

WARNING SIGNS

Here are some warning signs of suicide to watch out for:

- Talking or writing about death, dying, or suicide
- Talking about wanting to kill oneself
- Uncontrolled anger or rage, being unforgiving or seeking revenge
- Acting in reckless or risky ways
- Excessive drinking or drug abuse
- Hopelessness or feeling that there is no way out, no way to feel happy
- Feeling there's no reason for continuing to live
- Cutting oneself off from loved ones and friends
- If the person talks about harming him or herself or tries to get pills, guns, or other harmful items

Suicidal thoughts and feelings or the desire to harm oneself are sometimes caused by problems that seem like they can't be fixed. Suicide is not the answer. If anyone you know has a plan to hurt themselves and especially if he or she has the means to do it (for example: "I have a gun and will shoot myself"), you should try to be supportive and listen to what he or she has to say. You should also try to get him or her to get rid of all lethal weapons so that, if he or she has a sudden impulse to kill him or herself, it will not be as easy to act on it. Remain calm and encourage him or her to seek treatment. Ask him or her to agree not to do anything until he or she talks to a professional. Offer to make the initial call for a depressed or suicidal person because often this first step is the hardest part of getting help. If he or she can't promise to call for help when they start feeling suicidal, you should call 911 immediately.

SUBSTANCE ABUSE AND PROBLEMATIC DRINKING

It's common for troops attempting to cope with upsetting traumatic stress reactions to "self-medicate" by drinking or abusing drugs. Substance abuse

> ## In Case of Emergency
>
> In case of emergency or for more information, contact the National Suicide Prevention Lifeline at 800-273-TALK (8255) (En Español: 888-628-9454) or www.suicidepreventionlifeline.org.
>
> This hotline now has a special feature for U.S. military veterans. To call for yourself, or someone you care about, dial 800-273-TALK (8255) and press 1. Your call is free and confidential. Family members and other military personnel are welcome to call this special line for more information.

often signifies readjustment problems, as a person uses drugs or alcohol to numb out the difficult thoughts, feelings, and memories related to their war zone experiences. People with PTSD, especially men, are more likely to have alcohol abuse or dependence problems. When a person wants to avoid the memories or feelings related to combat, alcohol or drugs may seem to offer a quick solution, but they actually lead to more problems in the long run.

Alcohol

Alcohol use and excessive drinking can easily become problematic after you return from deployment. As you read earlier, drinking is often used by service members as a way to avoid intolerable thoughts or feelings. Alcohol does affect your body and slows down brain activity. In small amounts it reduces your arousal level and can help you relax. This can seem to help you feel more at ease. But alcohol only buys time by temporarily enabling you to avoid thoughts and feelings. It only puts them off; it doesn't make them go away. More importantly, this temporary relief can come at a very high price. The aggression, impulsivity, and intellectual disruption caused by alcohol can harm your marriage, other relationships, and job performance. Finally, alcohol use increases your risk of suicidal and homicidal behavior.

Warning Signs

For many people, drinking to cope can lead to a spiral of abuse. At the same time, a vast majority of people in our society drink. Sometimes it can be difficult to know if your drinking is actually a problem. Here are some signs of trouble that can help you determine whether you should seek help:

- Having thoughts that you should cut down on your drinking
- Feeling guilty or bad about your drinking
- If your drinking causes others to become annoyed with you or to criticize how much you drink
- If drinking frequently becomes excessive
- If drinking becomes automatic; you find you are drinking with dinner, after work, after dinner . . . without ever thinking about it
- If you need a drink in the morning to calm your nerves
- If drinking causes problems with work, family, school, or other regular activities

Isaac is afraid of what he's seeing in Kathleen. She often apologizes about her outbursts and the fact that she's drinking every day, sometimes to the point of passing out. Isaac has had it with the alcohol. It always makes everything worse.

During deployment to the war zone, alcohol is not easily available. Once troops return home where alcohol is readily available, many find that their intake increases considerably. This easy access can tempt you to turn to alcohol instead of seeking healthy ways to cope with readjustment problems. Social drinking is an acceptable outlet, but only if you're in control. When the need for alcohol begins to control your behavior, it's time to seek help. If you think you might have a problem with alcohol, talk to your primary care physician or a chaplain. They can help get you started on the road to recovery. Alcoholics Anonymous (AA) provides widespread access to peer support for problem drinkers, so help is available in virtually every community.

What to Do if Someone with a Drinking Problem Won't Get Help

Because drinking is acceptable in our culture, it can be hard to distinguish between social drinking and problem drinking. It can be hard to

---

TIPS FOR DRINKING RESPONSIBLY

If you choose to drink, here are some tips to help you drink responsibly:

- Don't ever drink when you're sad or upset.
- Set limits ahead of time on how many drinks to have and stick to it.
- Avoid hard liquor and shots.

---

see that you have a problem. Remember, if a person doesn't want help, you can't force them to get it. However, there are some things you can do to help:

- Stop covering for the person with the problem and let him or her experience the consequences of his or her drinking.
- Don't make false threats. Do what you say you will do.
- Don't punish the person with the problem. Instead, protect yourself from having to deal with his or her problem.
- Find out about resources and services that can help so you are prepared if the person does decide to get help.
- The first step can be very hard. Help the person seek help when he or she says they are ready.

SMOKING

Excessive smoking is very frequent among veterans, at least partly because smoking is also used as a way to cope with stress. At least one study of service members deployed to Iraq reported evidence that smoking has increased among deployed troops. The reasons service members gave for their smoking included boredom, social influences, and stress. Smoking is not a healthy form of coping. Smoking has been shown to cause both short- and long-term serious health problems, such as emphysema, lung cancer, cardiovascular (heart) disease, as well as other physical problems such as reduced performance during physical training, lung capacity, and heart rate levels.

Because smoking is such a serious health hazard, smoking cessation programs are available at VA hospitals and other medical facilities. These programs often use behavioral approaches such as counseling and therapy, as well as medications, such as nicotine patches. We urge you to take advantage of these resources, especially if your smoking is excessive or out of control or if you've begun to have smoker's cough, shortness of breath, or see signs that you have less physical stamina than before.

Drugs

As with alcohol and tobacco, other drug use can become a problem after you've been exposed to war zone traumatic events. In addition to the use of illegal drugs, over the past several years the U.S. population has increased its use of prescription drugs for nonmedical reasons. Below we discuss both illegal and prescription drug abuse.

Illegal Drugs. Illegal drugs that are being used by returning troops as a coping mechanism for wartime trauma include **methamphetamine** (meth), marijuana, ecstasy, and cocaine, among others. Known on the street as "speed," "meth," "crank," "crystal meth," and "glass," methamphetamine is a central nervous system stimulant, or an "upper." Like cocaine, it produces alertness and elation, along with a variety of problematic reactions such as changes in brain function, emotional problems, and nerve damage. Also like cocaine, it is highly addictive. When meth is mixed with alcohol, it increases the chances of sudden death.

Marijuana, also called "pot," "weed," "grass," "ganja," and "hash," is the most commonly abused illegal drug in the United States. It causes a high, but also impairs your ability to drive, causes troubles with memory and your ability to learn information, and reduces your body's ability to fight off disease.

MDMA (3,4 methylenedioxymethamphetamine), also known as **ecstasy** or X, is a drug that has skyrocketed in use among young Americans. Ecstasy has both stimulating and psychedelic properties (meaning it causes hallucinations). During the first hour after taking this drug you may experience a general sense of well-being, decreased anxiety, and feelings of affection toward others. But these apparent benefits can come at a very high price. Despite MDMA's erroneous reputation for being "safe," with continued use it can cause permanent brain damage and other serious neurological effects, such as striking increases in body temperature, chills, sweating, muscle cramping, and heart and kidney failure.

Prescription Drugs. As mentioned above, prescription drugs are now also being misused by many people, including service members. Similar to illegal drug use, misuse of prescription drugs is a form of drug abuse and can also lead to substance dependence and other problems. There are three types of prescription drugs most often misused:

Opioids. Opioids, which have a numbing affect on the body, are used as painkillers. Common opioids include codeine, oxycontin, morphine, and methadone.

Anxiolytics. These drugs, which include **barbiturates, benzodiazepines**, sedatives, and tranquilizers, are central nervous system depressants, meaning they act to help you feel calm and relaxed or to help you sleep. Common anxiolytics include Xanax, Ativan, Valium, and Halcion.

Stimulant medications. These medications are typically used to treat conditions such as **ADHD** (attention deficit hyperactivity disorder). When misused, they can give you a high similar to speed. Common stimulants include Ritalin, Adderall, and Dexedrine.

WARNING SIGNS

The following are signs that indicate you or someone you know may have a drug problem:

- Change in sleeping patterns
- Sudden mood swings
- Bloodshot eyes, bruises
- Uncontrollable and impulsive behavior
- Slurred speech
- Sudden aggressive outbursts
- Sudden or dramatic weight loss or gain
- Neglected appearance/poor hygiene, sick more often

- Hiding use; lying and covering up, secretive behavior, locked doors
- Sense that the person will "do anything" to use again regardless of consequences
- Loss of interest in previously enjoyed activities
- Emotional instability or depression
- Hyperactive behavior
- Missing work/school or not completing necessary projects
- Avoiding eye contact
- Going out every night
- Change in friends or clothing or appearance
- Unusual smells on clothing or breath
- Money or valuables missing
- Disappearances for long periods of time

Drug problems, whether the drugs abused are prescription medications or illegal drugs, can be treated. However, no single type of treatment works for all drugs and all individuals. In some cases a person may be using multiple drugs, which means that multiple addictions must be taken into account in treatment. Some drugs, such as sedatives/tranquilizers or stimulants, should not be abruptly stopped because this can cause serious medical complications that may be life threatening. As with the other mental health problems we have discussed thus far, both therapy and medications are used to successfully treat drug problems.

SUBSTANCE ABUSE AND PTSD

Many service members with PTSD also have problems with substance abuse. Some say that substance abuse needs to be dealt with before you can deal with PTSD symptoms. Some say that you need to get treatment for PTSD before you can deal with the substance abuse. Since it's really difficult to disentangle these two conditions, we strongly urge that you seek treatment for both at the same time. Substance misuse is often an attempt on the part of a service member to treat the symptoms of PTSD on his or her own. Self-medication with alcohol or drugs is a very bad idea for two reasons. First, it doesn't work. Second, it adds another problem (the substance abuse) on top of the problems caused by PTSD or depression. Many substance abuse counselors know how to collaborate with mental health practitioners. If you're not offered joint treatment for both PTSD/depression and substance abuse, you should request it. Many VA Medical Centers have formal programs that address both simultaneously.

There's a new program to help treat substance abuse and PTSD at the same time. Dr. Lisa Najavits has developed a cognitive-behavioral approach called Seeking Safety. It focuses first on safety. A therapist helps you to become "safe" in your relationships, the way you think and feel, and the way you act, by teaching you coping skills. Then the therapist helps you to refocus on ideals that you may have lost touch with during the time when PTSD and substance abuse took over your life. The effectiveness of this therapy has been demonstrated.

VIOLENCE AND ABUSE

In Chapter 6 we discussed the anger that many troops experience after returning from a war zone. Anger can sometimes turn into violence or physical abuse. In intimate relationships it may also be expressed as emotional and/or verbal abuse. Emotional and verbal abuse can be as damaging to relationships as physical abuse. Abuse can take the form of controlling behavior, threats, swearing, criticism, throwing things, conflict, pushing, grabbing, and hitting. If you were abused as a child, you are more at risk for becoming a perpetrator of domestic violence. The partners of service members with PTSD are more likely to experience violence and abuse, which may create marital problems, parenting problems, and adjustment problems within the family. They are also more likely to become the victims of domestic violence and abuse.

WARNING SIGNS

Here are a few warning signs that may lead to domestic violence:

- Controlling behaviors
- Excessive jealousy
- Blaming others for problems or conflict

- Radical mood changes
- Verbal abuse such as humiliating, manipulating, blaming, confusing

As we discussed in Chapter 9 on reconnecting, relationship enhancement programs can help improve communication and educate you on how to prevent conflict from turning into abuse (see the Resources section for more information). Newer findings suggest that the best way to deal with domestic abuse is for both partners to work together in therapy. However, if safety is an issue, you should seek professional help immediately. Couples therapy should begin as soon as possible, but only after safety concerns have been successively addressed.

OTHER ANXIETY DISORDERS

In Chapter 11, we discussed PTSD, which is the most common anxiety disorder experienced by troops after time in a war zone. However, there are several other anxiety disorders that can also develop during deployment to war. A thorough discussion of all of these other anxiety disorders is beyond the scope of this book, but it's important for you to have some general knowledge about them so you can recognize them if they occur. Here we provide a brief overview of the most common. Anxiety disorders can be successfully treated with cognitive-behavioral therapy and/or with medication.

Generalized Anxiety Disorder (GAD)

Service members who have PTSD are irritable, overly watchful, and on edge. They often startle easily. If you have GAD, you are also anxious, nervous, and worried, but you would usually have other symptoms as well. People with GAD worry and are anxious all the time, whereas those with PTSD tend to become anxious only when they fear that they're in a threatening situation. People with GAD show signs of restlessness, unrealistic worries, tense muscles, dry mouth, and physical signs such as frequent need to urinate and feelings of a lump in the throat. A person with GAD worries excessively, always expecting the worst, and is overly concerned about everyday things such as family, work, health, or financial issues.

PHOBIAS

Phobia means fear. If you have a phobia, you get upset when you believe you're going to be exposed to the specific thing that you fear. Some people who suffer from phobias exhibit the avoidant behaviors and arousal symptoms typical of PTSD. These symptoms might be brought on by things in the environment that remind them of dangerous war zone exposures. The most common types of phobia are **simple phobia** (fear of blood or heights), **social phobia** (fear of social situations), and **agoraphobia** (fear of leaving the safety and security of home to go to public places such as shopping malls). The best way to distinguish a phobia from PTSD is the presence or absence of numbing symptoms. If numbing symptoms are present, it's most likely PTSD. If they're absent, it's probably a phobia. Numbing symptoms include the lack of feeling negative or positive emotions, lack of interest in activities you used to enjoy, or the avoidance of relationships.

PANIC DISORDER

Panic disorder can mimic PTSD in many ways. The main symptom of panic disorder is **panic attacks**, which are attacks of fear that occur unexpectedly and without any apparent trigger. Symptoms of a panic attack include a pounding heart, weakness, and sweating. An attack usually lasts for about ten minutes and, unlike phobias, can happen at any time. Other symptoms include numbness and tingling, feeling like you are smothering or choking, fear of going crazy, fear of dying, and a fear of doom in the near future. The big difference between panic disorder and PTSD is that with panic disorder, the panic attacks usually occur out of the blue for no rhyme or reason. Intense PTSD reactions, on the other hand, usually occur when a person fears that he or she is in a life-threatening situation.

The first thing to do if you suspect you have an anxiety disorder is to go see your primary care physician, who will refer you to further help if you need it. Talking with a trusted friend, religious leader, or attending a support group can also provide support, but it's not a substitute for assessment and treatment by a mental health professional. Stress management techniques such as relaxation breathing, yoga, and meditation can also help with the behavioral and emotional reactions that come with anxiety disorders, but again, they are no substitute for treatment.

PHYSICAL HEALTH PROBLEMS

Service members exposed to traumatic events in a war zone are more likely to experience physical injuries, which we discuss in the next chapter. In addition, deployed troops who experience trauma often report more physical health issues, such as headaches, nausea, or other stomach problems. These may be related to war zone stress. Chronic pain may also result following trauma or physical injury during traumatic combat. Such injuries complicate war zone stress reactions and PTSD because the pain and discomfort also serve as constant reminders of the traumatic experience. For example, your headaches may remind you of a close call from an IED explosion, which was followed by days of headaches.

Some research suggests that there may be a direct relationship between the development of physical health problems following trauma and the onset of PTSD. Depression and other anxiety disorders also increase your risk for physical health problems. Other medical problems that are associated with PTSD involve the **cardiovascular system** (circulatory problems, heart problems, and symptoms of cardiovascular trouble), the **digestive system** (stomach pain, diarrhea and constipation, and gastrointestinal issues, such as irritable bowel syndrome), the **endocrine system** (problems with hormones or glandular issues mostly involving the pituitary gland, thyroid, adrenal glands, ovaries, testes, and pancreas), and the **musculoskeletal system** (problems with muscles and joints).

Problems with each of these health systems can cause a large variety of diseases and many more symptoms than we can cover here. Although PTSD, depression, or other psychiatric disorders may cause some of the following symptoms, they may also indicate that you have a medical problem. A few of the signs of these types of physical problems include:

- Fatigue
- Pain
- Sleep problems
- Muscle cramps

- Your heart beating rapidly
- Shortness of breath
- Unusual chest pain in your left chest, abdomen, arm, or back
- Feeling like you are being squeezed under your breastbone

If you've been through a traumatic event during your time at war and are experiencing some of these physical symptoms, we advise you to visit your primary care physician. Make sure you inform your care provider of your other trauma-related symptoms so he or she can better determine if you need further evaluation.

As we said in the beginning of this chapter, we've offered this information to help increase your awareness of the various types of mental health, drug, and physical problems that can sometimes develop following experiences in the war zone. As you can see, there are many issues to consider, and each can be quite complex. We urge you to seek information or assistance from your primary care physician or other health professional if you've begun to experience any of these problems.

13

DEALING WITH INJURY

While she was deployed, Kathleen often spoke to Isaac of the injuries she saw her fellow Soldiers suffer during her tour. Isaac told Kathleen that he recently read in the paper that there was now a 90-percent survival rate for service members with injuries; up from 75 percent in previous conflicts. Often when service members were injured, they were able to receive medical treatment in less than thirty minutes. Isaac told Kathleen that he too had begun to see young former service members with amputations and artificial limbs in his daily rounds at the hospital, and also back in the civilian workforce as part of the staff.

As of October 2007, in the conflicts in Afghanistan and Iraq, over 3,800 service members had lost their lives and over 27,000 had been wounded, many of whom were unable to return to duty. Advances in technology have enabled the military to provide troops with combat gear (such as body armor and Kevlar helmets) capable of protecting vital organs when they're attacked. At the same time, these technological advances have paved the way for more devious and destructive weapons that can overcome protective gear and fortifications, leaving troops still vulnerable to serious physical and psychological injuries.

Although most troops wounded in the war zone survive their injuries, these injuries, such as traumatic brain injury (TBI), spinal cord injuries, loss of limb(s), and loss of eyesight, can be serious and potentially incapacitating. Isaac is right; among the 90 percent of wounded troops who now survive injuries, many are left with serious disabilities.

LOSS OF LIMB OR EYESIGHT

Resentment, anger, fear, helplessness, hopelessness, depression, and anxiety are some of the feelings you may experience when you lose a limb or other part of your body. In addition, amputees or service members who lose some or all of their eyesight may also experience grief due to their loss and the trouble it causes in their relationships (including sexual intimacy issues). Sometimes they begin to dislike their bodies, or experience **phantom limb pain**. Many service members with amputations and other bodily losses must also deal with severe levels of pain. They often report problems with sleep, such as difficulty falling asleep, waking during the night, and nightmares. Service members who were wounded in action are also more likely to experience PTSD, depression, and other psychiatric problems that we discussed in Chapters 11 and 12.

If you're also suffering from emotional problems caused by deployment, you will likely have a harder time adjusting to the loss of a limb or your eyesight. Getting support from your family, friends, and others is crucial, as it will help you better adjust to life with an artificial limb, no eyesight, or other disabling injury. Therefore, attention to the mental health of a service member who has lost a limb or sight is a very important part of any rehabilitation program. Resolving any problematic emotional issues is the only way to help troops begin to function again in daily life.

Alex's amputation was creating more emotional stress than physical hardship. His mother's constant babying was creating a rift between the two of them. Alex just wanted to be left alone and to be able to do things on his own again without her harping at him every minute. At least his brother, Sam, seemed to understand and was helping to make it easier for Alex to *maneuver about the house on his own. His niece and nephew were growing more accustomed to seeing Alex with his **prosthetic** limb and Alex had learned to invite and answer their questions.*

*The doctors at the hospital were providing Alex with great physical therapy. However, his mother refused to come along with him to learn more about how best to help him. She seemed to think that "mother knows best" and didn't realize how difficult she was making things. Despite this, Alex was making significant progress. He had returned to college and was working with his **vocational rehabilitation therapist** to help determine what type of career would be best in view of his altered physical condition.*

Here are some things to keep in mind when you (or a loved one) are coping with the injury or physical loss of a limb or eyesight:

- Stabilizing the medical condition usually needs to come first.
- If a service member uses psychological defenses, such as denial, at first it's best not to challenge these defense reactions.
- The service member needs to regain as much independence as possible.
- Dealing with pain and sleep issues can help the recovery process.
- Support groups can be very helpful to both the injured person and his or her family.
- Maintain hope that treatment will work.

Family support and involvement is vital. Family and friends should become prepared to face the injuries of their returning service member. As with other unfamiliar, upsetting, or frightening situations, adults should prepare children for what they will see and feel. Often, children's imaginations about injuries are worse than reality. Discussing things like the nature of the injury, what bandages, tubes, or machines will be present, and what the hospital room looks like can help children understand and cope better. Seeing a loved one injured and in pain is very difficult, but be careful not to take out your anger, frustration, or fear on the medical staff caring for him or her. It won't help your loved one; in fact, it will likely make him or her feel worse.

Symptoms of anxiety and depression are common and should be expected after a traumatic amputation or loss of eyesight. However, you should watch for signs such as constant despair, crying and no wish to live, or for symptoms that last for more than three to six months. Symptoms that continue to worsen can turn into full-fledged PTSD, depression, or other psychiatric disorders. At Walter Reed Army hospital, every amputee receives a psychiatric evaluation and follow-up. Sometimes you might be doing okay in a very supportive hospital environment and then get in trouble after your discharge home. If your symptoms do continue or get worse, you should seek mental health assistance at your local VA medical facility or Vet Center, or contact your primary care physician.

SPINAL CORD INJURIES

Spinal cord injury is also occurring among a number of veterans of the current conflicts. Spinal cord injury can affect all of the body's systems. It can create a wide variety of problems with movement, function, pain, and other types of feeling. Injury to the lower part of the spinal cord can lead to **paraplegia**, which means that the lower part of your body is paralyzed, and injury to the neck can lead to **quadriplegia** (also called **tetraplegia**), in which your arms, lower body, and upper body are paralyzed. Recovery is complicated and may take a long time. It requires a combination of physical treatment, mental health care, family support, and often job assistance and other social services.

TRAUMATIC BRAIN INJURY (TBI)

Kathleen was constantly irritable and impatient, easily flaring into bouts of rage. She continued to drink to try to stop thinking about the war, but her drinking was making her regular headaches even worse. She was occasionally dizzy for no reason and found herself becoming sensitive to every little noise. Light also seemed to bother her. Isaac had a hard time reading or studying at home because Kathleen was constantly turning down the lights.

It turned out that in addition to problematic drinking Kathleen's symptoms were the result of a traumatic brain injury (TBI) caused by a bombing of her convoy while deployed. TBI affects many troops following deployment to the current war. In fact, 60 to 80 percent of service members who have injuries from some form of blast may have TBI. This type of injury is often caused by blasts from roadside bombs, VBIEDs, and often involves

PHYSICAL INJURY: PROCEDURES AND THINGS TO KNOW

When you're injured, the military handles the notification of your primary next of kin, or your main contact. Sometimes the military will also notify your secondary next of kin, but usually this only occurs in cases of death, not physical injury. In most cases, service members sustain injuries because they're either **wounded in action (WIA)** or, if the injury didn't occur in battle, it may be classified as **disease and non-battle injury (DNBI)**. If your injury is serious and the attending physician determines it's essential to your recovery, your primary next of kin may be issued **Invitational Travel Orders (ITOs)** so they can be with you. Their travel expenses are paid by the military (contact the hospital for information) and they are housed at a local hotel, with a military family or, if available, at a **Fisher House**. Wounded service members are re-evaluated every two weeks to determine whether their family's presence continues to be necessary to their recovery.

Wounded service members are treated at a military medical hospital and are assigned case managers to work with them during their recovery period. These case managers are also there to help family members. Many military hospitals also house a Family Assistance Center as well as provide chaplains, social workers, and other supports for wounded troops and their families, and we encourage you to make good use of these resources. Eventually you will transition from the military hospital to medical retirement, to the VA, or to separate from the military. The Department of Defense has a mandatory Transition Assistance Program (TAP) (see www.transitionassistanceprogram.com for more information) to help you through this process. It's a good idea to discuss this notification and transition process with your family before you leave for deployment, so they know what to expect.

invisible head injury in which there is no bruise or visible wound. TBIs are categorized as mild, moderate, or severe, and they're diagnosed according to how severe the injury was at first (for example, immediate loss of consciousness), not how severe the symptoms (such as headaches and dizziness) are afterward. Eighty percent of all traumatic brain injuries are categorized as mild TBI, while 20 percent are moderate to severe.

TBI is caused by explosions that produce dangerous blast waves of high pressure that basically rattle your brain inside your skull. Helmets cannot protect against this type of impact. These types of blast waves can also cause concussions leading to blindness, deafness, and loss of consciousness. This damage, damage that remains unseen, can have long-term consequences. It's very common for service members with mild TBI to show few symptoms and also to believe that they have not experienced any detrimental head trauma.

Symptoms associated with mild TBI, often referred to as a **concussion**, include:

- Headaches
- Dizziness
- Emotional problems, such as impatience or impulsiveness
- Cognitive problems, such as trouble concentrating, making decisions, or thinking logically
- Trouble remembering things, amnesia
- Depression, anxiety, and moodiness
- Apathy (lack of interest or concern), not caring
- Inability to sleep
- Lower tolerance for lights and noise
- Anger, agitation, and irritability

Although at first Isaac was surprised to hear that Kathleen was suffering from TBI, the more he learned about it, the more it explained things. Kathleen's TBI was not easily recognizable. The injury that initially caused it was not something that Kathleen thought of as serious, and if asked, she likely would not have mentioned it. She had survived the incident with very minor injuries and hadn't even hit her head on anything. However, the mere impact of the explosion caused her brain to bang into the inside bony surface in the front of her skull. Her constant headaches and her change in temperament were the only signs she exhibited. Because the VA had been seeing so many of this type of injury, when

Kathleen visited the primary care clinic to get some sleep medication, they had her complete a short screening instrument for TBI. Her screen came up positive and further testing and assessment led to the diagnosis of mild TBI.

TBI can be complicated to diagnose because troops injured in this manner can develop emotional or behavioral issues, such as irritability, depression, and out-of-control behaviors, which seem to change their personality. In Kathleen's case her drinking problem masked things further. These changes often coexist with or are mistaken for the changes caused by common posttraumatic stress reactions. It's also important to recognize that some troops may develop both TBI and PTSD, which we'll discuss shortly.

Most troops make a full and uncomplicated recovery from mild brain injuries and return to their previous level of functioning in three to six months. However, a small portion develop chronic and persistent symptoms such as headaches and insomnia, memory, attention, and cognitive problems. These injured service members require specialized care from medical professionals skilled in treating TBI. This specialized care usually focuses on helping patients reach the highest level of functioning possible through rehabilitation and education.

Symptoms associated with moderate to severe TBI include:

- Persistent headache
- Repeated vomiting or nausea
- Convulsions or seizures
- Inability to awaken from sleep
- **Stupor**, an unresponsive state that a person can be jarred out of
- **Coma**
- **Vegetative state**, which is similar to a coma but the person continues to have a sleep-wake cycle and periods of alertness
- **Persistent vegetative state (PVS)**, in which an individual stays in a vegetative state for more than a month

Although moderate to severe TBI can lead to serious and profound neurological and behavioral deficits (brain damage), some service members make remarkable recoveries. About half of these severely head-injured patients will need surgery to remove a collection of blood, stop bleeding, or treat severe bruising of the brain. Moderately to severely injured patients need rehabilitation that involves personally tailored treatment programs in physical therapy, occupational therapy, speech/language therapy, psychology/psychiatry, and social support. Further research is needed (and is currently being done) to find more effective ways to treat moderate to severe TBI.

PTSD VERSUS TBI

As you just read, TBI, especially mild TBI, can be very hard for a doctor to diagnose. Service members routinely complete screens for PTSD when they return from deployment and those with TBI often also meet criteria for PTSD on these screens. Because blast injuries often "erase" or obliterate memories of what occurred shortly before and shortly after the blast, you may not recall the injury that caused the TBI, nor have any documentation that it occurred. On the other hand, PTSD involves vivid memories of the trauma. That's why assessment of these two disorders among returning troops may be complicated. Further assessment may show that some individuals do have PTSD, others have TBI, and still others have both. When both PTSD and TBI are present, it appears that they have usually developed from two different events. As you know, many things can happen during a long deployment.

If you have TBI and PTSD, doctors and clinicians need to take both conditions into account during treatment. Individuals with TBI may be too sensitive to benefit from some medications used for PTSD. There are also questions about how much troops with TBI can benefit from cognitive behavioral therapies, although there have been some promising results in this regard. Your family also needs to be closely involved and educated about how to best help you. Because of the attention and memory problems involved in TBI, it may be beneficial to include family at doctor's appointments in order to help make sure all information is retained.

PSYCHOLOGICAL AND
EMOTIONAL IMPACT OF INJURY

As you know now, experiencing physical injury puts you at higher risk than other service members for developing PTSD and other trauma-related problems. If you're injured, it's important that you get medical attention, not just for your physical recovery and health, but also for your mental health. When the focus is exclusively on treatment of physical problems, such as broken bones, burns, and other serious injury, it's easier for both you and your doctor to avoid discussing any emotional issues that need attention. You may have to make a concerted effort to bring attention to your emotional needs, but it's well worth it.

Physical injury has profound effects on the lives of service members and their families. The physical injury itself produces a whole set of challenges about how best to cope with the emotional impact of the injury, your new physical limitations, possible disfigurement, pain, and the psychological trauma of the initial injury itself. The injury can also serve as a reminder of the traumatic experience or experiences that you have been through. This can make things even more difficult to handle. Your readjustment to civilian life will be much easier if you deal with both the emotional and physical impacts of your injury.

COPING TIPS

When you're severely injured, you and your family will have a lot to learn and many issues to cope with. None of you have had a chance to prepare for this event. Your roles will have to change, and your family will have competing demands on their time, which can cause them to neglect taking care of themselves properly. Here are some tips for coping with this difficult situation:

- Use normal supports (family, friends, etc.) as well as professional supports to get you through.
- Remember you're the same person you were before the injury. It may help to think of yourself as a whole person who just happens to have a missing or injured body part.
- Focus on learning new ways to do the things you enjoyed before; sometimes you may need to be creative.
- If you're learning to use a prosthesis, remember your body image will likely improve once you feel more comfortable with it.
- Stay involved with people you already know and like.
- Join a support group where you can meet others with similar injuries who live full and happy lives. It will help you realize that you can do the same.

- Talk with important people in your life about your feelings, including anger, fear, and frustration. Also listen to how these people feel now that you're injured.
- Your family must be sure to take time to relax, rest, and take care of their own needs.
- Introduce new ideas or changes slowly, so everyone has a chance to figure out how they will cope.

FINANCIAL AND LEGAL ISSUES

Seriously injured service members are assigned a case manager to help them and their families deal with logistical, financial, and other issues that arise. When you experience an injury that has disabling effects of any kind, you and your family may need some extra help with financial and benefits issues, or even some form of legal assistance. For assistance with such things as wills or advance directives, powers of attorney, or other legal support, these resources can help:

- American Bar Association's Legal Assistance for Military Personnel (LAMP): www.abanet.org/legalservices/lamp/home.html
- U.S. Army Judge Advocate General's Corp (JAG): www.jagcnet .army.mil/legal

Further benefits and disability information can be found through VA benefits (VBA) or at www.disabilityinfo.gov.

WORKING AFTER YOUR INJURY

You may also be looking for help with rehabilitation and/or getting back to work. The Department of Veterans Affairs works closely with the Department of Labor to help provide assistance and training to disabled veterans. Vocational rehabilitation helps connect former service members with employers as well. The VA's Compensated Work Therapy Program brings transitional and permanent jobs to veterans who are returning to the workforce following medical rehabilitation. For eligible veterans, this partnership can provide vocational rehabilitation that combines work and training for new job skills. The program also strongly emphasizes the use of community agencies to help veterans meet their individual needs. (See the Resources on page 241 for more places to seek help.)

FAMILY AND OTHER CAREGIVERS

When a service member sustains a serious injury during deployment, his or her family must learn how to cope with it. Usually, medical personnel, such as nurses, psychologists, and clinicians, and support groups are widely available to help you do just that. If your loved one is seriously or permanently injured, this will cause role changes within your family and will certainly add to the stress of readjustment. It's sometimes more difficult for partners than for parents to adjust to the new reality of having an injured service member at home. The transition from the hospital to the home is particularly difficult. Family distress is usually highest in the first year of transition. Personality, emotional, and behavioral changes are often harder for family and friends to deal with than physical, intellectual, or cognitive changes. Family members need to try hard not to be overprotective. Your service member should be allowed (and encouraged) to become as independent as possible. People need to take healthy risks so they can feel they are in control and have a useful place in society.

Caregiver burden is a term used to describe the mental, emotional, and physical cost of caring for someone. When a service member is injured and disabled, whether the injury is visible or invisible, his or her partner, parent, or other family member will likely need to assume more responsibilities for the household and family while helping their injured service member through rehabilitation and recovery. This can create considerable physical, financial, and emotional strain. The caregiver may sometimes feel angry and resentful about all the new demands caused by their loved one's injury. Caregiver burden can sometimes lead to depression and anxiety. Here are some tips to help lighten caregiver burden:

- Take breaks and time for yourself.
- Join a support group.
- Try to keep your sense of humor.
- Seek out spiritual support.
- Remember that your injured service member is also struggling to deal with this difficult situation.

SEEKING FURTHER ASSISTANCE

If you continue to have trouble dealing with the emotional impact of your injury, there are services available that can help. You may first want to discuss your adjustment problems with your primary care physician, but you can also turn to a social worker, counselor, or other therapist who specializes in treating injury-related readjustment issues. We also encourage you to connect with other people who have been through the same challenge you are now facing. They can bring new perspectives to your concerns as well as share tried and true coping strategies. Most importantly, they can help you see that you, too, will get through this difficult time and adjust successfully.

TRAUMATIC INJURY PROTECTION INSURANCE (TSGLI)

All service members are eligible for SGLI, a low-cost group life insurance for service members on Active Duty (and Ready Reservists, members of the National Guard, cadets and midshipmen of the four service academies, and members of the Reserve Officer Training Corps). Those who are enrolled in SGLI are automatically covered by TSGLI insurance unless they specifically decline coverage. This insurance provides a payment to service members and their families during recovery from injuries causing loss of limbs, eyesight or speech, or other traumatic injuries. The insurance offers a lump sum payment from $25,000–100,000, depending on the extent of the service member's injury during Operations Iraqi Freedom or Enduring Freedom. This coverage is retroactive to October 7, 2001. Visit www.insurance.va.gov/sgliSite/legislation/TSGLIFacts.htm, or dial toll-free telephone: 800-419-1473 for more information.

14

COMMUNITY SUPPORT

Approximately three million service members, plus their families, out of a U.S. population of 303 million are directly affected by the current war in Iraq and Afghanistan. In spite of wide-reaching, graphic news coverage, blogs, email, and other forms of communication, war doesn't appear to have affected the daily lives of the general public, only the troops and their close family and friends. This may be because the United States is currently functioning with an entirely volunteer military force.

It was not always this way. In the past, entire communities were transformed during time of war. For example, in World War II, the traditional role of women was dramatically altered as they went to work in factories in order to support the war effort. The **Selective Service draft** brought the war to families from all sectors of society across the entire country. These factors kept the reality of war and the possibility of deployment at the forefront of everyone's mind. Until recently, war was a personal concern of all Americans. Now, it seems that the immediacy of war only touches our brave volunteers and those closest to them.

However, if we look a little closer, we can see that war does, in fact, affect our entire community. Furthermore, the community has a major impact on troops and families who must deal directly with deployment and readjustment stress. Although most of this book is written for service members and their families, in this chapter we are speaking directly to members of the general public as well. Our goal is to underscore the crucial interplay between returning troops, military families, and the community as a whole. Successful post-deployment readjustment for our troops and their families should be a community concern. However, both troops and community members need to take some responsibility for making readjustment a success.

HOW WAR AND RETURNING TROOPS IMPACT THE COMMUNITY

The community is impacted by war because when service members return home from deployment, they begin to resume their roles not only with their close family and friends, but in their communities as well. A returning service member may be a National Guard Soldier or Airman, returning to his or her previous occupation in order to work side by side with civilians who have no idea what it's like to have been deployed. He or she may be a Reservist returning to school and interacting with fellow students and professors who know nothing about deployment and readjustment stress. This lack of knowledge makes things difficult for everyone. The returning troop often winds up feeling misunderstood and isolated, and his or her community doesn't know how to be supportive and helpful during the service member's reintegration. It can be especially problematic when community service providers are uninformed about reintegration stressors, because it limits their ability to help returning troops or their families, who are trying to overcome challenges such as physical disabilities, financial issues, children's difficulties at school, family readjustments, and more.

Service members often return home before they have time to readjust and resettle, and are expected to be back to work, functioning normally, before they've had time to feel comfortable back in their communities. These service members may be ending a four-year military commitment, retiring after years of service, or entering the civilian workforce for the first time. They may be National Guard or Reservists whose varied war zone experiences have changed their sense of belonging and level of comfort about being a part of the community who also remain in the military and may be redeployed at any time.

If the community is not prepared for the common post-deployment readjustment challenges that troops must tackle, and it doesn't create a supportive environment, then that community makes readjustment more difficult for troops when they come home. Service members are returning to civilian life after constant immersion in destruction, atrocities, and violence for months on end. They often have little patience for our usual complaints about the price of milk or other things that seem so petty after all they've been through. Troops are often changed by deployment, and it's important for the community to appreciate how war can affect them.

A major distinction between the past and present is that there's stronger community support for our military service members now than there was following the war in Vietnam. In general, the American public has learned from its mistakes following Vietnam; it now recognizes that our troops deserve support despite political disagreements about the policies that led to war in the first place. Words of gratitude and support from the community are a good place to start. The crucial next step is for communities to understand the post-deployment challenges faced by troops and their families so that it can play a greater role in helping them through the readjustment process.

HOW THE COMMUNITY IMPACTS
RETURNING TROOPS AND THEIR FAMILIES

The troops who have served overseas might be your neighbor, your former or current teacher, your firefighter, or your dry cleaner. Our military force is made up of people from all walks of life, both male and female, old and young. These people have made great sacrifices for our country, placed their lives in danger, and sometimes come home with physical or psychological problems. They certainly deserve whatever assistance and support we can give them.

RETURNING TO WORK

For some veterans, going back to work is hard because of changes within themselves and sometimes because of changes in the workplace. Following the excitement of deployment, the old job may seem boring or meaningless. Post-deployment stress reactions, such as feeling irritable or "on edge," having trouble sleeping or concentrating, or problems relating to people can make going back to work very difficult or even seem impossible. Some troops worry that an employer (or future employer) might not want to work with somebody who's dealing with symptoms of PTSD or other war zone stress reactions. This can also be problematic when Reserve troops are seeking a new job. Employers may be reluctant to hire a Guard or Reserve member whom they fear will soon be redeployed. As we discussed in Chapter 3, a recently returned Active Duty service member may be getting his or her first civilian job—or first one in many years—and may find it very difficult to find a job or start a new (nonmilitary) career. Here is some advice on how employers and coworkers can make returning to work and reintegration in general easier for our troops.

Employers. Employers (as well as employees) should be aware of the rights and responsibilities to which they are obligated under law. Because approximately half of our deployed forces are Guard and Reservists, it's even more important that employers know their obligations to members of our national defense. Employers are required by law to allow employees who are in the Reserves to return to their jobs without penalty if they're called to active duty. Military command usually welcomes open communication, and employers should feel free to contact military commanders for assistance with concerns or conflicts between military duty and civilian employment. If you're unsure who to talk with, contact your local ESGR representative (see following page) for help in making this bridge at 800-336-4590, or go to www.esgr.org.

The **Uniformed Services Employment and Reemployment Rights Act (USERRA)** is written to make sure that members of the uniformed services are allowed to return to their civilian employment when they finish their tour of duty. Their return to employment should be at the same status and pay level at which they would have been if they'd continued to work during this time.

The **Employer Support of the Guard and Reserves (ESGR)** is a Department of Defense organization made up of volunteers who help inform employers about USERRA and how to most effectively work with deploying service member employees. ESGR also helps troops and employers resolve conflicts and misunderstandings without legal action. ESGR personnel include ombudsmen who provide troops with confidential assistance and act as impartial advisors when problems arise.

Above and beyond their responsibilities under the law, employers' support of their military employees is vital to their successful reintegration. If you're educated and prepared for what to expect when a service member who works for you returns from deployment, it will make things easier for both of you. Knowing that reintegration takes time and being familiar with the common reactions to the trauma of war can help explain the initial behavior of a returning service member and can also help you be patient with him or her. It can help you know what to say and do when interacting with someone who's recently been deployed. Since social support is so important in overcoming trauma and stress and we spend so much of our time at work, the social support of employers and coworkers is really a critical part of a returning service member's successful reintegration.

Employers can also help support the troops by helping their families. You can offer flexible work hours for military spouses before, during, and following deployment. You can recognize that the spouse's workload at home may have doubled during this time period, and be understanding if he or she struggles at work sometimes or needs some extra time off.

Coworkers. Coworkers can also be a big help to service members during their reintegration. Remember that it will take some time for troops to readjust to life back home. Also remember that you will never be able to completely understand what someone who has been in a war zone has been through. Try to appreciate their readjustment challenges described in this book. They may be short-tempered or edgy for a while, but don't take it personally. It's a normal part of their readjustment process. Don't feign interest in their deployment experiences; be genuine and ask about them, but be clear about your limits, about what and how much you can listen to. Any support you can offer will be very helpful. Finally, be sensitive to coworkers who have a loved one deployed and the issues their families are facing.

LAW ENFORCEMENT AND EMTS

Because the readjustment process can be a rocky and emotional time and issues such as substance abuse and aggressive behavior sometimes result, service members can find themselves losing their tempers too easily. This can lead to interactions with law enforcement and/or medical emergency personnel once they return home. If you work in one of these professions, be prepared to ask whether the angry individual was recently deployed and, if he or she was, try to be understanding in order to calm things down before the situation spirals out of control.

TEACHERS AND EDUCATORS

Those troops returning to school may not be able to handle the same course loads that they could before deployment. Reintegration takes time. It's important for professors and other instructors to recognize this and be flexible. It's also helpful if fellow students who've also been deployed try to connect with recently returned troops on campus. They can share readjustment problems at school and offer each other support. Many colleges have a veteran representative or a veterans club that can help.

Children with parents who are or have been deployed may need special consideration from their schools. Teachers, administrators, school nurses, and guidance counselors need to be sensitive to the potential impact of both separation and reunification on children and the emotional or behavioral problems they can cause. This may be further complicated (especially for children of military Reservists living in rural areas) when the child with difficulties is the only student in the entire school who's faced the stress related to a parent's deployment. All too often, it doesn't occur to a teacher or other school officials that a student's problems stem from a parent's military service. For this reason, it's helpful to inform teachers about what's happening at home so they can monitor children's behavior during a parent's deployment and after he or she has returned home. We want to emphasize that most children are resilient and will generally seem no different than usual. If, however, a good student starts to flunk exams or a well-behaved student becomes a classroom management problem, it's time to ask about a parent's military status.

WHAT SERVICE MEMBERS
AND FAMILIES CAN DO

Here are some ways that service members and their families can tap into community support to help ease the readjustment process:

- Participate in Readiness and Reintegration briefings that the military offers. These meetings provide information that will help you with deployment and reintegration and inform you about resources in the community of which you might not be aware.
- Tell teachers, guidance counselors, and principals that your child's parent will be, is, or was deployed. Point them to information available through military family and youth programs that can help them to understand the issues kids face.
- Make the first move. Contact Children and Youth programs, ESGR, and other resources that can help with any reintegration issues you might face.
- Following deployment, enroll in VA (both for health care and benefits) *even if you don't currently have any concerns*.

HOW COMMUNITY MEMBERS
CAN HELP TROOPS AND THEIR FAMILIES

We hope that community members will be sensitive to the potential problems we've described when interacting with someone trying to readjust to civilian life after deployment. Given the sacrifices made by military personnel, it's not too much to ask community members to educate themselves about the challenges faced by returning troops and their families.

Think about the reality of war. Take a moment in your busy schedule to think about the fact that there is a war going on and how it has affected individuals, families, and communities. Think about what troops and their families are going through. Think about all of the children who are separated from their parents and about all of the partners who must now take full responsibility for their households while also worrying endlessly about whether their loved ones will return safely home. Consider how reunited couples must get reacquainted or learn to deal with the returned partner's agitation, silent withdrawal, or continual nightmares.

Reach out. Stop to thank service members for risking their lives. Welcome them home. Ask them how they are doing. As we've already mentioned, the process of readjusting to civilian life takes time and can be difficult. Recognize that your overtures of support may be rejected or dismissed by a curt, "you just wouldn't understand"—and don't take it personally. You could also join an existing community service designed to help troops through this difficult time or, if one doesn't exist in your community, consider creating one. In order to find existing groups in your area, check with your local Family Assistance Center (www.guardfamily.org), which is funded by the National Guard Bureau yet serves *all* service members and their families. You can also check with the volunteer services at a local VA medical center.

Put yourself in their shoes. In a world where we are bombarded by information overload, we regularly tune out the ceaseless news reports about the war. Take a minute to put yourself in the shoes of those who have put their lives in danger. If you don't know someone directly, imagine what it's like to come home to a family whom you haven't seen in months, or a family who will never be able to understand what you went through in the war zone. Or think of what it would be like to be a wife who hasn't seen her husband, or a teenager who hasn't seen his dad, for months on end. And this is only the beginning of the hardships associated with deployment. After troops return home, they must face a whole new set of challenges and problems.

Educate yourself on the available resources. Take some time to become familiar with the services and resources that exist to help veterans and their families so you can help point a friend in the right direction should the need arise. It can make a real difference if you can provide useful information when asked. Service members as well as their family members will undoubtedly first turn to those they know for help and advice, and you may be that individual. Be ready to know what to say when asked.

Learn about PTSD. Excessive news reports can cause family and friends to think "this must be PTSD!" when actually their loved one is having a normal post-deployment stress reaction. Instead of jumping to conclusions, educate yourself on the symptoms of PTSD with the understanding that it takes more than a few PTSD symptoms to have the full disorder. In other words, it's important to recognize that there is a difference between full PTSD, some PTSD symptoms, and normal post-deployment stress reactions.

COMMUNITY-BASED NETWORKS

In some communities across the nation, individuals have come together to do whatever they can to make the transition from the war zone to the home front easier for both troops and their families. The identities of these groups vary by region. They network with one another about the various services that already exist and identify problem areas that need attention in that community or gaps that need to be filled. In some areas, state agencies have provided new services specifically designed for veterans and their families, such as information phone lines. Others have made efforts to increase the awareness of their staff regarding the challenges that service members and their families face. In other areas, organizations that already serve veterans like VA, ESGR, State Departments of Veterans Affairs, military family programs, chaplains, State Guard units, and the United Way have stepped up and are working together to provide support. These individuals and organizations understand the challenges that reintegration can present. They understand that, in addition to institutional programs supported by the Departments of Defense, Veterans Affairs, and other organizations, there is still much more that can be done.

Community networks such as this might exist in your neighborhood. If so, find out how you can learn more. If not, you can help make a difference by starting a conversation today. Organizations such as the local United Way, Military Family Support Groups, and VA medical centers are always in need of volunteers. If you're already a member of a community group, bring up the topic of the needs of military members and their families following their return from deployment. You can make a difference.

A COMMUNITY CASE STUDY IN VERMONT

In 2005, a group of people consisting of chaplains, Family Readiness Group personnel, and top command of the Vermont National Guard approached the VA National Center for Posttraumatic Stress Disorder and the Vermont Veterans Affairs Medical Center for help. They wanted to be better prepared to deal with potential problems among returning troops who had seen heavy action in the Sunni triangle of Iraq. They were also concerned that service members and their families did not have adequate support systems in the community. The Vermont National Guard wanted to provide services and support in order to ease the readjustment process for troops and their families.

During our initial group meetings, we realized that the first order of business was to hold a training program for commanders, community service personnel, and medical providers who work with veterans or their family members so that they would be prepared to meet the challenges of readjustment in this new cohort. It was evident that there was a great need for more information and support for service members and their families.

Our group began to grow as people in the community learned about its existence. Soon the group also included people from the Vet Centers, the Vermont State Guard, representatives of the Employer Support for the Guard and Reserves (ESGR), and other local area providers. Vermont state officials, including the governor and staff from the state Agency for Human Services, became involved. Religious leaders, the partners of deployed troops, local veteran groups, and military family members also joined us, creating a grass roots foundation that enabled us to put together a sustainable and far-reaching community of individuals united by their determination to make the readjustment process as good as it could be for returning troops.

In less than two years, this collaboration has grown into a formal statewide network. We established an identity and mission and took the name **Vermont Military, Family & Community Network (MFCN)**. Our network is now paired with the Agency of Human Services in Vermont and is growing to meet service members', families', and community needs. We have expanded, creating six local task forces across the state. The National Guard's Family Assistance Centers located across the state serve as hubs from which all services are provided. A civilian and a military liaison colead each of the six task forces. Our goals are to increase networking between currently existing services; communicate and share common problems; identify gaps in services; help overcome barriers to care and support; convey useful educational information to medical and service providers; pave the way for continuing partnerships among different agencies; and educate troops, their families, and community members on the issues associated with reintegration.

Any organization or individual who wants to help in any small way is encouraged to join. At a minimum, MFCN members are on email lists so they can learn about educational events in their area. Others are much more involved and help organize local training events, promote awareness months, post flyers, advertise the network's services, and encourage awareness and participation in the community. The network continues to grow as new people join from many walks of life, united by their desire to help returning veterans. In fact, the MFCN has even attracted people from the neighboring states of New Hampshire, New York, Maine, and Massachusetts.

The core group has held conferences and trainings for leaders, community providers, and anyone who wants to help veterans and their families. Over eighty commanders, practitioners, service members, family members, and family program personnel attended our initial training event in November 2005. In 2005–2006, we held two additional trainings for providers, two Friday evening family trainings at National Guard armories, and held presentations at several community events across the region. The main focus of these trainings was to educate attendees on common posttraumatic stress reactions and human resilience, what to expect during reintegration, how long it takes troops and families to readjust, what types of problems to watch out for, and what resources and services are available. Evaluations of these trainings were unanimously favorable. Many people stopped to give personal thanks for our collaborative efforts and the information we provided.

Because many troops, family members, and even service providers themselves didn't know about what other services were available, the MFCN has filled a major gap for returning troops and their families. The MFCN has partnered with VT 211, a statewide telephone hotline that provides information and a referral service (www.vermont211.org) for a wide array of services for veterans and their families. A vast number of services that existed previously are now tied together in the 211 database, to which more resources are regularly added. To check if your state has a 211 information line, visit www.211.org. The MFCN is in constant communication with community providers in order to keep them abreast of services and resources that are available.

In June of 2006, we held the first of several planned statewide conferences: "Returning from the War Zone to the Home Front." This event was for community service members, health care providers, and anyone else interested in helping veterans and their families with reintegration. The Governor of Vermont and the adjutant general of the Vermont National Guard attended and addressed the group. Nationally renowned author Kristin Henderson appeared at our first two statewide conferences to discuss her book *While They're at War: The True Story of American Families on the Home Front*.

At our second statewide event in October 2006, we began to see some of the effectiveness of our program. The education we provided in our trainings had begun to pay off. Communication between the military, community service providers, agencies, and others had significantly improved. We continue to meet regularly in order to expand the services that the MFCN provides. Service providers and family members are finding it easier than ever to access the information they need and to get social support or professional assistance when they need it. They're also beginning to know one another, know whom to call to find out answers, and know where to send referrals. The process continues.

Our experience in Vermont shows that a comprehensive approach that combines collaboration between military and civilian service providers, information gathering, training, and network creation and enhancement is a highly effective way to provide troops and their families the information and support they need in order to successfully readjust to life after returning from deployment.

WAYS COMMUNITY MEMBERS
CAN HELP SUPPORT RETURNING TROOPS

Here are some ideas that can help you show support for troops working through the transition back into civilian life:

- Watch a documentary film about the war or what it's like to be at war (e.g., *The War Tapes*, *After the Fog*) so you have an idea of what returning troops have been through.
- Learn about services that exist at the VA for returning troops and their families so you can point them in the right direction if asked.
- Learn if your area has an information and referral line (such as Vermont 211) and find out the kinds of services to which they can refer veterans and their families.
- Help to create a local handyman-type assistance service in your area to help families during deployment while a partner is away, or following return from deployment in order to help during the returning service member's readjustment to life at home.
- Offer assistance to friends or neighbors with child care or household tasks.

- Thank service members and their families for their sacrifices.
- Don't pressure those who have been deployed to talk, but also don't be afraid to ask and provide opportunities for them to talk if they want.
- If you belong to an organization with the means to help veterans (such as a law firm) discuss the possibility of providing some services pro bono.
- Try not to make judgment statements about returning troops and avoid telling them what they "should" do.
- Donate to organizations that help service members and their families.
- Don't tell a service member or family members that "everything will be okay" or that "they are lucky it wasn't worse."
- If you belong to a church, start a support group or sponsor activities around the holidays for military families who may be missing a loved one who has been deployed.

15

FOR THOSE FACING
UNIQUE CHALLENGES

Many people associate being involved in a military situation or warfare with being on the front lines, facing daily combat. The truth is that a variety of different roles are played in these situations by many different kinds of people. In the current conflicts in Iraq and Afghanistan, many service members do face daily combat, but others take on supportive roles in their war duties that involve other dangers. Women are more involved in the current military and face more dangers than they have in any previous conflict. Still other troops are deployed to work in peace-keeping situations. Civilians are playing a larger role in war than ever before, such as private contractors who haul supplies, build schools, fix utilities, and much more. Special consideration should be given to ethnic minorities, who face some special challenges both in the war zone as well as after deployment. At home, the military family focus is usually on the partner and children of a deployed service member while the parents and extended family, who face their own challenges, tend to get less attention than they deserve.

In this final chapter, we focus on some of the unique challenges that confront members of these above-mentioned groups and offer some advice on handling them. The bottom line is that everyone who spends time in a war zone—military or civilian—as well as the people close to them, is touched by the experience.

NON-COMBAT ROLES

Regardless of your specific assignment or duty description, everyone serving in Iraq and Afghanistan is engaged in hazardous duty. Every service member serving in these areas receives hazardous duty pay. Conventional war had an established front line with "combat arms" individuals in the front fighting the battle and support troops in "the rear with the gear." This is not the case in Iraq and Afghanistan. Because of this, we've made an intentional effort throughout this book to use the term *war zone exposure* rather than *combat exposure*. Now, more than ever before, any service member who is deployed may experience severe life-threatening traumatic war stressors.

For example, female troops, who are still not authorized to be officially assigned to certain levels of some of the combat arms branches, frequently find themselves faced with violence and bloodshed in combat situations. They patrol dangerous communities, drive trucks, and lead convoys. Reservists, who may be trained in specialties other than direct combat, also often find themselves surrounded by death and destruction. Additionally, at times Reservists are asked to take on unfamiliar roles— roles for which they haven't been fully prepared, which may put them in a more dangerous position. There are many scenarios in which "non-combat" personnel are faced with dangerous duties and repetitive levels of stress that can cause trauma.

Some people assigned to roles inside the wire experience guilt because they are in a relatively safe environment and may feel they haven't truly served because other service members "had it worse" than they have. They mistakenly believe that they haven't endured enough war zone stress to have emotional, behavioral, and psychological problems. Some even feel that they aren't entitled to have such problems. To make matters worse, back at home, rumors are often tossed around that one unit didn't *really* experience war, or didn't have it as bad as another unit. The reality is that in the current wars, all military roles and assignments expose troops to traumatic stressors serious enough to cause psychological distress and noticeable problems when they return home.

It's important to remember that all service members deployed to a war actually share many of the same experiences: the separation from family and friends, the dangerous environments and continual state of fear or hypervigilance, and waiting for the next attack. Each role in a military mission contributes to the mission's success. That's why we urge you to discourage any negative comparisons you may hear being circulated, and remind everyone that each service member, regardless of his or her role in the war, has made a big sacrifice.

SPECIAL ISSUES
FOR FEMALE SERVICE MEMBERS

Women currently make up about 15 percent of the American active military. They must confront and overcome many—if not all—of the same challenges faced by their male counterparts. They must live and function under the same conditions, and have shown time and again that they can successfully master almost all of the same jobs. However, as any woman in the military knows, there are unique challenges to face when you are a female in a traditionally male environment.

Although many women feel at ease within their units, some do not. Many military women are the target of tactless and vulgar jokes made by male service members as well as sexual harassment and unwanted advances. While men may also be victims of military sexual trauma, it's a much bigger problem among women.

After deployment, women who serve may have to face some different issues than their male counterparts. If you're married or in a relationship, gender roles may play out differently. If you're a parent, you may have had a more primary role in the parenting of your children, as opposed to the more traditional role that male troops often play in parenting (although this too is changing). This means you may have a harder time readjusting to the home front because you need to undergo a more extreme role change and/or feel a greater need to reestablish connections with your children.

In the general population, women are more likely to seek treatment than men, but this doesn't appear to be the case for military women. The prevailing macho culture of strength in the military may create a more complicated barrier for women who would otherwise wish to seek professional mental health assistance. Generally speaking, service members avoid seeking help because they mistakenly see it as a sign of weakness, and this appears to be even truer for women who have served. Some women feel a need to show that they can "out-macho" the men and handle any problems on their own. In addition, there seems to be a tendency for young women to avoid Veterans Affairs hospitals and medical centers because they mistakenly perceive them as places for "old male war heroes." All of these factors work to deter women from seeking services they need and deserve.

As members of a conspicuous minority in the military, women often must confront many of the typical challenges that all minorities face. Stereotypes are hard to break. One VA woman veterans' specialist told us that she was at work behind a desk one day when a young couple approached her. She turned to the man and asked if he'd recently been deployed. The woman quickly corrected her, saying, "No, miss. I'm the one who was recently deployed to Iraq!" This goes to show that even someone who is highly attentive to the unique challenges that women service members face can make a stereotypical mistake.

Although women normally don't serve in units involved in direct combat, the very nature of guerilla warfare often puts their lives at risk and exposes them to violence and bloodshed. Whereas women have always been involved in combat, they have traditionally held more supportive roles, such as nurses. Now, beginning with the first Gulf war, women are frequently playing the same roles as their male counterparts and often end up in the direct line of fire. As a result, we're just beginning to gain a full understanding of how women are affected by their war zone experiences and how their reactions might differ from those of men. Thus far, research suggests that women are coping with their stressful experiences during deployment as successfully as men. Rates of PTSD, depression, and anxiety disorders are no different between the genders. It remains unclear, however, exactly how or if reintegration problems with family, children, work, and community will differ between women and men.

WHERE SHOULD
WOMEN TROOPS TURN FOR HELP?

It's important to know that VA services have been changing to become more women friendly. All VA Medical Centers and Vet Centers now have a woman veteran coordinator to help female veterans with VA benefits and health care. Although all service members—both men and women—are offered the same benefits, services, and resources we have discussed throughout this book, here are two places in VA that put women's concerns first:

VA FOR WOMEN, CENTER FOR WOMEN VETERANS

Ensures that women veterans have access to VA benefits and services on par with male veterans; that VA programs are responsive to gender-specific needs of women veterans; that outreach is performed to improve women veterans' awareness of services, benefits, and eligibility criteria; and that women veterans are treated with dignity and respect. The Web site also includes answers to the twenty-five most frequently asked questions by women vets (www1.va.gov/womenvet/page.cfm?pg=14). Visit their Web site at: www1.va.gov/womenvet/index.cfm.

WOMEN'S MENTAL HEALTH CENTER

For women who are having more severe issues, this residential program at the VA Medical Center in Palo Alto, California, includes the Women's Trauma Recovery Program, the goal of which is to promote the psychological well-being of women veterans by providing individual and group therapy as well as psychoeducational classes and seminars. Call them at 650-493-5000, or visit their Web site at www.womenvetsPTSD.va.gov.

SPECIAL ISSUES FOR
ETHNIC MINORITY SERVICE MEMBERS

The war zone experience itself can be more difficult for minority service members because of racial or cultural prejudices. In today's world, troops of Arab descent in particular are often the focus of unwanted and prejudicial attention or frank harassment because they "look like" the enemy. If you are of Arab descent, you may feel socially excluded by members of your unit, emotionally demoralized, and conflicted about waging war against people with whom you share an ethnic and cultural heritage.

You may also find readjusting to life after war particularly challenging. In addition to dealing with all of the stress reactions we've discussed throughout this book, past research shows that ethnic minority veterans may tend to be at greater risk for developing PTSD following deployment to a war zone. During the Vietnam War, minority troops were most likely to have the heaviest combat exposure. (It's not clear whether this will remain true for the current wars.) In addition, the race-related stress you may encounter during your deployment or at home can contribute to psychological distress. Finally, ethnocultural factors may influence how the symptoms of PTSD are expressed. For example, it seems that troops of Hispanic descent tend to have more bodily symptom complaints. Medical providers need to consider factors like these when assessing troops for psychiatric problems. In addition to diagnostic assessment issues, some minority groups may be less likely to seek treatment for problems because of language barriers, cultural pressures, or fear of other biases.

Treatment for mental health problems in minority veterans should also take ethnic and cultural factors into account. The cultural or ethnic identity of the service member, the acceptability of certain treatments, possible interactions of some ethnic foods with certain medications, complications caused by possible cultural identification with the enemy, and cultural expectations regarding the seeking of mental health assistance must all be addressed. For more information regarding specific challenges for different ethnic or racial minorities, visit the VA National Center for PTSD's Web site, where you'll find fact sheets and educational videos: www.ncptsd.va.gov/ncmain/providers/fact_sheets/treatment/ treatmt_specific.jsp and www.ncptsd.va.gov/ncmain/providers/training/ trn_video_ethnic.jsp.

PEACEKEEPERS

Peacekeeping can involve American military personnel, UN peacekeepers, or other civilian personnel. Those who are in place to help maintain peace are also often exposed to traumatic situations, such as being threatened with physical harm or being killed. You may be placed in situations where you are personally vulnerable to attacks, must helplessly witness human death and suffering, or are unable to prevent ongoing violence and abuse. You too must deal with your subsequent psychological responses, which can include intrusive thoughts, avoidance, numbing, and hyperarousal symptoms. In addition, you may find it hard to carry out orders when you've been commanded to maintain a neutral stance and not intervene, even when faced with provocations, threats, or intolerable situations.

Peacekeeping assignments are complicated, and the operational demands may fluctuate significantly. Sometimes you may be bored by inactivity. At other times you may be overwhelmed by danger and uncertainty. It's also not unusual for peacekeepers to experience burnout, where you lose your motivation or ability to perform as before. It's important to remember that peacekeepers experience a number of traumatic stressors and, like other military personnel, are at an increased risk for developing conditions like PTSD.

PRIVATE CONTRACTORS

In the conflicts in Iraq and Afghanistan, private contractors are provid-ing more services than ever before in a war. It's contractors—rather than troops—who prepare meals, work in **PX**s (Post eXchanges or military retail stores), and provide other products and services. The destruction and devastation occurring in the Middle East demands that services be provided to improve conditions and raise the standard of living to an acceptable level for the native inhabitants. Contractors are constructing buildings, restoring electricity, providing clean water, and training local police. Consequently, the reconstruction of Iraq has led to the hiring of a huge number of private contractors. Because these tasks are very dangerous, private contractors are being paid a great deal of money to provide these services.

Some contractors are former military personnel, and some are war veterans. Many others are regular civilians who haven't been ade-quately prepared and trained to face and deal with the bloodshed, atrocities, destruction, and death they must witness while carrying out their duties. The lure of high salaries has persuaded them to risk death and injury despite these dangers. Just like military members in support roles, these contractors often find themselves in the middle of full combat situations. As of June 30, 2007, over 1,000 contractors have lost their lives in the war. Many more have been physically injured or psychologically traumatized. These contractors are often at great risk for developing PTSD because they haven't been fully prepared, adequately educated about what to expect, or trained to effectively deal with the critical and time-sensitive situations in which they sometimes find themselves.

Unlike military members and their families, contractors are not offered the services, support, and resources they may need (unless they are also veterans) following their "deployment." There's no universal assistance for the contractors who return, and none for their families. However, most of the same issues we've discussed throughout this book apply to contractors as well as to military members. The families of contractors will go through similar emotional cycles and face many of the same challenges. This is compounded by the lack of preparation and support before, throughout, and following contractors' time spent overseas. Some contractors have insurance policies that don't cover, or only partially cover, emotional and behavioral health. To make matters even worse, some contractors find themselves no longer employed and without adequate health insurance when they return to the United States.

WHERE SHOULD
PRIVATE CONTRACTORS TURN FOR HELP?

Many educational materials about the issues and challenges of war, which are prepared for military personnel, also apply to contractors and are widely available online and in libraries and bookstores (including this book!). Education about stressors and what to expect following war zone exposure may help you cope effectively with war-related stress reactions and help you see that you are not losing your mind.

You may have heard of **employee assistance programs (EAP)**. Many companies provide these types of free programs to help employees who are having trouble functioning at work for any reason. EAPs usually provide education, referrals, counseling, and therapy in order to help employees work through personal, family, or financial problems as well as mental health or substance abuse problems that are affecting their job performance. Although your company will usually know whether you used EAP services, the content of therapy sessions is strictly confidential. Your employer must get signed permission from you before they have access to any information about the assistance you received from the EAP. If you're experiencing readjustment problems, ask your personnel or human resources department if your company offers this type of program.

Another good resource is your primary care physician. He or she may be able to help you understand what you're going through and refer you to further resources and services. It's also worth mentioning that people and organizations who help service members usually want to help anyone who has been adversely impacted by war. In other words, some of the resources we've mentioned for service members will be available to you as well because they are willing to help out a fellow citizen who is experiencing traumatic stress reactions following time in a war zone. Obviously military and VA resources are not available (unless you're also a veteran), but other resources might be available through your health insurance or other state services. It's a good idea to check this out. Finally, don't forget that most health insurance covers behavioral or mental health problems, so be sure to investigate your coverage.

PARENTS AND EXTENDED FAMILY

Because the emphasis is usually on partners and children, the parents of troops are often overlooked during the reintegration process. But parents are family, too, and mothers and fathers of deployed service members experience a wide range of emotions, from pride, to fear, to feeling that everything is unreal. Parents who've spent years raising a son or daughter may now find themselves helpless to assist or protect them following deployment.

If your child is married, information about his or her military or medical status can only be communicated to you through his or her partner because of military (and sometimes medical) privacy restrictions. You may be angry or very dissatisfied about this if you feel that your child's partner doesn't share enough information with you. As we discussed in Chapter 3, family friction can develop, which interferes with open and honest communication. It's obviously much better if parents and partners can support one another. It's also best if you can discuss homecoming and other post-deployment issues with your child and his or her partner well in advance of demobilization to be clear about everyone's expectations. When you do communicate, we suggest you avoid email. Email messages usually lack key information that is present in open discussions, such as the tone of voice and important nonverbal cues, so email can be easily misconstrued. Speaking in person or over the phone will help prevent miscommunications.

Parents of single service members have other issues to keep in mind. You should have a power of attorney so you can help your child handle issues that might arise while he or she is deployed. You should also consider making sure you have a passport in case you need to travel someplace to be with your child. It takes about six weeks to get a tourist passport, so it's better to be prepared. Finally, newscasts, more often than not, will upset you. Don't watch too much news coverage. It's better if you can learn about your child's experiences directly from him or her (or through his or her partner).

It's difficult to be the parent of a deployed service member. Coping is often difficult. Remember that even if your child was deployed from another part of the country, you can still use local support and assistance. Family Assistance Centers (FACs) were created by the National Guard Bureau with the explicit purpose of helping all service members and all families wherever they live. You can find one located in an area near you at www.guardfamily.org.

To get through this difficult time, it's important to take care of yourself. This means making sure you eat right, exercise, and get a full night's sleep. It's okay to feel sad and fearful, but try to not put your life on hold as you continue to worry about your child. Recognize that you're not the only one who's going through this, and see if you can find additional support from other parents who are going through the same difficult experience. Send care packages to your child and keep busy.

Although homecoming is a time for celebration, you should also keep in mind the demanding and exhausting experiences that your child has been through. Keep your expectations in check and give him or her time to readjust to home life. Be available, but don't press your child to talk or to participate in family affairs until he or she is ready.

A FINAL NOTE

Throughout this book, we've offered you the best advice we know on a variety of challenges many service members face when they return from the war zone. We took you through a tour of the entire emotional cycle of deployment and gave both you and your loved ones a sense of what it's like to be left at home during deployment. We discussed several experiences that occur in theater and told you the stories of three service members and their families to illustrate some of the common challenges you may encounter during homecoming and for the first year afterward. Our goal is to offer this book as a useful tool that will help you reintegrate successfully when you get home.

Now that you've read it, you're aware of the myths and realities of homecoming. You're prepared for the fact that the initial "honeymoon" period, which occurs right after you get home, doesn't last. You recognize that you and your loved ones have changed during separation and that you need to take time to reconnect. You know that being in the military—and particularly in a war zone—has changed your mindset and that you must leave your "battlemind" behind in order to reintegrate smoothly with your family and friends. If you are redeployed, your Battlemind should be applied again. You can rest assured that most of the reactions you're having now that you're back are actually shared by many other troops and commonly occur in anyone who goes through a traumatic experience.

Again, we caution you about the barriers to care that many service members face—in particular, the barrier that stigma creates. The courage you possess, which allows you to effectively serve in the military, shouldn't get in the way if you need help with reintegration. Use your courage and strengths to recognize that not all problems can be solved on your own. When it's time to use teamwork in order to overcome an emotional or behavioral problem, a mental health professional is the best person to have on your team. Don't let concerns about image or reputation stand in the way; in the end, you and your family will suffer for it. Effective treatments exist for problems like PTSD, depression, substance abuse, and out-of-control anger. Use them.

We hope you're now able to recognize the symptoms that indicate that you, or someone you know, may be experiencing PTSD or other emotional issues, traumatic brain injury, or other physical and emotional pain. We encourage you to use the coping tips we offer for these problems—they really can help you successfully reintegrate into your family and your community. We also encourage you to look to your community for resources and services that will make this time of readjustment easier for both you and your loved ones. Enroll in your local VA, even if you don't think you'll ever need their services. That way, if you ever find yourself at the VA, you'll already have completed your paperwork and established records of your experiences and health status following deployment. Take advantage of the free five years of health coverage VA offers all war zone veterans (this coverage increased from two to five years in 2008). Because veterans health care is somewhat separate from veterans benefits within the VA system, also visit the Veterans Benefits Administration to see about other benefits such as education, work training, retirement, etc. Both the VA and your community may offer a host of services of which you may not be aware until you do some investigating. Consult the Resources section of this book for contact information for other organizations and the like that can help you. The Internet is also a good source of information. If you don't have a computer at home, visit your local library and do some scouting around online.

Experiences during war are often traumatic and life changing. Being prepared for what to expect during and after deployment will help you and your family successfully readjust to home life and also enable you to help others you know who are struggling. As we've mentioned before, most service members will return from deployment and reintegrate

Honoring Our Injured and Deceased

As of November 2007, over 38,164 U.S. service members who served in Iraq and Afghanistan have been physically wounded. Many of these troops suffer with disabling injuries—both physical and psychological—such as PTSD, traumatic brain and spinal cord injuries, amputations, and more.

In addition, a total of 3,859 U.S. servicemen and women have given their lives during service for their country. We take a brief moment here to give honor and tribute to these brave Soldiers, Airmen and women, Marines, Sailors, and others. We also pay homage to their families and friends who suffer as a result of these sacrifices.

into the civilian world without any major problems. However, if you do need some extra assistance, it's usually only a phone call away. We believe it's important for you and your family to be prepared for the worst that can happen, but to also remember that usually things will work out fine. Remember that serving your country during a time of war also brings positive consequences. Triumphing over the challenges you've faced has likely increased your self-confidence, leadership skills, patriotism, and personal growth. It can bring a new sense of meaning to your life and appreciation for all things that surround you.

We thank you and your family for the sacrifices you make for our country.

GLOSSARY

Acute stress reactions: See war zone stress reactions.

ADHD (Attention Deficit Hyperactivity Disorder): A behavior disorder characterized by hyperactivity, inattention, and impulsivity.

Agoraphobia: The fear of leaving the safety and security of home to go to public places, such as shopping malls.

Anticipatory grief: A grief reaction that occurs in anticipation of an impending loss, usually of a family member or friend.

Anxiety disorder: A condition in which severe and persistent anxiety interferes with daily functioning.

Anxiolytics: Medications that help you to calm down and relax.

Barbiturates: A class of drugs that slow down your central nervous system (brain and nerve impulses), causing drowsiness and relaxation.

Benzodiazepines: Family of depressant medications used therapeutically to produce sedation, induce sleep, relieve anxiety and muscle spasms, and to prevent seizures.

Brief psychodynamic therapy: A therapy that focuses on unconscious processes that are believed to be expressed. This therapy intends to help a person gain control over these repressed thoughts and feelings.

Burnout: A problem in which an individual loses their motivation or ability to perform as before.

Cardiovascular system: The organ system that includes the blood, the heart, and blood vessels.

Casualty: A military person lost through death, wounds, injury, sickness, internment, capture, or through being missing in action.

Cognitive behavioral therapy (CBT): Psychotherapy that focuses on changing negative or faulty patterns of thinking into accurate, desirable ones.

Cognitive processing therapy (CPT): A therapy, involving a written narrative and cognitive restructuring, that focuses on trauma-related thought patterns as well as the intense emotions that occur following a trauma.

Cognitive restructuring: A therapy technique in which you identify negative, irrational beliefs and replace them with more balanced, rational statements.

Coma: A profound state of unconsciousness in which the person cannot be awakened.

Combat stress reactions: See war zone stress reactions.

Comorbid: The presence of more than one disorder.

Concussion: The most common form of brain injury, also called mild traumatic brain injury. Often the injured person loses consciousness for a brief period of time and has little or no memory of the event.

Counseling: Treatment that is focused on the here and now and provides advice on how to deal or cope with situations and feelings.

Demobilization: A period of time when troops deprocess and unwind following deployment.

Deployment: A troop movement resulting from a Joint Chiefs of Staff/Unified Command Deployment Order for thirty continuous days or greater to a land-based location outside the United States.

Digestive system: The group of organs that break down foods into chemical components that the body can absorb and use for energy as well as for building and repairing cells and tissues.

Disease and non-battle injury (DNBI): An injury or other health issue that is not incurred in battle.

Ecstasy: Also known as *MDMA (3,4 methylenedioxymethamphetamine)*, a chemically modified amphetamine that has hallucinogenic as well as stimulant properties.

Employee assistance programs (EAP): A counseling service for employees and their eligible dependents who may be experiencing personal or workplace problems.

Endocrine system: The system of glands in the human body that is responsible for producing hormones.

Evidence-based clinical practice guidelines: A set of guiding rules that are created to help clinicians and other health care providers treat a mental illness; rules that are based on expert research findings.

Exposure Therapy: A form of behavior therapy in which you confront feelings or phobias or anxieties about a traumatic event and relive it in the therapy situation Also known as Prolonged Exposure Therapy.

Eye Movement and Desensitization Therapy (EMDR): A therapy that involves elements from both exposure and cognitive therapy. It involves thinking about the traumatic event while simultaneously moving your eyes back and forth.

Family Assistance Center (FAC): A part of the National Guard family program, under the National Guard Bureau, that provides readiness and reintegration assistance to all military family members and troops from all branches of service.

Fisher House: A "home away from home" made available to families of military patients. This housing is sometimes provided free to families of wounded service members.

Flashback: A psychological phenomenon in which you have a sudden, usually vivid, recollection of a past experience.

Forward operating base (FOB): A secured forward position that is used to support tactical operations.

Health care proxy: A legal document that allows an agent to make health care decisions in the event that you are incapable of executing such decisions.

Hindsight bias: The tendency to believe, after learning of an outcome, that you could have foreseen it.

Honeymoon period: Happens often for couples during the first weeks of homecoming when partners are extremely happy to see one another, things seem perfect, and you are separated from real world issues and responsibilities.

IEDs (improvised explosive devices): Conventionally known as "bombs."

Intrusive thoughts: Unwelcome, involuntary thoughts, images, or unpleasant ideas that may become obsessions, are upsetting or distressing, and can be difficult to manage.

Invitational Travel Orders (ITOs): Orders that can be issued by command to allow family to come visit a wounded service member because it is deemed helpful to the service member's recovery.

Logistical supply area (LSA): Also sometimes called logistical support areas, these are large military facilities that serve as depots, division headquarters, rest and relaxation areas, and support to FOBs.

MDMA (3,4 methylenedioxymethamphetamine): Also known as *Ecstasy*, a chemically modified amphetamine that has hallucinogenic as well as stimulant properties.

Medical Holding Company (MHC): Facilities, for Active Duty service members who cannot be immediately returned to full duty, that provide support, and manage the health, welfare, and training of service member-patients to facilitate their care and proper disposition.

Methamphetamine (meth): A commonly abused, potent stimulant drug that is part of a larger family of amphetamines.

Military Reserve: (also see *Reserve Component*), Armed forces that are not on Active Duty but can be called in an emergency. The Reserve Components are also referred to collectively as "the Guard and Reserves." However, the term "Reservist" often refers specifically to members of the Reserve as opposed to the National Guard. The National Guard forces are under state control unless federally activated and the Reserve branches are under federal control and usually trained in a specialty of some kind.

Military sexual trauma (MST): Sexual assault or harassment that occurs in a military setting.

Military occupation specialty (MOS): The category of career specialty for a U.S. military member.

Multiple deployments: When a service member is deployed more than one time, usually in the same conflict.

Musculoskeletal system: The skeleton and its associated bones, the ligaments, tendons, and the muscles.

National Guard: U.S. military Reserves recruited and under the control of the states and subject to call to duty by either the state or a federal activation in time of national disaster or war.

Opioids: Powerful chemical substances that are administered to relieve severe pain.

Panic attacks: Sudden periods of intense anxiety, fear, and discomfort that are associated with a variety of somatic and cognitive symptoms.

Paraplegia: Complete paralysis of the lower half of the body including both legs, usually caused by damage to the spinal cord.

Peer counseling: Counseling or advice provided usually in groups by others who have been in the same situation and are not necessarily professionals. These peer counseling groups are often moderated by a professional.

Persistent vegetative state (PVS): A vegetative state lasting more than a month, where the person has lost his or her thinking abilities and awareness of their surroundings, but still has normal sleep patterns.

Phantom limb pain: The sensation of pain or other unpleasant feelings in the place of a missing limb.

Post-deployment: The six to twelve months after you return home from war, during which you and your family must readjust to life at home together.

Post Deployment Health Assessment (PDHA): A screening process that service members must complete following deployment to a war zone in order to determine the presence of any physical or mental health issues.

Post Deployment Health Re-Assessment (PDHRA): A screening process similar to the PDHA that is completed three to six months after return from deployment.

Posttraumatic Stress Disorder (PTSD): An anxiety disorder that can occur after exposure to a terrifying event, most often characterized by the repeated re-experience of the ordeal in the form of frightening, intrusive memories, and brings on hypervigilance and a deadening of normal emotions.

Pre-deployment: The period between the day you receive your deployment orders and the day you leave for your post.

Prosthesis: An artificial device to replace or augment a missing or impaired part of the body, such as an artificial limb.

Prosthetic: Term used to describe an artificial extremity, such as an arm or leg.

Psychotherapy: Also known as *therapy*, treatment that goes beyond counseling to offer increased awareness by mastering conflicts and overcoming patterns that have previously impacted thoughts, feelings, and actions.

Psychoeducation: Materials and information provided in order to teach people about mental health issues and coping skills.

PX (post exchange): A military retail store.

Quadriplegia: Also known as *tetraplegia*, describes the complete or incomplete paralysis from the neck downwards, affecting all four limbs and the trunk.

Readjustment and renegotiation: The first few months of reintegration after return from deployment when you need to readjust to civilian life and renegotiate your roles at home.

Reserve Component: (also see *Military Reserve*), The Reserve Components of the Armed Forces of the United States are the Army National Guard, Army Reserve, Naval Reserve, Marine Corps Reserve, Air National Guard, Air Force Reserve, and the Coast Guard Reserve. The National Guard is distinctive from the Reserve branches in that Guard forces are under state control but can be federally activated, while Reserves are under federal control and usually trained in more specific specialties.

Selective serotonin reuptake inhibitors (SSRIs): A group of medications used to treat depression by increasing the amount of the neurotransmitter serotonin in the brain.

Selective Service draft: A government act that stated that adult males were required to register for military service and could not hire someone to go as their replacement if they were selected for duty.

Serotonin: A neurotransmitter that helps with the body's regulation of mood.

Simple phobia: Also called specific phobia, simple phobia is characterized by strong, irrational, involuntary fear reactions to a particular object, place, or situation.

Social phobia: A fear of people or social situations.

Stress Inoculation Training: A cognitive-behavioral approach for stress management that teaches you a variety of skills for alleviating stress and achieving personal goals.

Stupor: An unresponsive state that a person can be jarred out of.

Survivor guilt: A mental condition that results from the belief that you have done wrong by surviving a traumatic event.

Tetraplegia: Also known as *quadriplegia*, describes the complete or incomplete paralysis from the neck downwards, affecting all four limbs and the trunk.

Theater: The specific geographic area where armed war takes place.

Therapy: Also known as *psychotherapy*, treatment that goes beyond counseling in order to offer increased awareness by mastering conflicts and overcoming patterns that have previously impacted thoughts, feelings, and actions.

Traumatic grief: Grief that is compounded by the fact that the loss was due to a traumatic event (for example, murder).

The Uniformed Services Employment and Reemployment Rights Act (USERRA): This act prohibits discrimination against persons because of their service in the Armed Forces Reserve, the National Guard, or other uniformed services.

VBIEDs (vehicle born improvised explosive devices): "Bombs" that are attached to a moving vehicle.

Vegetative state: Similar to a coma, but the person continues to have a sleep-wake cycle and periods of alertness.

Vocational rehabilitation therapist: Therapists who assist disabled, ill, or injured workers to access, remain in, and return to work.

War zone stress reactions: Also known as combat stress reactions or acute stress reactions, these are reactions that commonly occur after spending time in a war zone and include things like nightmares and feeling hypervigilant.

Wounded in action (WIA): Service members who have been injured while fighting during war time.

REFERENCES

CHAPTER 1

American Psychological Association Presidential Task Force on Military Deployment Services for Youth, Families and Service Members. "The Psychological Needs of US Military Members and Their Families: A Preliminary Report." 2007. www.apa.org/releases/MilitaryDeploymentTaskForceReport.pdf.

Brewin, C. R., B. Andrews, and J. D. Valentine. "Meta-analysis of Risk Factors for Posttraumatic Stress Disorder in Trauma-exposed Adults." *Journal of Consulting and Clinical Psychology* 68, no. 5 (2000): 748–66.

Doyle, M. E. and K. A. Peterson. "Re-entry and Reintegration: Returning Home after Combat." *Psychiatric Quarterly* 76, no. 4 (2005): 361–70.

MacDermid, S. M. "Coming Home: An Army Reserve Unit Returns Home from War, Report from the Military Family Research Institute." PowerPoint presentation, 2006.

MacDermid, S. M. "Multiple Transitions of Deployment and Reunion for Military Families, Report from the Military Family Research Institute." Powerpoint presentation, 2006.

National Military Family Association. "Report on the Cycles of Deployment: An Analysis of Survey Responses from April through September 2005." www.nmfa.org/site/DocServer/NMFACyclesofDeployment9.pdf?docid=5401.

Pincus, S. H., R. House, J. Christenson, and L. E. Adler. "The Emotional Cycle of Deployment." *U.S. Army Medical Department Journal* 8, (August 2001): 4/5/6.

Scranton, D., director. *The War Tapes*, documentary film, 2006.

Slate. "The Sandbox" 2007. http://gocomics.typepad.com/the_sandbox/.

Swan, R., et al. *Deployment and Family Separation: An Annotated Bibliography*. West Lafayette, IN: Military Family Research Institute, 2002.

CHAPTER 2

Force Health Protection & Readiness. "Deployment Tips." Accessed on 11/8/2007. http://fhp.osd.mil/deploymentTips.jsp.

Hendersen, K. *While They're at War: The True Story of American Families on the Homefront.* New York: Houghton Mifflin, 2006.

Hoge, C. W, C. A. Castro, S. C. Messer, D. McGurk, D. I. Cotting, and R. L. Koffman. "Combat Duty in Iraq and Afghanistan, Mental Health Problems, and Barriers to Care." *New England Journal of Medicine* 351, no. 1 (2004): 13–22.

Hoge, C. W., J. L. Auchterlonie, and C. S. Milliken. "Mental Health Problems, Use of Mental Health Services, and Attrition from Military Service after Returning from Deployment to Iraq or Afghanistan." *Journal of the American Medical Association* 295, no. 9, (2006): 1023–32.

icasualties.org. "Iraq Coalition Casualty Count." 2007. http://icasualties.org/oif/.

Kang, H. K. "VA Health Care Utilization Among OIF/OEF Veterans: FY 2002-FY 2007" 2nd Qtr. Report from the War Related Illness and Injury Center. PowerPoint presentation, 2007.

Milliken, C. S., J. L. Auchterlonie, and C. W. Hoge. "Longitudinal Assessment of Mental Health Problems Among Active and Reserve Component Soldiers Returning from the Iraq War." *Journal of the American Medical Association* 298, no. 18 (2007): 2141–48.

CHAPTER 3

Craven, J. *After the Fog*, documentary film, 2006. Kingdom County Productions, Vermont.

Hendersen, K. *While They're at War: The True Story of American Families on the Homefront.* New York: Houghton Mifflin, 2006.

Milliken, C. S., J. L. Auchterlonie, and C. W. Hoge. "Longitudinal Assessment of Mental Health Problems Among Active and Reserve Component Soldiers Returning from the Iraq War." *Journal of the American Medical Association* 298, no. 18 (2007): 2141–48.

VA National Center for PTSD. "Returning from the War Zone: A Guide for Families of Military Personnel." 2005. www.ncptsd.va.gov/ncmain/ncdocs/manuals/nc_manual_returnwarz_gp.html.

CHAPTER 4

Battlemind.org. "Military Operational Medicine Research Program." 2007. www.battlemind.org.

CHAPTER 5

McNulty, P. "Reported Stressors and Health Care Needs of Active Duty Navy Personnel during Three Phases of Deployment in Support of the War in Iraq." *Military Medicine* 170, no. 6 (2005): 530–35.

Ursano, R. J. and C. S. Fullerton. "Cognitive and Behavioral Responses to Trauma." *Journal of Applied Social Psychology Special Issue: Traumatic Stress: New Perspectives in Theory, Measurement, and Research: II.* 20, no. 21, Pt 1 (1990): 1766–75.

VA National Center for PTSD. "Returning from the War Zone: A Guide for Military Personnel." 2005. www.ncptsd.va.gov/ncmain/ncdocs/manuals/nc_manual_returnwarz_vet.html.

VA National Center for PTSD. "Common Reactions After Trauma." 2007. www.ncptsd.va.gov/ncmain/ncdocs/fact_shts/fs_commonreactions.html.

Whealin, J. M. "Warzone-Related Stress Reactions: What Families Need to Know." In *Iraq War Clinician Guide, 2nd ed*. VA National Center for PTSD (2002): 202–3. www.ncptsd.va.gov.

CHAPTER 6

Gerlock, A. A. "An Anger Management Intervention Model for Veterans with PTSD." *National Center for PTSD Clinical Quarterly* 6, no. 3 (1996): 61–4.

Novaco, R. W. "Anger Treatment and Its Special Challenges." *National Center for PTSD Clinical Quarterly* 6, no. 3 (1996):56–60.

Street, A. and J. Stafford. "Military Sexual Trauma: Issues in Caring for Veterans Fact Sheet." 2007. www.ncptsd.va.gov/ncmain/ncdocs/fact_shts/military_sexual_trauma.html.

Taft, C. T. and B. L. Niles. "Assessment and Treatment of Anger in Combat-Related PTSD." In *Iraq War Clinician Guide, 2nd ed*. VA National Center for PTSD (2002): 70–4. www.ncptsd.va.gov.

VA National Center for PTSD. "Anger and Trauma Fact Sheet." 2006. www.ncptsd.va.gov/ncmain/ncdocs/fact_shts/fs_anger.html.

CHAPTER 7

Conant, E. "The Military: Faith Under Fire." *Newsweek*, May 7, 2007.

Currier, J. M., J. M. Holland, and R. A. Neimeyer. "Sense-making, Grief, and the Experience of Violent Loss: Toward a Mediational Model." *Death Studies* 30, no. 5, (2006): 403–28.

Drescher, K. D., M. W. Smith, and D. W. Foy. "Spirituality and Readjustment Following War Zone Experiences." In *Combat Stress Injury Theory, Research, and Management*, ed. C. R. Figley and W. P. Nash. 486–512. New York: Routledge, 2006.

Kubany, E. S. "Thinking Errors, Faulty Conclusions, and Cognitive Therapy for Trauma-Related Guilt." *National Center for PTSD Clinical Quarterly* 7, no. 1 (1997): 6–8.

CHAPTER 8

Bartone, P. T. and M. G. Ender. "Organizational Responses to Death in the Military." *Death Studies* 18, no. 1 (1994): 25–39.

Brandsma, J. and L. Hyer. "Resolution of Traumatic Grief in Combat Veterans." *National Center for PTSD Clinical Quarterly* 5, nos. 2–3 (1995): 14–6.

Callahan, E. J. "Psychological Intervention for Unresolved Grief." *National Center for PTSD Clinical Quarterly* 5, nos. 2–3 (1995): 11–13.

Pennebaker, J. W. "Writing about Emotional Experiences as a Therapeutic Process." *Psychological Science* 8, no. 3 (1997): 162–66.

Pivar, I. "Traumatic Grief: Symptomology and Treatment for the Iraq War Veteran." In *Iraq War Clinician Guide, 2nd ed*. National Center for PTSD (2002): 75–99. www.ncptsd.va.gov.

Pivar, I. L. and N. P. Field. "Unresolved Grief in Combat Veterans with PTSD." *Journal of Anxiety Disorders* 18, no. 6 (2004): 745–55.

Raphael, B. and N. Martinek. "Assessing Traumatic Bereavement and Posttraumatic Stress Disorder." In *Assessing Psychological Trauma and PTSD*, ed. J. P. Wilson and T. M. Keane. New York: Guilford, 492–512, 1997.

Shapiro, E. R. "Grief and Trauma in Family Developmental and Cultural Context." *National Center for PTSD Clinical Quarterly* 5, nos. 2–3 (1995): 1–6.

Shear, M. K., A. Zuckoff, N. Melhem, and B. J. Gorsack. "The Syndrome of Traumatic Grief and Its Treatment." In *Psychological Effects of Catastrophic Disasters: Group Approaches to Treatment*, ed. L. A. Schein, H. I. Spitz, G. M. Burlingame, and P. R. Muskin. 287–334. Binghamton, NY: Haworth, 2006.

Shear, M. K. and K. Smith-Caroff. "Traumatic Loss and the Syndrome of Complicated Grief." *PTSD Research Quarterly* 13, no. 1 (2002): 1–7.

Worden, J. W. "Four Tasks of Mourning." *Grief Counseling and Grief Therapy, 2ⁿᵈ ed.* New York: Spring Publishing, 1991.

Wendt Center for Loss and Healing, 2006. www.wendtcenter.org/grief/four _tasks.htm.

CHAPTER 9

Cozza, S. J., R. S. Chun, and J. A. Polo. "Military Families and Children During Operation Iraqi Freedom." *Psychiatric Quarterly* 76, no. 4 (2005): 371–78.

Dekel, R., Z. Solomon, and A. Bleich. "Emotional Distress and Marital Adjustment of Caregivers: Contribution of Level of ImpAirment and Appraised Burden." *Anxiety, Stress and Coping* 18, no. 1 (2005): 71–82.

Flack, W. F., B. T. Litz, F. Y. Hsieh, D. G. Kaloupek, and T. M. Keane. "Predictors of Emotional Numbing, Revisited: A Replication and Extension." *Journal of Traumatic Stress* 13, no. 4 (2000): 611–18.

Houser, B. "Children and Deployment." Presentation at Strengthening Community Support for our Military Families Conference. Colchester, VT, November 2007.

Lauterbach, D., C. Bak, S. Reiland, S. Mason, M. R. Lute, and L. Earls. "Quality of Parental Relationships among Persons with a Lifetime History of Posttraumatic Stress Disorder." *Journal of Traumatic Stress* 20, no. 2 (2007): 161–72.

Litz, B. T. and M. J. Gray. "Emotional Numbing in Posttraumatic Stress Disorder: Current and Future Research Directions." *Australian and New Zealand Journal of Psychiatry* 36, no. 2 (2002): 198–204.

Riggs, D. S., C. A. Byrne, F. W. Weathers, and B. T. Litz. "The Quality of the Intimate Relationships of Male Vietnam Veterans: Problems Associated with Posttraumatic Stress Disorder." *Journal of Traumatic Stress* 11, no. 1 (1998): 87–101.

Ruscio, A. M., F. W. Weathers, L. A. King, and D. W. King. "Male War-Zone Veterans' Perceived Relationships with Their Children: The Importance of Emotional Numbing." *Journal of Traumatic Stress* 15, no. 5 (2002): 351–57.

CHAPTER 10

Corrigan, P. W. and N. Rüsch. "Mental Illness Stereotypes and Clinical Care: Do People Avoid Treatment Because of Stigma?" *Psychiatric Rehabilitation Skills* 6, no. 3 (2002): 312–34.

Corrigan, P. W. "Don't Call Me Nuts: An International Perspective on the Stigma of Mental Illness." *Acta Psychiatrica Scandinavica* 109 (2004): 403–4.

Hoge, C. W., C. A. Castro, S. C. Messer, D. McGurk, D. I. Cotting, and R. L. Koffman. "Combat Duty in Iraq and Afghanistan, Mental Health Problems, and Barriers to Care." *New England Journal of Medicine* 351, no. 1 (2004): 13–22.

CHAPTER 11

Friedman, M. J. *PTSD and Acute Post-Traumatic Reactions*. Kansas City, MD: Compact Clinicals, 2006.

Hamblen, J. "What is PTSD? A Handout from the National Center for PTSD. "VA National Center for PTSD (2006). www.ncptsd.va.gov/ncmain/ncdocs/handouts/hand out_What_is_PTSD.pdf.

Slone, L. B. and M. J. Friedman. "Treatment of War-related Posttraumatic Stress Disorder." In *Encyclopedia of Stress, 2nd ed.*, ed. G. Fink. 865–68. Burlington, MA: Academic Press, 2007.

VA National Center for PTSD. A Supplemental Take-Home Module for the NAMI Family-to-Family Education Program: Understanding and Coping with PTSD, NAMI. 2007.

VA National Center for PTSD. "PTSD and Problems with Alcohol Use Fact Sheet." 2006. www.ncptsd.va.gov/ncmain/ncdocs/fact_shts/fs_alcohol.html.

CHAPTER 12

Boos, C. J. and A. M. Croft. "Smoking Rates in the Staff of a Military Field Hospital Before and After Wartime Deployment." *Journal of the Royal Society of Medicine* 97, no. 1 (2004): 20–22.

Hudenko, B. H. "The Relationship Between PTSD and Suicide Fact Sheet." 2006. www.ncptsd.va.gov/ncmain/ncdocs/fact_shts/fs_suicideprof.html.

Hurd, R. "Endocrine Glands." Medline Plus Medical Encyclopedia. www.nlm.nih.gov/medlineplus/ency/article/002351.htm.

Kessler, R. C., A. Sonnega, E. Bromet, M. Hughes, and C. B. Nelson. "Posttraumatic Stress Disorder in the National Comorbidity Survey." *Archives of General Psychiatry* 52, no. 12 (1995): 1048–60.

Kessler, R. C., P. Berglund, O. Demler, R. Jin, and E. E. Walters. "Lifetime Prevalence and Age-of-Onset Distributions of DSM-IV Disorders in the National Comorbidity Survey Replication." *Archives of General Psychiatry* 62, no. 6 (2005): 593–602.

King, D. W., L. A. King, C. T. Taft, K. C. Koenen, A. P. Pless, and L. J. Stalans. "Risk Factors for Partner Violence Among a National Sample of Combat Veterans." *Journal of Consulting and Clinical Psychology* 73, no. 1, (2005): 151–59.

Najavits, L. M. *Seeking Safety: A Treatment Manual for PTSD and Substance Abuse*. New York: Guilford, 2002.

National Institute on Drug Abuse. "NIDA Info Facts Marijuana." 2006. www.nida.nih.gov/Infofacts/marijuana.html.

National Institute on Drug Abuse. "NIDA Info Facts Methamphetamine." 2006. www.drugabuse.gov/infofacts/methamphetamine.html.

National Institute on Drug Abuse. "Drugs of Abuse Information" 2007. www.drugabuse.gov/drugpages.html.

National Institute on Drug Abuse. "Research Report: MDMA (Ecstacy) Abuse." 2006. www.drugabuse.gov/ResearchReports/MDMA/default.html.

National Institute on Drug Abuse. "Research Report: Treating Prescription Drug Addiction." 2006. www.nida.nih.gov/ResearchReports/Prescription/prescription7.html.

National Institutes on Mental Health. "Anxiety Disorders." 2007. www.nimh.nih.gov/publicat/anxiety.cfm.

Norris, F. H., L. B. Slone, C. K. Baker, and A. D. Murphy. "Early Physical Health Consequences of Disaster Exposure and Acute Disaster-related PTSD." *Anxiety, Stress and Coping: An International Journal* 19, no. 2 (2006): 95–110.

Partnership for a Drug-Free America. "Signs Someone is Using Drugs or Alcohol." 2007. www.drugfree.org/Intervention/Articles/Signs_Someone_Is_Using.

RTI International. "2005 Department of Defense Survey of Health Related Behaviors Among Active Duty Military Personnel." 2006. www.ha.osd.mil/special_reports/2005_Health_Behaviors_Survey_1–07.pdf.

Schnurr, P. P. and B. Green. "Understanding Relationships Among Trauma, Posttraumatic Stress Disorder, and Health Outcomes." In *Trauma and Health: Physical Health Consequences of Exposure to Extreme Stress*, ed. P. P. Schnurr and B. Green. 247–75. Washington, DC: American Psychological Association. 2004.

Walser, R. D. 2002. "Stress, Trauma, and Alcohol and Drug Use. In *Iraq War Clinician Guide, 2nd ed.*, 195–96. National Center for PTSD. www.ncptsd.va.gov.

CHAPTER 13

Acquired Brain Injury Outreach Service. "Supporting the Family After Brain Injury." 2007. www.health.qld.gov.au/abios/documents/support_worker.pdf.

Defense and Veterans Brain Injury Center. "Defense and Veterans Brain Injury Center Brochure." 2004. www.dvbic.org.

Gil, S., Y. Caspi, I. Z. Ben-Ari, D. Koren, and E. Klein. "Does Memory of a Traumatic Event Increase the Risk for Posttraumatic Stress Disorder in Patients with Traumatic Brain Injury?: A Prospective Study." *American Journal of Psychiatry* 162, no. 5 (2005): 963–69.

Glasser, R. "A Shock Wave of Brain Injuries." *The Washington Post*, April 8, 2007. B01. www.washingtonpost.com/wp-dyn/content/article/2007/04/06/AR2007040601821.html.

Gourick, J. and D. Gentleman. "The Emotional and Behavioral Consequences of Traumatic Brain Injury." *Trauma* 6, no. 4 (2004): 285–92.

Houston, S. "Body Image, Relationships and Sexuality after Amputation." 2006. www.amputee-coalition.org/easyread/first_step_2005/altered_states-ez.html.

Koren, D., Y. Hilel, N. Idar, D. Hemel, and E. M. Klein. "Combat Stress Management: The Interplay between Combat, Physical Injury, and Psychological Trauma." In

Combat Stress Injury: Theory, Research, and Management, ed. C. R. Figley and W. P. Nash. 119–35. New York: Routledge, 2007.

Koren, D., D. Norman, A. Cohen, J. Berman, and E. M. Klein. "Increased PTSD Risk with Combat-related Injury: A Matched Comparison Study of Injured and Uninjured Soldiers Experiencing the Same Combat Events." *American Journal of Psychiatry* 162, no. 2 (2005): 276–82.

The Mayo Clinic. "Traumatic Brain Injury." 2007. www.mayoclinic.com/health /traumatic-brain-injury/DS00552/DSECTION=2.

National Military Family Association, Inc. "Resources for Wounded or Injured Service Members and Their Families Fact Sheet." 2006. www.nmfa.org.

National Institute of Neurological Disorders and Stroke. "Traumatic Brain Injury Information Page." 2007. www.ninds.nih.gov/disorders/tbi/tbi.htm.

O'Donnell, M. L., M. C. Creamer, P. Pattison, and C. Atkin. "Psychiatric Morbidity Following Injury." *American Journal of Psychiatry* 161, no. 3 (2004): 507–14.

Scurfield, R. M., and S. Tice. "Acute Psycho-social Intervention Strategies with Medical and Psychiatric Evacuees of 'Operation Desert Storm' and Their Families. Operation Desert Storm Clinician Packet." White River Junction, VT: VA National Center for PTSD, 1991.

Summerall, E. L. "Traumatic Brain Injury and PTSD Fact Sheet." 2007. www.ncptsd .va.gov.

Thombs, B. D., J. A. Fauerbach, and U. D. McCann. "Stress Disorders Following Traumatic Injury: Assessment and Treatment Considerations." *Primary Psychiatry* 12, no. 3 (2005): 51–55.

VA National Center for PTSD. *Iraq War Clinician Guide, 2nd ed.* 2002. www.ncptsd.va.gov.

Vasterling, J. J., S. P. Proctor, P. Amoroso, R. Kane, T. Heeren, and R. F. White. "Neuropsychological Outcomes of Army Personnel Following Deployment to the Iraq War." *Journal of the American Medical Association* 296, no. 5 (2006): 519–29.

CHAPTER 14

Fairbank, J. A., M. J. Friedman, J. de Jong, B. L. Green, and S. D. Solomon. "Intervention Options for Society, Communities, Families, and Individuals." In *Trauma Interventions in War and Peace: Prevention, Practice, and Policy*, ed. B. L. Green, M. J. Friedman, J. T. de Jong, S. D. Solomon, T. M. Keane, J. A. Fairbank, B. Donelan, and E. Frey-Wouters. 57–72. New York: Kluwer Academic/Plenum, 2004.

Hendersen, K. *While They're at War: The True Story of American Families on the Homefront.* New York: Houghton Mifflin, 2006.

CHAPTER 15

Friedman, M. J., P. G. Warfe, and K. M. Gladys. "UN Peacekeepers and Civilian Field Personnel." In *Trauma Interventions in War and Peace: Prevention, Practice, and Policy*, ed. B. L. Green, M. J. Friedman, J. T. de Jong, S. D. Solomon, T. M. Keane, J. A. Fairbank, B. Donelan, and E. Frey-Wouters. 323–48. New York: Kluwer Academic/Plenum, 2004.

Risen, J. "Contractors Back from Iraq Suffer Trauma from Battle." *New York Times,* July 5, 2007. www.nytimes.com/2007/07/05/us/05contractors.html.

RESOURCES FOR TROOPS
AND THEIR FAMILIES

ADOLESCENTS

See *Children*

ADVOCATES

These resources offer help with applications for benefits, compensation claims, trouble obtaining services, and more.

Legislative Staff Members

Most members of the House and Senate have a designated veteran representative who can help with veteran's issues that fall through the cracks. Contact your local representative's office for further information by referencing your local phone book.

National Alliance on Mental Illness (NAMI)

NAMI now also provides a veterans' resource center.
Colonial Place Three
2107 Wilson Blvd., Suite 300
Arlington, VA 2220-3042
Toll-free: 800-950-NAMI
Email: info@nami.org
Web site: www.nami.org

Transition Assistance Program (formerly State Benefits Advisors)

Assistance for service members with access to care, enrollment in VA health care, and more. One advisor is designated for each state.
Call your local Family Assistance Center to locate your advisor, or visit www.dodtransportal.dod.mil/dav/lsnmedia/LSN/dodtransportal/op.htm

Veterans Service Organizations (VSOs)

Provide a wealth of free services to veterans and can help you navigate the system.
See *Veterans Service Organizations* for more.

ALCOHOL ABUSE RECOVERY

See *Substance Abuse Recovery*

ANGER

See *Domestic Violence*

BATTLEMIND

Battlemind.org
Site offers a series of trainings to help service members and families deal with the stressors of deployment.
Web site: www.battlemind.org

BENEFITS

Also see *VBA: Veterans Benefits Administration* in the VA special section at the end of the Resources
Also see *Advocates*

Military.com

An organization that connects service members, military families, and veterans to all the benefits of service— government benefits, scholarships, discounts, lifelong friends, mentors, great stories of military life or missions, and much more. Free membership.
Web site: www.military.com/Benefits/0,14972,00.htm

BEREAVEMENT

Operation Comfort

A nationwide network of mental health professionals and agencies that provide counseling free of charge.
Phone: 866-632-7868
Web site: www.operationcomfort.com

Patriot Guard Riders (PGR)

A diverse amalgamation of motorcycle riders from across the nation with an unwavering respect for those who risk their lives for America's freedom and security. PGR honors this country's deceased veterans by attending their funeral services as invited guests of the family—to show a sincere respect for our fallen heroes—via Flag Lines, Honor Salutes, and motorcycle escorts. PGR also has a program called Help on the Home Front—which coordinates PGR involvement in send-off and welcome home events, and visits to and events for our returning or wounded heroes.
Email: contact@patriotguard.org
Web site: www.patriotguard.org

Tragedy Assistance Program for Survivors (TAPS)

Offers grief support for deaths that occurred in line of duty.
Toll-free: 800-959-TAPS (8277)
Web site: www.taps.org

Vet Centers

Offer veterans and their families free counseling and outreach, usually provided by other veterans. There are 207 centers across the nation.
Toll-free: 800-905-4675
Web site: www.vetcenter.va.gov

BOOKS

See *Educational Materials/Resources*

CAREERS

See *Employment*

CHILDREN

The American Academy of Pediatrics

Videos: "When Parents Deploy," children with deployed parents speaking about their experiences, and "Mr. Pie and Friends."
141 Northwest Point Boulevard
Elk Grove Village, IL 60007-1098
Phone: 847-434-4000
Web site: www.aap.org/sections/unifserv/deployment/ysp-resources.htm

Coaching Young Families

A pilot program that the National Guard started that provides outreach and education to newly married couples and couples with young children. See if there is one in your area by contacting your local Family Assistance Center.
Web site: www.guardfamily.org

Guard Family Youth

The National Guard program to help youth of guard Soldiers and Airmen.
Web site: www.guardfamilyyouth.org

Military Child Education Coalition

This site shows you how to identify children facing deployment and help them get through it.
108 East FM 2410, Suite D
P.O. Box 2519
Harker Heights, TX 76548-2519
Phone: 254-953-1923
Web site: www.militarychild.org

Military Student

A wonderful Web site for youth. They can click on different options and even email a peer their age.
Web site: www.militarystudents.org

Child Care Aware

National Association of Child Care Resource and Referral Agencies
Phone: 800-424-2246
Web site: www.childcareaware.org

Operation Military Child Care

Provided by National Association of Child Care Resource and Referral AgenciesSubsidies for licensed child care for children up to twelve years old, based on family income. For support for employment, education, or special medical circumstance needs.
Phone: 800-424-2246
Email: OMCC@NACCRRSA.org
Web site: www.naccrra.org/Military Programs

Talk, Listen, Connect

A DVD provided by Sesame Workshop and Wal-Mart to help children cope with feelings, challenges, and concerns experienced during deployment.
Web site: www.sesameworkshop.org/tlc

COUNSELING/THERAPY

Also see *VA Medical Centers* and *Vet Centers* in the VA special section at the end of the Resources
Also see *Support Groups*

The following resources will help you find a counselor or therapist.

Military OneSource

Phone: 800-342-9647
Web site: www.militaryonesource.com
The Center for Mental Health Services Locator Provides you with information on how to locate a therapist and about mental health services and resources. Useful for professionals, consumers and their families, and the public.
Web site: www.mentalhealth.samhsa.gov/databases

The Anxiety Disorders Association of America

Offers a referral network.
8730 Georgia Ave., Suite 600
Silver Spring, MD 20910
Phone: 240-485-1001
Web site: www.adaa.org/Getting Help/FindATherapist.asp

The Association for Advancement of Behavioral and Cognitive Therapies (ABCT, formerly AABT)

A professional organization that maintains a database of CBT therapists.
305 7th Avenue, 16th Fl.
New York, NY 10001
Phone: 212-647-1890
Web site: https://abct.org/members/Directory/Clinical_Directory.cfm

Deployment Health Clinical Center

Toll-free: 1-800-796-9699

Employee Assistance Program (EAPs) Listings

EAPs are counseling services for employees and their eligible dependents who are experiencing personal or workplace problems.
Web site: www.eaplist.com/?l2s_trk=Google

Give an Hour

A nonprofit organization that is establishing a national network of mental health professionals to offer one hour a week of free counseling/therapy for military members and their families.
P.O. Box 5918
Bethesda, MD 20824-5918
Web site: www.giveanhour.org

Military chaplains and other religious leaders

Also provide counseling and can be located through your military establishment or community.

National Institute of Mental Health Information Center

Toll-free: 1-866-615-6464

SOFAR

This Boston area-based organization offers pro bono psychotherapy services to OEF/OIF veterans and their families.
Web site: www.sofarusa.org

CRISIS/RELIEF

Also see *Financial*

These organizations can help you find information on food, shelter, and housing, or in an emergency. You can find assistance at the following places if you can demonstrate the need for funds for emergency travel, automobile repair, urgent health, and welfare, etc.:

Armed Forces Relief Trust (including Guard and Reserves): www.afrtrust.org
Army Emergency Relief: www.aerhq.org
Navy-Marine Corps Relief Society: www.nmcrs.org
Air Force Aid Society: www.afas.org
Coast Guard Mutual Assistance: www.cgmahq.org

American Red Cross

Offers worldwide communication and support, interest free loans, and more.
Phone: 877-272-7337
Web site: www.redcross.org/services/afes/0,1082,0_321_,00.html

Food Allowance

Web site: www.military.com/benefits/military-pay/basic-allowance-for-subsistence

Housing Allowance

Web site: http://perdiem.hqda.pentagon.mil/perdiem

The Fisher House program

A unique private-public partnership that supports America's military in their time of need. The program donates "comfort homes," built on the grounds of major military and VA medical centers. These homes enable family members to be close to a loved one at the most stressful times—during the hospitalization for an unexpected illness, disease, or injury.
1401 Rockville Pike, Suite 600
Rockville, MD 20852
Phone: 301-294-8560
Toll-free: 888-29-8560
Web site: www.fisherhouse.org

DD214

See *Forms*

DAY CARE

See *Children*

DENTAL

The VA provides a six-month benefit covering free dental following a deployment. See VBA for more information or call your local VA.

DEPARTMENT OF VETERANS AFFAIRS

See special VA Services section at the end of the Resources

United Concordia (Tricare Dental: Active Duty Dental)

(to compare with VA dental benefits)
Web site: www.ucci.com

DEPLOYMENT

Department of Labor Employee Benefits Security Administration

Answers to FAQs for reservists called to Active Duty.
Toll free: 866-444-EBSA
Web site: www.dol.gov/ebsa/faqs/faq_911_2.html

Deployment LINK

Health care news for deployed personnel and their families.
Web site: http://deploymentlink.osd.mil

Family Readiness Centers

(Deployment Resource for Guard and Reserves)
Toll free: 888-607-8773
Web site: www.defenselink.mil/ra/html/familyreadiness.html

Homecoming: Resilience after Wartime

Materials from the APA to help returning service members and their families.
Web site: www.apahelpcenter.org/featuredtopics/feature.php?id=43

Military Homefront

The official Department of Defense Web site for reliable quality of life information designed to help troopsand their families, leaders, and service providers.
Web site: www.militaryhomefront.dod.mil

DISABILITY

Also see *Benefits, Injury,* and *Employment*

Military.com

Veteran Disability Compensation
Web site: www.military.com/benefits/military-pay/va-disability-compensation

VA's Compensated Work Therapy Program

These programs strive to maintain highly responsive long-term quality relationships with business and industry promoting employment opportunities for veterans with physical and mental disabilities.
Web site: www1.va.gov/Vetind

Vet Success

Presents information about the services that the Vocational Rehabilitation and Employment (VR&E) program provides to veterans with service-connected disabilities. It also provides information about vocational rehabilitation.
Web site: http://vetsuccess.symplicity.com

DOMESTIC VIOLENCE

National Toll-free Domestic Violence Hotline

Information and resource contact numbers on violence and anger in the home.
Toll free: 800-799-SAFE (7233)
Web site: www.ndvh.org

Controlling Anger Before It Controls You
An American Psychological Association online resource.
Web site: www.apa.org/topics/controlanger.html

EDUCATION

Also see *Benefits*

The Fund for Veterans' Education
College scholarships for veterans.
Web site: www.veteransfund.org

National Guard Virtual Armory
Click the "education" tab for information on college reenrollment issues and educational benefits.
Web site: www.virtualarmory.com

Military Child Education Coalition
108 East FM 2410, Suite D
P.O. Box 2519
Harker Heights, TX
Phone: 254-953-1923
Web site: www.militarychild.org

Service member Opportunity Colleges (SOCs)
Toll-free: 800-368-5622
Web site: www.soc.aascu.org

U.S. Department of Education
Federal Student Aid Programs
Web site: www.ifap.ed.gov/dpcletters/GEN0113.html

GI Bill
Active Duty service members and veterans can receive a monthly benefit that can be used for tuition, books, fees, and living expenses while earning a degree or certification (including undergraduate and graduate degrees), or attending trade school.
Toll-free: 888-442-4551
Web site: http://edu.military.com/gibill

EDUCATIONAL MATERIALS/RESOURCES

Books and Guides for General Audience
Armstrong, Keith, Suzanne Best, and Paula Domenici. *Courage after Fire: Coping Strategies for Returning Soldiers and Their Families.* Berkeley, CA: Ulysses Press, 2005.

Cantrell, Bridget and Chuck Dean. *Down Range: To Iraq and Back.* West Concord, MN: Wordsmith Books, 2005.

Henderson, Kristin. *While They're at War: The True Story of American Families on the Homefront.* New York: Houghton Mifflin, 2006.

Military Family Research Institute (MFRI). *Deployment Support Resources Guide.*

MFRI provides a special collection of resources that focus on employment issues. Several of these resources focus specifically on deployment and how it affects military families. Other resources are targeted more toward helping children deal with war.
Web site: www.cfs.purdue.edu/mfri/pages/military/deployment_support.html

Sherman, Deann and Michele Sherman. *Finding My Way: A Teen's Guide to Living with a Parent who has Experienced Trauma.* Edina, MN: Seeds of Hope Books, 2005.

VA National Center for PTSD. *Returning from the War Zone: A Guide for Families.* See www.ncptsd.va.gov for a wealth of resources, including this guide.

Online Videos
American Academy of Pediatrics
Video of children with deployed parents speaking about their experiences, and more.
Web site: www.aap.org/sections/unifserv/deployment/ysp-resources.htm

Battlemind: Military members are taught a mindset to help them in the war zone that can sometimes be maladaptive if used when they return home. This site provides brochures and Powerpoint presentations with video clips discussing this mindset.
Web site: www.battlemind.org

Pentagon Channel video on war zone stress 30 min., PC format
Web site: www.usuhs.mil/usuhs/videocenter.html

VA National Center for PTSD Web site contains a wealth of videos for veteran and general audience. See www.ncptsd.va.gov/ncmain/publications/electronic/videos_gpv.jsp

Films
After the Fog: documentary film by Jay Craven.

Soldiers of Conscience: documentary film by Catherine Ryan and Gary Weinberg.

The War Tapes: documentary film by Deborah Scranton.

Vermont Fallen: a student documentary about Vermonters killed in Iraq.

EMERGENCY
See *Crisis/Relief*

EMPLOYMENT
Also see *Disability*

America Supports You
A DoD website to help with training and placement for veterans.
Web site: www.americasupportsyou.mil/AmericaSupportsYou/training_placement.html

Career Center for the Military Severely Injured Center
Toll-free: 888-774-1361
Web site: www.Military.com/support

Employer Support of the Guard and Reserves (ESGR)
1555 Wilson Blvd, Suite 200
Arlington, VA 22209-2405
Toll-free: 800-336-459
Web site: www.esgr.org

Department of Labor Veteran's Employment and Training Service (VETS)
Provides veterans, reservists, and National Guard members with information on the rights and benefits associated with securing employment.
Frances Perkins Building
200 Constitution Avenue, NW
Washington, DC 20210
Toll-free: 866-4-USA-DOL
Web site: www.dol.gov/vets

Hire Vets First
A career Web site for hiring veterans of America's military; matching employment opportunities with veterans. The President's National Hire Veterans Committee
U.S. Department of Labor
Veterans' Employment & Training Service
200 Constitution Avenue, N.W., Rm. S-1325
Washington, DC 20210
Phone: 202-693-4700
Web site: www.hirevetsfirst.gov

Military Assistance Program
Information and interactive resources for military relocations, job searching, and money management.
Web site: www.defenselink.mil/mapsite

Military Spouse Career Center
Career advice for military spouses.
Web site: www.military.com/spouse

Military Spouses' Career Network
Web site: www.mscn.org

Operation Transition
A Web site sponsored by the Department of Defense to help military members transition into the civilian workforce. It provides the Transition Bulletin Board (TBB), an automated system that contains a listing of job want ads and other useful information for service members and their partners.
Web site: www.dmdc.osd.mil/ot

National Partnership for Workplace Mental Health
Delivers educational materials to employers and employees on a broad range of mental health topics, provides a forum for businesses to explore mental health issues and share innovative solutions, and serves as a clearinghouse of mental health information important to employers.
Web site: www.usuhs.mil/csts

Operation Healthy Reunions
A program of Mental Health America. Provides specific information for Guard and reservists returning to work.
Web site: www.mentalhealthamerica.net /reunions/infoReturnWork.cfm

Transition Assistance
The largest single source of transition assistance information and tools for today's separating military.
Web site: www.taonline.com

Turbo Tap
Transition assistance (TAP)
Web site for Active Duty and Guard and Reserves.

Web site: www.transition assistanceprogram.com/register.tpp

U.S. Department of Labor
Employment Rights
Web site: www.dol.gov/elaws/userra.htm
Also check out this press release about employee benefits at www.dol.gov/ebsa /newsroom/pr011003.html

Vet Success
Presents information about the services that the Vocational Rehabilitation and Employment (VR&E) program provides to veterans with service-connected disabilities.
Web site: http://vetsuccess.symplicity.com

Vocational Rehabilitation (Voc Rehab)
Most state departments of human services have a vocational rehabilitation program or division to help persons with a disability find suitable work. See your local phone book for information.

FAMILY

Family Assistance Centers
Located at armories across the United States, these centers were created by the National Guard but exist to assist all members and families of all branches of military. For instance, if your son or daughter is deployed from Arkansas but you live in Miami, you can still go to any Florida FAC and receive assistance.
Also sometimes called Family Readiness Centers.
Web site: www.guardfamily.org

Army Community Services (ACS) and U.S. Air Force Services Agency
These services exist within the respective armed forces to provide family support and readiness, helping families to meet

the challenges of separations due to deployments, new assignments, and other disruptions associated with military lifestyle.
ACS Web site: www.armymwr.com/
U.S. Air Force Services Agency
Web site: www-p.afsv.af.mil

Family Readiness Program links:

www.militaryhomefront.dod.mil
www.myarmylifetoo.com
www.lifelines.navy.mil
www.usmc-mccs.org
www.uscg.mil/reserve

Air Force Crossroads

The official community Web site of the U.S. Air Force.
Web site: www.afcrossroads.com

Air Force Reserve Family Readiness

Toll-free: 800-223-1784,
ext. 7-1243 (ext. 7-0089 after duty hours)
Web site: www.afrc.af.mil/library/family.asp

Ameriforce Publishing

A leading publisher of military magazines, AmeriForce Publishing focuses on four very important aspects of military life: relocation, military family life, service in the Reserve or National Guard, and deployment issues.
Web site: www.ameriforce.net

Army Families Online

Information provided by the Army Well-Being Liaison Office.
Web site: www.armyfamiliesonline.org
Toll-free: 800-833-6622

Army MWR

Web site: www.armymwr.com

Army Family Team Building (AFTB)

A volunteer-led organization that provides training and knowledge to partners and family members to support the total Army effort.
Web site: www.armyfamilyteam building.org

Coast Guard ombudsman

A Coast Guard spouse or other volunteer who serves as the family liaison. An ombudsman understands and supports command policy and works with command and the Active Duty Coast Guard members and families to keep communication open.
Web site: www.uscg.mil/mlcpac/iscseattle/pw/ombudsman.htm

Defenselink

The U.S. Department of Defense military Web site.
Web site: www.defenselink.mil

Department of Defense Deployment Health & Family Readiness Library

This library provides service members, families, and health care providers a quick and easy way to find the deployment health and family readiness information they value.
Web site: http://deploymenthealth library.fhp.osd.mil/home.jsp

Family Matters

Web site: www.hooah4health.com/deployment/familymatters

Fleet and Family Support Division

Provides support to Sailors, families, and communities by offering policy guidance, field support, resources, and information services to people in need, their business partners, the

Fleet and Family Support Division, *continued*

Chain of Command, and their field activities. They accomplish this through planning, oversight, advocacy, and research.

Web site: www.npc.navy.mil/Command Support/CommunitySupportProgram Policies/fleet.htm

Hooah4Health.com

The U.S. Army health promotion and wellness Web site.

Web site: www.hooah4health.com

Lifelines

Navy Lifelines services network provides Sailors, Marines, and their families with answers.

Web site: www.lifelines.navy.mil

Marine Corps Community Services (MCCS)

MCCS exists to help Marine families wherever they may be stationed. It developed from merging the Corps old Morale, Welfare, and Recreation and Human Resources programs to help with family readiness.

Web site: www.usmc-mccs.org

Military Family Life Consultants

This program provides support and assistance to Active Duty Soldiers, National Guard and Reserves, military family members, and civilian personnel. Military and Family Life Consultants can help people who are having trouble coping with concerns and issues of daily life.

Phone: 1-800-646-5613

Email: terry.d.fullerton@healthnet.com

Web site: www.hoodmwr.com/ACS/sfrb_mflc.html

Military Home Front

The official Department of Defense Web site for reliable quality of life information designed to help troops and their families, leaders, and service providers. Whether you live the military lifestyle or support those who do, you'll find what you need.

Web site: www.militaryhomefront.dod.mil

MyArmyLifeToo.com

A portal of resources for Army families.

Web site: www.myarmylifetoo.com/skins/malt/home.aspx

National Alliance on Mental Illness (NAMI)

Colonial Place Three
2107 Wilson Blvd., Suite 300
Arlington, VA 22201-3042
Toll-free: 800-950-NAMI
Email: info@nami.org
Web site: www.nami.org

National Guard Children and Youth Program

Provides resources and information for youth as well as information on educational funds and scholarships.

Web site: www.guardfamilyyouth.org

National Guard Bureau Family Program

Information on programs, benefits, resources, and more for families, military members, volunteers, educators, and others.

Web site: www.guardfamily.org

Navy Moral, Welfare and Recreation

Web site: www.mwr.navy.mil

Operation Comfort

A nationwide network of mental health professionals and agencies that provide counseling to families with deployed member free of charge.

Toll-free: 866-632-7868
Web site: www.operationcomfort.com

Reserve Affairs

Information on all matters that involve the Reserve Components, including the Army National Guard, Army Reserve, Naval Reserve, Marine Corps Reserve, Air National Guard, Air Force Reserve, and Coast Guard Reserve.
Web site: www.defenselink.mil/ra

Veterans and Families Coming Home

This site provides information for families, employers, and communities to help support homecoming veterans in their transition from military to civilian life. Resources and readings are provided as well as information on preparing for homecoming.
Web site: www.veteransandfamilies .org/home.html

Virtual Family Readiness Program

Tools to facilitate and enable the establishment, communications, and maintenance of online FRGs between volunteers and Soldier families regardless of their locations. Offers instant messaging, blogs, kids postcards, video email, in-case-of emergency family plans, and much more.
Web site: www.armyfrg.org

FILMS

See *Educational Materials / Resources*

FINANCIAL

Also see *Veterans Affairs Benefits* and *Disability*

American Red Cross Military Members and Families

Web site: www.redcross.org/services /afes/0,1082,0_477_,00.html

Defense Finance and Accounting Service (DFAS)

Military Pay Site
Web site: www.dod.mil/dfas

FAQs on Debt

Web site: www.dfas.mil/military pay/debt/frequentlyaskedquestions.html

Military Assistance Program

Information and interactive resources for military relocations, job searching, and money management.
Web site: www.defenselink.mil/mapsite

MYPAY

Web site to check your LES.
Web site: https://mypay.dfas.mil mypay.aspx

Personal Finance Assistance for Vets

Web site: www.transition assistanceprogram.com/portal/ transition/lifestyles/Personal_Finances

State Department of Veterans Affairs

Each U.S. state has its own state department of Veterans Affairs that offers a variety of services to veterans, including financial assistance. Check your local phone book for contact information.

FORMS

The National Archives

If DD214s are lost, veterans (or the next of kin of deceased veterans) can get a duplicate copy by completing a form found here.
Web site: www.archives.gov/ research/index.html

VA Enrollment Form

Web site: https://www.1010ez.med .va.gov/sec/vha/1010ez

VA Forms
Web site: www.va.gov/vaforms

GENERAL RESOURCES

Deployment Health and Family Readiness Library

Provides service members, families, leaders, health care providers, and veterans an easy way to find deployment health and family readiness information.
Web site: http://deploymenthealth library.fhp.osd.mil/home.jsp

Military OneSource

(user id: military; password: onesource)
Designed to help military members, veterans, and families deal with life issues for free twenty-four hours a day, seven days a week, 365 days a year. You can call in and speak to a master's level consultant who can answer almost any question, no matter how big or small.
Toll-free (in the U.S.): 800-342-9647
Toll-free (outside the U.S.): (country access code) 800-342-9647 (dial all 11 numbers)
International toll-free: 800-464-8107.
Web site: www.militaryonesource.com

State Department of Human Services (or Health and Human Services)

Each U.S. state has some form of department of human services that can assist state residents with a variety of domestic issues. Check your local phone book for information.

State Departments of Veterans Affairs

Each U.S. state has its own department of veterans affairs to help service members who live there. You can find them in your local phone book.

State Guard

About half of the U.S. states have an additional back up force of military personnel for the National Guard called the State Guard mostly composed of retired military members. Sometimes called the State Militia, the State Guard serves many community functions and can be a wonderful resource.
Web site: www.sgaus.org/States.htm

United States 211 Information and Referral Systems

Many U.S. states now have a 2-1-1 comprehensive referral phone line. By dialing 211, state residents are provided with helpful information regarding a variety of state and community services available to them.
Web site: www.211.org

GRIEF

See *Bereavement, Counseling/ Therapy*

GUIDES

See *Educational Materials/ Resources*

GUILT

See *Counseling/Therapy*

HEALTH/MEDICAL

Also see the VA special section at the end of the Resources

Major health resources are listed first, followed by alphabetical health topic listings that are more specific.

TRICARE (Active Duty Medical)

Phone: 877-874-2273
Customer Service: 800-600-9332
Web site: www.tricare.osd.mil
Also see www.military.com/kwlp08 ?ESRC=ggl_mem_ben_tric_kw.kw

My Health Vet

The VHA Health Portal created for you, your family, and for VA employees. This new health portal will enable you to access health information, tools, and services anywhere in the world that you can access the Internet.
Web site: www.myhealth.va.gov

Deployment Health and Family Readiness Library

This site provides service members, families, leaders, health care providers, and veterans an easy way to find deployment health and family readiness information.
Web site: http://deploymenthealth library.fhp.osd.mil/home.jsp

Healthfinder.gov

A guide to reliable health information sponsored by the Office of Disease Prevention and Health Promotion.
Web site: www.healthfinder.gov

American College of Gastroenterology

Provides information, support groups, recipes, product information, and reference articles.
P.O. Box 342260
Bethesda, MD 20827-2260
Phone: 301-263-9000
Web site: www.acg.gi.org

American College of Rheumatology

Fact sheets about a variety of muscle, back, joint, and other problems.
1800 Century Place, Suite 250
Atlanta, GA 30345-4300
Phone: 404-633-3777
Web site: www.rheumatology.org/public/factsheets/index.asp

American Pain Foundation

A nonprofit organization serving people with pain through information, advocacy, and support.
201 North Charles Street, Suite 710
Baltimore, MD 21201-4111
Toll-free: 888-615-PAIN (7246)
Email: info@painfoundation.org
Web site: www.painfoundation.org

Courage to Care Campaign

Courage to Care is an electronic health campaign for professionals serving the military community, as well as for military and families.
Web site: www.usuhs.mil/psy/courage.html

Department of Defense Deployment Health Clinical Center

Pdhealth.mil: This site was developed as a resource for clinicians, veterans, and their families.
Walter Reed Army Medical Center
Bldg. 2, 3rd Floor, Room 3G04
6900 Georgia Avenue NW
Washington, D.C. 20307-5001
Toll-free: 800-796-9699
Web site: www.pdhealth.mil

The Endocrine Society

Information on endocrine research and clinical treatment of endocrine disorders.
8401 Connecticut Ave., Suite 900
Chevy Chase, MD 20815
Toll-free: 888-363-6274
Web site: www.endo-society.org

Hooah4Health.com

The U.S. Army health promotion and wellness Web site.
Web site: www.hooah4health.com

International Foundation for Functional Gastrointestinal Disorders (IFFGD)
Provides information, support groups, information, and reference articles.
P.O. Box 170864
Milwaukee, WI 53217-8076
Phone: 414-964-1799
Toll-free: 888-964-2001
Email: iffgd@iffgd.org
Web site: www.iffgd.org

National Heart Lung and Blood Institute
A variety of information on heart and vascular disease.
Phone: 301-592-8573
Email: nhlbiinfo@nhlbi.nih.gov
Web site: www.nhlbi.nih.gov/health public/heart/index.htm

HOUSING

Also see *Crisis/Relief*

The Fisher House program
1401 Rockville Pike, Suite 600
Rockville, MD 20852
Phone: 301-294-8560
Toll-free: 888-294-8560
Email: info@fisherhouse.org
Web site: www.fisherhouse.org

Housing Allowance
Web site: http://perdiem.hqda.pentagon.mil/perdiem
Military.com Home Buying
Web site: www.military.com/Finance/HomeBuying

VA Home Loans
Web site: www.homeloans.va.gov

HOMELESSNESS

Homeless Veterans
Offers a wide range of services to help homeless veterans.
Web site: www1.va.gov/homeless

INJURY

Also see *Disability*

Army Wounded Soldier and Family Hotline
Toll-free: 800-984-8523
Email: wsfsupport@conus.army.mil

Career Center for the Military Severely Injured Center
Web site: www.Military.com/support

The Fisher House program
1401 Rockville Pike, Suite 600
Rockville, MD 20852
Phone: 301-294-8560
Toll-free: 888-294-8560
Email: info@fisherhouse.org
Web site: www.fisherhouse.org

Wounded Warrior Project
Seeks to assist those men and women of our armed forces who have been severely injured during the conflicts in Iraq, Afghanistan, and other locations around the world.
7020 AC Skinner Pkwy,
Suite 100
Jacksonville, FL 32256
Phone: 904-296-7350
Toll-free.: 877-TEAM-WWP
Web site: www.woundedwarrior project.org/index.php

INSURANCE

Also see *Benefits*

Family Service Members' Group Life Insurance (FSGLI)
Web site: www.insurance.va.gov/sgliSite/FSGLI/sglifam.htm

**Service Members' Group
Life Insurance (SGLI)**
Web site: www.insurance.va.gov/
index.htm

**Traumatic Injury Protection
Under Service Members'
Group Life Insurance
(TSGLI)**
Web site: www.insurance.va
.gov/sgliSite/TSGLI/TSGLI.htm

JOBS

See *Employment*

LEAVE

Check the amount of leave you have
at MyPay
Web site: https://mypay.dfas.mil/
mypay.aspx

LEGAL ISSUES

American Bar Association's Legal
Assistance for Military Personnel
(LAMP)
Web site: www.abanet.org/legal
services/lamp

**U.S. Army Judge Advocate
General's Corp (JAG)**
Web site: www.jagcnet.army.mil/
legal

U.S. Department of Justice
Information on rights as provided by
Uniformed Services Employment and
Reemployment Rights (USERRA) and
the Service members Civil Rights Act
(SCRA). Provides protection to those
called to Active Duty. Offers legal
information on rental agreements,
income tax payments, and more. Can
also help you reduce preservice consumer
debt and mortgage interest rates.
Web site: www.usdoj.gov/crt/military/
index.html

**Judge Advocate General
United States Air Force**
Web site: http://hqja.jag.af.mil

U.S. Coast Guard Legal
Web site: www.uscg.mil/legal/index.htm

**Navy and Marines
Judge Advocate General's Corps**
Web site: www.jag.navy.mil

MWR (MORALE, WELFARE AND RECREATION)

See *Recreation*

MARRIAGE

See *Relationships*

MEDICAL

See *Health/Medical*

MENTAL HEALTH SERVICES

See *Counseling/Therapy*

MILITARY BRANCHES

U.S. Air Force
Web site: www.af.mil

**U.S. Air Force Reserve
Command**
Web site: www.afrc.af.mil

U.S. Air National Guard
Web site: www.ang.af.mil

U.S. Army
Web site: www.army.mil

U.S. Army National Guard
Web site: www.arng.army.mil/
default.aspx

U.S. Army Reserve
Web site: www.armyreserve
.army.mil/ARWEB

U.S. Coast Guard
Web site: www.uscg.mil

U.S. Coast Guard Reserve
Web site: www.uscg.mil/reserve

U.S. Marines
Web site: www.usmc.mil

U.S. Navy
Web site: www.navy.mil

U.S. Navy Reserve
Web site: www.marforres.usmc.mil

MOVIES

See *Educational Materials/Resources*

PAIN

See *Health/Medical*

PARENTS

See *Family*

PETS

Military Pets Foster Project
Connects military pet owners who are
about to deploy with foster homes for
their pets.
P.O. Box 563
N. Myrtle Beach, SC 29597
Phone: 843-249-5262
Web site: www.netpets.org/netp/
foster.php

PHYSICAL HEALTH ISSUES

See *Health/Medical*

POSTTRAUMATIC STRESS DISORDER (PTSD)

VA National Center for PTSD
Offers extensive information on stress-
related health problems, coping,
educational materials, and more for a
variety of audiences, including veterans
and their families, providers, researchers,
and others.
Phone: 802-296-6300
Web site: www.ncptsd.va.gov

RECREATION

Morale, Welfare and Recreation (MWR)
Provides activities such as arts and crafts,
bowling, golf, and clubs for service
members and their dependents.
Air Force: www.afsv.af.mil
Army: www.armymwr.com
Coast Guard: www.uscg.mil/mwr
Navy: www.mwr.navy.mil
Marine Corps: www.usmc-mccs.org

RELATIONSHIPS

Also see *Counseling/Therapy*

MPREP
A military version of relationship
counseling that has been used in
trainings to help couples improve
their relationships. General
information can be found at
www.prepinc.com or contact your
local Family Assistance Center at
www.guardfamily.org.

Military Spouse Career Center
Web site: www.military.com/spouse

Military Spouse Support
Web site: www.milspouse.org

RELOCATING

Also see *Transition Assistance*

Military Assistance Program
Web site: www.dod.mil/mapsite

SEXUAL TRAUMA

WomenSafe Hotline: 800-388-4205
National Sexual Assault Hotline:
800-656-HOPE (4673)

VA Military Sexual Trauma Coordinator
Toll-free: 800-827-1000

Military Sexual Trauma on Miltary.com
Web site: www.military.com/benefits/veterans-health-care/sexual-trauma

The Rape, Abuse & Incest National Network
Toll-free: 800-656-HOPE (4673)
Web site: www.rainn.org

SLEEP

Sleepnet.com
Links to sleep disorder centers across the United States.
Web site: www.sleepnet.com/slplabs.htm

SPOUSES

see *Relationships*

SUBSTANCE ABUSE RECOVERY

The resources in this section are for both alcohol and drug abuse recovery. Also check online or see your local phone book for AA meetings or NA meetings.

Alcohol and Drug Treatment Center Referral
Toll-free: 1-800-821-4357

NIDA Alcohol and Drug Abuse Recovery Resources
Web site: www.nida.nih.gov/medstaff.html

Substance Abuse and Mental Health Services Association (SAMHSA)
Links to online directories of service providers; professional, program, and budget information; as well as substance abuse and mental health information.
Web site: http://dasis3.samhsa.gov

The Partnership for a Drug-Free America
Information about helping people with drug or alcohol problems, finding treatment, and staying clean.
405 Lexington Avenue, Suite 1601
New York, NY 10174
Toll-free: 866-281-9945
Web site: www.drugfree.org/Intervention

SUICIDE PREVENTION

National Suicide Prevention Lifeline
Toll-free: 800-273-TALK (8255), press 1 for military/veteran specific assistance
Web site: www.suicidepreventionlifeline.org

Suicide Hotline
800-784-2433

SUPPORT GROUPS/PEER SUPPORT

The Anxiety Disorders Association of America (ADAA)
Offers a self-help group network.
Phone: 240-485-1001
Email: self-help@adaa.org
Web site: www.adaa.org/GettingHelp/SupportGroups.asp

The National Alliance on Mental Illness (NAMI)
Has information on advocacy for those with mental illness, including affiliates who provide family support groups in different states.
Colonial Place Three
2107 Wilson Blvd., Suite 300
Arlington, VA 22201-3042
Toll-free: 800-950-NAMI
Email: info@nami.org
Web site: www.nami.org

VA Vet Centers
Web site: www.va.gov.rcs

TEACHERS

Military Impacted Schools Association
This Web site is great for teachers, parents, youth, and partners.
1600 Highway 370
Bellevue, NE 68005
Toll-free: 800-291-MISA (6472)
Web site: www.militaryimpacted schoolsassociation.org

TEENAGERS

See *Children*

THERAPISTS/THERAPY

See *Counseling / Therapy*

TRANSITION ASSISTANCE

Also see *Employment*

Transition Assistance Guide for Demobilizing Members of the Guard and Reserves
This site allows you to download a guide full of information on transitioning.
Web site: www.dodtransportal.dod.mil /dav/lsnmedia/LSN/dodtransportal/tag dmgr.htm

TRAUMATIC BRAIN INJURY (TBI)

Department of Defense Deployment Health Clinical Center (DHCC)
Walter Reed Army Medical Center
Bldg. 2, 3rd Floor, Room 3G04
6900 Georgia Avenue NW
Washington, D.C. 20307-5001
Phone: 202-782-6563
Toll free: 866-559-1627
Web site: www.pdhealth.mil/TBI.asp

Defense and Veterans Brain Injury Center
A multi-site medical care, clinical research, and education center funded by the Department of Defense.
Toll-free: 800-870-9244
Web site: www.dvbic.org

National Brain Injury Information Center
1-800-444-6443

Transition Assistance
Assists in the smooth transition of military personnel, civilian employees, and family members from government service.
Web site: www.dodtransportal.dod .mil/dav/lsnmedia/LSN/dod transportal/op.htm

TRAVEL

Armed Forces Vacation Club
Toll-free: 800-724-9988
Web site: www.afvclub.com

Space-Available and Space-Required Travel
Web site: www.militarypay.com/ SpaceAvailableTravel.html

U.S. Army MWR
Special offers on travel.
Web site: www.armymwr.com

Operation Hero Miles
Americans are using frequent flyer miles to support our injured service members and their families. Provides free airline tickets for reuniting hospitalized Soldiers and family.
Web site: www.heromiles.org

The Fisher House program
A unique private-public partnership that supports America's military in their time of need. The program donates "comfort

homes," built on the grounds of major military and VA medical centers. These homes enable family members to be close to a loved one at the most stressful times—during the hospitalization for an unexpected illness, disease, or injury.
1401 Rockville Pike, Suite 600
Rockville, MD 20852
Phone: 301-294-8560
Toll-free: 888-294-8560
Web site: www.fisherhouse.org

VA MEDICAL CENTERS

See VA special section at the end of the Resources

VET CENTERS

See VA special section at the end of the Resources

VETERANS AFFAIRS, DEPARTMENT OF (VA), VETERANS BENEFITS ADMINISTRATION (VBA), AND VETERANS HEALTH ADMINISTRATION (VHA)

See VA special section at the end of the Resources

VETERANS SERVICE ORGANIZATIONS (VSOS)

Directory of Veterans Service Organizations
A site provided by Office of the Secretary of Veterans Affairs that lists and allows searches of the VSO directory (see below).
Web site: www1.va.gov/vso/index.cfm

Veterans Service Organizations (VSOs) Directory
A listing of veterans' service organizations.
Web site: www1.va.gov/vso/index.cfm ?template=view

American Legion
Web site: www.legion.org

AMVETS
4647 Forbes Boulevard
Lanham, MD 20706-4380
Phone: 301-459-9600
Toll-free: 877-726-8387
Web site: www.amvets.org

Disabled American Veterans (DAV)
3725 Alexandria Pike
Cold Spring, KY 41076
Phone: 859-441-7300
Toll-free: 877-I Am A Vet (426-2838)
Web site: www.dav.org

Iraq and Afghanistan Veterans of America
The nation's first and largest group dedicated to the Troops and Veterans of the wars in Iraq and Afghanistan.
Web site: www.iava.org

Iraq War Veterans Organization, Inc.
P.O. Box 571
Yucaipa, CA 92399
Web site: www.iraqwarveterans.org

The Military Order of the Purple Heart
A special organization for special patriots that works to promote history, education, fraternity, service, and patriotism.
5413-B Backlick Road
Springfield, VA 22151-3915
Phone: 703-642-5360
Toll-free: 888-668-1656
Web site: www.purpleheart.org

Paralyzed Veterans of America
The Paralyzed Veterans of America has worked to secure health care and benefits for veterans of the armed forces living with spinal cord injury and disease (SCI/D) and funded research into finding care and cure since its founding.

Paralyzed Veterans of America,
continued
801 Eighteenth Street, NW
Washington, DC 20006-351
Toll-free: 800-424-8200
Email: info@pva.org
Web site: www.pva.org

Veterans of Foreign Wars (VFW)
Web site: www.vfw.org

Vietnam Veterans of America (VVA)
A congressionally chartered not-for-profit organization exclusively dedicated to improving the condition of Vietnam-era veterans and their families.
Web site: www.vva.org

Vietnam Veteran Wives (VVW)
Membership with VVW is now open to those veterans and family members interested in helping veterans and veteran issues. They offer claims consultation and the opportunity to interact with other veterans and wives of veterans suffering from PTSD, and much more.
Web site: www.vietnamveteranwives
.com/index.html

VIDEOS

See *Educational Materials/*
Resources
Also see *Children*

WOMEN

VA Women Veterans Program Manager (WVPM)
Coordinates the provision of comprehensive health care services to women veterans and plans for the establishment of new specialty or primary programs as well as the expansion of existing programs to meet the needs of women veterans.
Web site: www.va.gov/wvhp

The Rape, Abuse & Incest National Network
National Sexual Assault Hotline:
800-656-HOPE (4673)
Web site: www.rainn.org
WomenSafe Hotline: 800-388-4205

THE U.S. DEPARTMENT OF VETERANS AFFAIRS SPECIAL SECTION

VA Services
The VA provides medical, dental, emotional well-being, behavioral health services, and other benefits to Soldiers/Airmen, including Guardsmen and Reserves. Free services for military-related problems for the first two years following deployment, and copay based on eligibility after two years. The VA has many community based outpatient clinics (CBOCs) in addition to their medical centers.
VA has three sections:
- Health (VHA) Veterans Health Administration
- Benefits (VBA, other than health) Veterans Benefits Administration
- Veterans Cemetery: 800-697-6947, www.cem.va.gov
VA nationwide toll-free number:
800-827-1000
Web site: www.va.gov

VHA: Veterans Health Administration
We urge you to complete VA Form 10-10EZ to sign up for VA health care services even if you think you'll never use these services!
Phone: 877-222-VETS (8387)
Web site: www1.va.gov/health

VA Medical Centers

The largest health care system in the ·
United States, with facilities located in
every state. Find a facility or community-
based clinic (CBOC) near you at:
www1.va.gov/directory/guide/
home.asp
Each medical center has:

- An OEF/OIF Program Manager to
  help all recent returnees
- Health and Mental Health Services
- A Women Veterans Program Manager
- Social Work Services

VA facilities locator Web site

www1.va.gov/directory/guide/home.asp
Here you can find a VA facility close to
you. In addition to VA Medical Centers,
VA also provides Community Based
Outpatient Clinics (CBOCs).

Vet Centers

Readjustment Counseling Service
Toll-free: 800-905-4675
Vet Centers assist veterans and their
families toward a successful postwar
adjustment, offering readjustment
counseling (including PTSD treatment),
bereavement, alcohol and drug, trauma,
marriage and family, and benefits
counseling as well as job services and
help obtaining services at the VA and
community agencies. There are no
copayments or charges for Vet Center
services, and services are completely
confidential.
Web site: www.va.gov/rcs

My HealtheVet

The VHA Health Portal created for you,
your family, and for VA employees. This
new health portal will enable you to
access health information, tools, and
services anywhere in the world that you
can access the Internet.
Web site: www.myhealth.va.gov

VA National Center for PTSD

The center of excellence for research
and education on the prevention,
understanding, and treatment of
PTSD. Although we provide no
direct clinical care, our purpose
is to improve the well-being and
understanding of American veterans.
Our Web site provides extensive
information on stress-related
health problems.
Email: ncptsd@va.gov
PTSD Info Line: 802-296-6300
Web site: www.ncptsd.va.gov

VA Women's Veterans Program Manager (WVPM)

Coordinates the provision of
comprehensive health care services
to women veterans and plans for
the establishment of new specialty
or primary programs as well as the
expansion of existing programs to
meet the needs of women veterans.
Web site: www.va.gov/wvhp

VBA: Veterans Benefits Administration

Veterans benefits include those
listed below and many more. There's
a separate enrollment form that's
much longer and detailed than the
health care 10-10EZ. VSO officers
and other advocates can help you
complete it.
Benefits: Civilian Health and Medical
Program of the Department of Veterans
Affairs (CHAMPVA), Death Pension,
Dependency Indemnity Compensation,
Direct Deposit, Disability Compensation,
Disability Pension, Education, Home
Loan Guaranty, Life Insurance, Vocational
Rehabilitation and Employment.
Toll free: 800-827-1000
Web site: www.vba.va.gov

Compensation and Benefits Page:
Information on how to submit a
compensation claim for PTSD.
Web site: www.vba.va.gov/bln/21

Education (GI Bill): 888-442-4551

Income Verification and Means Testing:
800-929-8387

Life Insurance: 800-669-8477

Telecommunications Device for the Deaf
(TDD): 800-829-4833

**Seamless Transition Office now
VA/DoD Outreach Office**
The VA has created this Web site for
returning Active Duty, National Guard,
and Reserve service members of
Operations Enduring Freedom and
Iraqi Freedom.
Web site: www.seamlesstransition.va.gov

VetSuccess.gov
Presents information about the services
that the Vocational Rehabilitation and
Employment (VR&E) program provides
to veterans with service-connected
disabilities.
Web site: http://vetsuccess.symplicity.com

ACKNOWLEDGMENTS

There are many people we want to thank who helped make this book possible. This includes those who have sacrificed to serve in our military, including their families, and those who help the men and women who serve. Thank you to Chaplain Jim MacIntyre and his wife Ruby MacIntyre, Vermont National Guard Adjutant General Michael Dubie, Gen. Jonathan Farnham, Col. Jonathan Coffin, Col. Brad Jensen, Maj. Randy Gates, Chaplain Charlie and Barbara Purinton, Chaplain Cal Kemp, and Lynn Bidell of the VT National Guard; Dr. Andy Pomerantz Chief of Psychiatry, VA Medical Center White River Jct.; Col. Deborah Carter of the NH National Guard; Col. Carl Castro; Jackie Smith, former case worker for Sen. Patrick Leahy's Office; Jay Craven, filmmaker of the documentary *After the Fog*, and Bob Miller; Kathy Darte and Stephan Grenier of VA Canada; Lisa Harmon, for her help in checking our military facts and adding a true military perspective; Kristin Hendersen, author of *While They're at War*; Chaplain John Morris of the MN National Guard; James "Scotty" Scott and Barbara Thompson, DoD Family Policy; Director Deborah Scranton and the cast of *The War Tapes*; Dr. Sue Storti, John, and Felix from Rhode Island, and Col. Terry Washam now with the VHA/DoD Outreach office.

Thank you to Renée Sedliar for keeping us on task to produce this book as quickly as possible and get it into the hands of readers who need this information. And many thanks to Sue McCloskey, our writer, for her insights into the type of advice people need in order to better cope with the challenges that they face.

From Dr. Laurie B. Slone: I would like to thank both my Dad and my Mom for their constant encouragement and support, Eric for his support and understanding over the past months, my dear friends Marcy and Liz, and Kathleen for recognizing how hard I was working and keeping me motivated. Finally I would like to thank my co-author, Matt Friedman, who never ceases to be an inspiration. I am proud to have the pleasure of working with him and thankful to him for his patience while serving as my mentor.

From Dr. Matthew J. Friedman: I would like to thank my wife, Gayle Smith, nurse extraordinaire and in-country Vietnam vet who first taught me how to listen to vets and has been partner and inspiration ever since. Also, I thank all the friends, partners, and collaborators within the VA, military, Vermont, and National Center for PTSD communities who have encouraged and sustained my efforts for many years. Finally, my co-author, Laurie Slone, has put forth great effort to help needy returned troops and their families, this book being only one example of her energy and commitment.

The Military, Family, & Community Network of Vermont and the surrounding region (MFCN): In addition to the MFCN members already listed, we also thank the following members of the network for all they do.

Vermont National Guard: Mary Blow and the FAC leaders and FRG leaders (Michael Bourgeois, Wayne Boyce, Mary Bullis, Joyce Cloutier, Heather Hinkley [former], Louis Labelle, Kelli Langlois, Sharon Roberts), Tamra Augustino, The GWOTOS (Global War on Terror Outreach Specialists, now the Veterans and Family Outreach Program), JAG Ellen Abbot, Pat Boyden, Michael S. Currier, Chaplain Marty Fors, John P. Gill Jr., Llyod Goodrow, Ann Gorrigan, Jim Greene, Maj. Carl Hausler, Besty Houser, Gus and Ann Marie Klein, Ronnie Labounty, Maj. Bill McKern, Maj. (Mac) McLaughlin, Alaria O'Brien, Heather Powell, Glenn Riley, Marcy Smith, Miles Trudell.

Other MFCN members: Brent Bresette, Robin Castle, Clayton Clark, Jon Copans, VT State Governor Jim Douglas, Paula Gile, Rev. Robyn Green, Myra Handy, Diana Harrington, Sam Haskins, Mrs. Patrick Leahy, Mark Leo, Katherine Long, Denise Luck, Pamela Mather, Janko Mitric, Ray Paquette, Richard Reed, Melinda Rouille, John Tracy,

Keith Warren, Erin Weaver, VT 211 (MaryEllen Mendl, Sharon Tierra, Jim Tonkovich, and Cathy Nellis).

Vermont Agency of Human Services: Scott Johnson; Dave Cote; Sherry Burnette; all of the VT Field Service Directors and volunteers including: Wendi-Sue Allard, Lynn Boyle, Bob Brickey, Richard Giddings, Charles Gingo, Bob Hannan, Jane Helmstetter, Nora Jane Hier, Rever Kennedy, Sara Kobylenski, Greg MacDonald, Don Mandlekorn, Pam McCarthy, Ron Morissette, Mark Schroeter, Jeanne Neal, Sue Schmidt, John Swartz, Dave Yacovone.

VA: Jill Alger, Anselm Beach, Michael Casey, Sandra Davidson, Wendy DeCoff, VA Medical Center Director (retired) Mr. Gary DeGasta, Jim Dooley, Fred Forehand, David Frantz, Stan Gajda, Jessica Hamblen, Travis Jones, Michele Klevens, Steve Krasinski, Catherine Kutter, Dan Moriarty, Fran Norris, Chaplain Joseph O'keeffe, Maureen McClintock, Bob Rummel, Paula Schnurr, Tracy Stecker, Susie Stevens, Bobbie Surrott-Kimberly, George Troutman, Michael Casey, Elizabeth Goldstein, Rebecca Robinson, Cliff Trott, Ed Vega, Julia Whealin, Peggy Willoughby, Steve Willoughby.

INDEX

AA. *See* Alcoholics Anonymous

Abandonment, feelings of, 73–74, 128

Abuse, 182–183. *See also* Children: child abuse; Violence, interpersonal

Accountability, 58

ACS. *See* Army Community Services

ADHD. *See* Attention deficit hyperactivity disorder

Admitting problems, xiii, 136–138, 143

Adrenaline rush/train, 66, 72, 88, 90, 153

Afghanistan, 5, 11, 20(box), 22, 83, 187, 201, 225(box)

  non-combat roles in, 214–215

  private contractors in, 219–220

AFTB. *See* Army Family Team Building

Agency of Human Services, 140

Age of enlisted service members and officers, 20(box)

Aggression, 59, 74, 82, 83, 84, 92–93, 93–94, 119, 123–124, 160, 176, 206

  aggressive driving, 90–91 (*See also* Driving, non-defensive/defensive)

  expression of, 60–61

Agoraphobia, 184, 227

Air Force Reserve Family Readiness, 38

Alcohol and substance abuse. *See* Drinking alcohol; Substance abuse

Alcoholics Anonymous (AA), 177

Alex C. case history, 20–21, 24, 32, 36, 98–99

  homecoming, 42–43, 44–45, 45–46, 71, 88, 92, 119, 188–189

Alienation, 139

Ambushes, 1, 137

American Bar Association's Legal Assistance for Military Personnel (LAMP), 196

Amnesia, 192

Amputations, 38, 42, 44, 90, 111, 188, 188, 189, 225(box). *See also* Prostheses

Anger, 3, 7–8, 49, 55, 59, 66, 72, 73, 74, 75, 78, 82, 83–95, 108, 118, 119, 130, 175, 192, 206, 224

  coping with, 93–94, 131–132, 145

  displaced on wrong person, 84–85

  expression of, 87–88, 90–91

  and fear, 121, 123–124

  and grief, 109, 110, 111

  and posttraumatic stress disorder, 156, 159, 162, 168(box), 169

  reasons for feeling, 85

  recognizing, 92, 93–95

Anniversary dates, 94, 114

Anxiety, 3, 32, 33, 59, 70, 72, 74, 156, 166, 192

  anxiety disorders, 183–185, 230

  and gender, 216

Anxiolytics, 180, 227
Apathy, 192
Arab Americans, 218
Armed forces, members of, 20(box)
Army Community Services (ACS), 37
Army Family Team Building (AFTB), 37
Arousal levels, 83, 88, 94, 153, 155, 156,
    159, 176
Arrests, 82. See also Law enforcement
ASD. See Stress: Acute Stress Disorder
Atrocities, 100, 151, 219
Attention deficit hyperactivity disorder
    (ADHD), 180
Automatic reflexes, 71
Avoidance, 3, 7, 75, 109, 118, 122–
    123, 125, 139, 145(box), 176, 219
    of grief, 112(box), 114, 115
    and posttraumatic stress disorder,
        152–154, 156, 159, 160–162, 168
    of relationships, 185

Barbiturates, 180, 227
Battlemind, 44, 49, 56–64, 83, 94, 119,
    121, 127, 129, 223
    as acronym, 57(box), 63(box)
    creation of, 57
    spouse Battlemind, 62–64
Benzodiazepines, 180, 227
Betrayal, 85
Blame, 131, 132
Blindness. See Eyesight, loss of
Blogs, 33, 199
Body armor, 1
Boredom, 52, 71, 178, 202
Boys, 118. See also Children
Brain damage, 193. See also Injuries:
    traumatic brain injury
Brief psychodynamic therapy. See under
    Therapy/therapists
Burnout, 12, 102(box), 219, 227

Cardiovascular system, 185, 227
Caregiver burden, 197

Case histories. See Alex C. case history;
    Kathleen B. case history; Tony K.
    case history
Castro, Carl (Colonel), 56
Casualties, 21, 25(box), 29, 73, 85, 97,
    188, 225(box), 227. See also Deaths;
    Injuries
Casualty Affairs in the Army, 115(box)
CBT. See Cognitive behavioral therapy
Cell phones, 1, 33, 35, 77
Center for Mental Health Services
    Locator, 148
Chain of command, 22, 58
Chaplains, 61, 79, 95, 98, 100, 101, 105,
    107, 133, 139, 142, 148, 177, 208
    support for, 102(box)
Children, 1, 4, 7, 8, 17, 20(box), 33, 40,
    41, 44, 71, 75, 77, 98, 126, 131,
    141, 161, 208, 215
    angry reaction to normal behavior of,
        91–92
    and authority from abroad, 32
    child abuse, 142, 151, 182
    Children and Youth programs, 205
    communicating feelings, 128, 134
    coping with deployment, 30–32
    and death, 114
    disciplining, 4, 27
    and injuries of service member, 189
    overprotection of, 68, 77–78, 91, 120
    problems at school, 31, 118, 204–205
    reconnecting with, 127–128, 216
    security objects for, 118
    and separation, 117–118
Clichés, 81
Coast Guard Ombudsman, 37
Cocaine, 181. See also Substance abuse
Cognitive behavioral therapy (CBT) 165,
    167, 183, 195, 227
Cognitive Processing Therapy (CPT),
    165–166, 227
Cognitive restructuring, 165–166, 227
Colleges, 204

Coma, 193, 227

Combat experiences, 23

Combat gear, 187

Common stress reactions, 17, 78–82, 109, 118–123, 124

Communication, 13, 28–30, 32, 33–35, 37, 41, 45, 46, 54, 55, 61, 62, 63, 77, 94, 100, 120, 124, 135, 145

    communicating feelings, 128, 133, 134

    ground rules for, 76

    and listening, 132

    miscommunications, 222

    plan, 35

    See also Language

Comomorbid conditions, 171, 228

Compromise, 55, 58, 161

Concentrating, 71–72, 93, 107, 154, 169, 192, 202

Concussion, 192, 228

Confidentiality, 143

Conflict, 29, 59, 61, 68, 80, 93, 119, 121, 147, 203. *See also* Homecoming: and conflict within family

Contractors, 213, 219–221

Control issues, 58, 63, 68, 74, 96, 134, 161

    and abuse, 182

    and anger, 88, 93

    emotional control, 59–60

    fear of loss of control, 86–87

    and hypervigilance and over-protectiveness, 119, 120

    and injured service members, 197

    overcontrolling, 77–78, 84, 121

    and repressed thoughts and feelings, 166

    See also Helplessness

Convoys, 22–23, 25(box)

Coping strategies/skills, 8, 9, 30–32, 135, 141, 167, 168, 179, 182, 195–196, 224. *See also* Anger: coping with; Guilt feelings: coping with; Posttraumatic stress disorder: coping with

Counselors, 54, 79, 95, 100, 105, 128, 133, 147, 168, 182–183, 198, 205, 243. *See also* Getting help; Therapy/therapists

Couples therapy, 183

CPT. *See* Cognitive Processing Therapy

Crying, 115, 172, 189

Cultural differences. *See under* Deployment stage

Danger/threat, 9–10, 16, 22, 66, 69, 74, 91, 123, 153, 156

    dangerous activities during homecoming, 111

Deaths, 6, 9, 12, 21, 22, 23, 34, 41, 59, 72, 73, 75, 85, 99, 103–104, 106, 137, 152, 174, 175, 220

    finding meaning in death, 113(box), 115(box)

    killing and religious/moral beliefs, 97–98

    military assistance with, 115(box)

    number of deaths, 25(box), 225(box)

    See also Casualties; Grief

Debt, 52

Decision-making, 64, 78, 93, 131

    and trauma, 99

Defense Department, 142, 207

    Transition Assistance Program (TAP), 191

Demobilization, 47–49, 50, 51, 66, 228

Department of Veterans Affairs (VA), 89, 164–165, 191, 196, 207, 208, 211

    Compensated Work Therapy Program, 196

    Medical Centers, 25(box), 90(box), 135, 139, 140, 148, 167, 168, 179, 182, 190, 207, 208, 217

    National Center for PTSD, 144, 220

Department of Veterans Affairs, *continued*
  Vet Centers, 90(box), 95, 101, 105,
    135, 139, 140, 142, 148, 165, 167,
    191, 217
  Veterans Benefits Administration
    (VBA), 196, 224
  and women veterans, 217
Deployment stage, 2, 7–13, 14(box),
    19–38, 117, 150, 228
  and anticipation of returning home, 13
  being home on leave, 125
  changes due to, 39–40, 41, 42, 49,
    125–126, 203
  children coping with, 30–32
  common reactions to, 65–82
  and communicating with home,
    33–34, 35
  and cultural differences, 24–25,
    25–26, 65, 87
  and down time, 87
  effect on personal relationships, 8, 10,
    13, 15, 30. *See also* Homecoming:
    and relationships
  emotional cycle of, 2–18, 48
  and heat, 1, 9, 24
  impact on family, 7–9, 28–30, 54–55
  impact on troops, 9–10
  living conditions during, 1, 9, 24, 73
  multiple deployments, 11–12,
    25(box), 229
  planning for deployment, 3–5, 8,
    27–28, 35
  recovery and stabilization during,
    10–11, 12
  redeployment, 6
  and reservists, 14(box) (*see also*
    Reservists)
  three steps of, 7
Depression, 72, 73, 81, 90(box), 99,
    108(box), 117, 124, 172–173
  and anger, 84
  diagnosis of, 173
  and gender, 218

and grief, 109, 110(box), 115
  and injuries, 190, 193
  percentage of Americans having
    experienced, 149
  and posttraumatic stress disorder, 157,
    161
  treating, 173, 224
  warning signs, 172–173
Despair, 74, 97, 110, 172, 189
Detachment. *See* Emotions: emotional
    detachment/withdrawal
*Diagnostic and Statistical Manual of Mental
    Disorders* (DSM IV), 151
Diet, 69, 173, 218, 222
Digestive system, 185, 228
Discipline, 61. *See also* Children:
    disciplining
Disease and non-battle injury (DNBI),
    191, 228
Disillusionment, 101
Divorce, 111, 125, 135
DNBI. *See* Disease and non-battle injury
Domestic violence. *See* Violence,
    interpersonal
Drinking alcohol, 16, 49, 72, 78, 82,
    90(box), 94, 99, 112, 122–123,
    141, 175–178
  drinking responsibly, 178(box)
  and posttraumatic stress disorder, 156,
    159, 162, 168, 177
  and refusal to get help, 177–178
  social drinking, 177
  warning signs of abuse, 177
Driving, non-defensive/defensive, 61,
    72, 79, 90–91
Drugs. *See* Substance abuse
DSM IV. *See Diagnostic and Statistical
    Manual of Mental Disorders*

EAP. *See* Employment: employment
    assistance programs
Ecstasy drug (MDMA), 179–180, 228
Educators, 204

Effexor, 167

Email, 1, 33, 77, 222

Embarrassment, 89

Emergencies, 4

EMTs, 204

Emotions, 44, 52, 99, 112(box), 192, 197

   emotional control, 59–60, 131–132

   emotional detachment/withdrawal, 7, 32, 52, 53, 60, 66, 68, 75, 99, 107, 130, 139, 141, 160, 171

   emotional numbness, 73, 74–75, 122, 145(box), 153, 154, 155–156, 176, 184, 219

   emotional outbursts, 141

   emotional reactions after war zone, 67, 72–75

   and posttraumatic stress disorder, 155, 160–161

   See also Deployment stage: emotional cycle of; *individual emotions*

Employer Support of the Guard and Reserves (ESGR), 202, 203, 205, 2208, 208

Employment, 5, 14(box), 51–52, 71, 75, 77, 93, 138, 143, 156, 177, 202

   coworkers, 203–204

   after being injured, 196–197

   employers' obligations, 202–203

   employment assistance programs (EAP), 220–221, 228

Endocrine system, 185, 228

ESGR. *See* Employer Support of the Guard and Reserves

Evidence-based clinical practice guidelines, 165, 228

Exercise, 69, 114, 169, 173, 222

Exhaustion/fatigue, 7, 9, 94, 185

Expectations, 13, 39, 47, 48, 55, 64, 127, 134, 218, 222

Exposure therapy, 165, 228

Eye movement desensitization and reprocessing, 166, 228

Eyesight, loss of, 188, 189, 192, 198(box)

FACs. *See* National Guard: Family Assistance Centers

Faith. *See* Religion

Family Assistance Centers. *See under* National Guard

Family issues, 1, 2, 3, 6–7, 7–9, 10, 61, 127, 133–135, 195–196, 221–222

   changes in family, 125, 126

   conflict in extended families, 29

   contractors' families, 222

   family angry with service member, 124

   family counseling, 128

   family income, 161

   family sacrifices, 54–55, 124

   fear of anger and aggression of service member, 123–124

   getting help for service member, 140–141

   and grief of service member, 111–113

   and guilt feelings of service member, 100

   helping service member reconnect, 134–135

   and injured service member, 190, 197

   and posttraumatic stress disorder, 155, 158–163, 169

   primary contact in extended families, 29–30

   reassignment of residence, 15

   and stress reactions of service member, 80–81

   taking care of family needs, 197

   See also Deployment stage: impact on family; Homecoming; Postdeployment stage; Support issues: support for families

Fear, 7, 8, 10, 13, 34, 35–36, 66, 77, 86–87, 89, 96, 121, 123–124, 152

   fear concerning admitting mental health problems, 137–138, 141 (*see also* Mental health: stigma surrounding mental health problems)

Fear, *continued*
    and posttraumatic stress disorder, 154
    See also Phobias
Family Programs, 53, 129–130, 139. *See
    also* Support issues: support for
    families
Family Readiness Group (FRG), 27, 37,
    38(box)
Fight/flight/freeze responses, 86
Financial issues, 4, 7, 15, 28, 48, 52–53,
    63, 75, 120, 196
First Gulf War, 16, 216
Fisher House, 42–43, 228
Flashbacks, 70, 154, 169, 228
FOB. *See* Forward operating base
Following the rules, 84, 121
Forward operating base (FOB), 23–24,
    228
FRG. *See* Family Readiness Group
Friends, 62, 75–76, 77, 98, 100, 107,
    124, 128–129, 133–134, 169
    and changes in service member,
    128–129
Frustration, 93, 123, 130, 162

GAD. *See* Generalized anxiety disorder
Generalized anxiety disorder (GAD), 183
Gestures, 26
Getting help, 54, 60, 61, 63, 68–69, 74,
    80–81, 87, 95, 100, 101, 111, 121,
    134, 149, 176, 218
    barriers to, 136–149, 225
    and posttraumatic stress disorder, 155
    and red tape, 140
    telephone numbers for, 135
    and violent behavior, 133(box)
    when to seek professional help, 105,
    107, 114–115, 135, 178
    for women troops, 217
Grief, 72, 73, 74, 106–115, 168(box), 188
    and anger, 109, 110
    anticipatory grief, 8–9, 108(box), 227
    coping with, 113–114, 115

expression of, 109–111, 112(box),
    114
physical symptoms, 107
stages of, 109
traumatic grief, 73, 108–109,
    110(box), 111, 115, 231
Group therapy, 168
Guilt feelings, 9, 10, 24, 28, 33, 59, 60,
    72, 73, 82, 89, 96–105, 108, 156,
    162, 163, 166, 173, 177, 214
    and anger, 84
    coping with, 102–105
    expression of, 98–99
    and fear, 96
    and intentions, 98, 103
    and suicide, 174–175
    survivor guilt, 97, 105, 110(box), 231
Guerilla warfare, 22, 216
Guns. *See* Weapons

Headaches, 70, 72, 87, 163, 185, 191,
    193
Health issues, 157, 162–163, 179,
    185–186
    health care proxies, 5, 228
    health insurance, 220, 221
    integrated primary-behavioral health
    care, 157
    neurological problems, 180
    See also Mental health
Help. *See* Getting help
Helplessness, 74, 121, 151, 221
Henderson, Kristin, 210
Hindsight bias, 97, 98, 228
Hispanics, 218
Homecoming, 2, 39–55, 70–71
    and conflict within family, 51, 75, 76,
    92
    missing war buddies during, 57–58
    myths about, 39–47
    preparing for, 49
    and relationships, 41–42, 44–45, 59,
    64, 75–78, 84, 88, 100. *See also*

Deployment stage: effect on personal relationships
and talking about war experiences and feelings, 54, 60, 76, 79, 80, 81, 100, 102, 104, 109, 110(box), 116, 119, 129, 131, 133, 161, 168(box), 174, 197, 214, 224
welcome home parties, 47
See also Demobilization; Post-deployment stage
Hopelessness, 74, 110, 159, 172, 175
Household management plans, 3–5
Hypervigilance, 9, 17, 52, 57, 59, 66, 69, 70, 72, 87, 118, 119–122, 145(box)
and posttraumatic stress disorder, 153, 154, 156, 161

IEDs. *See* Improvised explosive devices
Improvised explosive devices (IEDs), 9, 22–23, 25(box), 61, 185, 229
Vehicle Borne IED (VBIED), 23, 41, 61, 99, 110(box), 190, 231
Information, 48, 49, 50, 71, 139, 196, 208, 210, 211(box), 224
medical information confidentiality, 142–143, 224
211 information lines, 211
Injuries, 44, 82, 111, 151, 185, 187–198
coping tips, 195–196
impact of, 195
procedures and things to know concerning, 191
and psychiatric evaluations, 190
psychological, 137, 225(box) (*see also* Mental health)
spinal cord injuries, 191, 225(box)
survival rates for, 188, 189
traumatic brain injury (TBI), 190–194, 225(box)
traumatic injury protection insurance (TSGLI), 198(box)
See also Amputations; Wounded in action

Insurance policies, 198(box), 221, 222
Internet, 33, 224
Intimacy, 15, 42, 49, 62, 63, 68, 76, 89–90, 127, 130–131, 162
Intrusive thoughts, 109, 219, 229
Invitational Travel Orders (ITOs), 42, 191, 201, 229
Iraq, 5, 11, 20(box), 22, 25(box), 83, 141, 164, 178, 187, 208, 225(box)
exodus of educated civilians, 26
non-combat roles in, 214–215
private contractors in, 219–220
Sunni Triangle in, 21
Irritability, 118–119, 154, 162, 193, 202
Isolation, 122, 126, 130, 141, 160, 168
ITOs. *See* Invitational Travel Orders

JAG. *See* U.S. Army Judge Advocate General's Corp
Jealousy, 47
Jobs. *See* Employment

Kathleen B. case history, 20, 21, 25–26, 27, 29–30, 35
homecoming, 45, 46–47, 48–49, 70, 72, 78, 87–88, 120–121, 177, 187
traumatic brain injury of, 190, 192–193
Kuwait, 5, 21, 24

Labor Department, 196
LAMP. *See* American Bar Association's Legal Assistance for Military Personnel
Language, 24, 25–26
Law enforcement, 82, 206
Legal issues, 5, 197
Lessons learned, 16
Letters, 35
Life insurance, 198(box)
Lifelines, 27, 37
Living wills, 4

Logistical supply area (LSA), 23–24, 229
Loneliness, 2, 6, 11, 26–27, 55, 75, 155
Loss, kinds of, 111
  loss of former self, 111, 155, 173
LSA. *See* Logistical supply area

Marijuana, 179
Marine Corps Community Services
    (MCCS), 38(box)
Marine Forces, 20, 38
MCCS. *See* Marine Corps Community
    Services
MDMA (ecstasy), 179–180, 228
Media, 8–9, 27, 33, 34, 222
  and mental health issues, 146
Medical Holding Company (MHC), 42,
    229
Medications, 145, 147, 149, 164, 167,
    173, 179–181, 194
Memories, 6, 68, 70–71, 79, 98, 122,
    139, 194
  erroneous memories and guilt feelings,
    97
  and posttraumatic stress disorder, 151,
    152, 154, 165, 168(box), 169, 170
  and traumatic grief, 109, 110(box)
Mental health, 14(box), 25(box), 48, 50,
    51, 63–64, 66, 68, 79, 81, 142,
    171–186, 188, 195, 217, 218, 221,
    224
  Center for Mental Health Services
    Locator, 148
  education about, 146–147
  mental health status and military
    commanders, 143
  percentage of people with
    psychological disorders, 149
  protesting inaccurate portrayals of
    mental health issues, 146
  risk factors, 150
  stigma surrounding mental health
    problems, 137–138, 141, 143, 144,
    146–147, 149, 150, 224

treatments for, 145, 147–148, 149, 220
  women's mental health center, 217
  See also Posttraumatic stress disorder
Methamphetamine, 179, 228
MFCN. *See* Vermont: Military, Family &
    Community Network
MHC. *See* Medical Holding Company
Military Family Support Groups, 209
Military occupation specialty (MOS), 21,
    229
Military OneSource, 38, 53, 90, 128, 139
Military Reserve, 5, 14(box), 229. *See
    also* Reservists
Military sexual trauma (MST), 86, 87,
    89–90, 162, 215, 229
  defined, 89
Mindset, 40, 56, 112(box). *See also*
    Battlemind
Minipress, 167
Minorities, 213, 215, 216, 218, 217–220
Mood swings, 72, 82
Moral dilemmas, 97–98
Morale, 33, 37
Morale, Welfare and Recreation, 38
Mortars, 23, 24
MOS. *See* Military occupation specialty
MST. *See* Military sexual trauma
Multiple Deployments, 11. *See*
    Redeployment
Musculoskeletal system, 185, 229
Music, 173
MWR. *See* Morale, Welfare and
    Recreation

Najavits, Dr. Lisa, 182
National Center for Posttraumatic Stress
    Disorder, 208
National Center for Victims of Crime,
    135
National Domestic Abuse Hotline,
    133(box), 135
National Guard, 3, 5, 14(box), 21, 30,
    36, 37, 83, 198(box), 203, 228

Family Assistance Centers (FACs), 8, 11, 27, 30, 38(box), 128, 130, 160, 208, 212, 222, 228
   Family Program, 129–130
   Vermont National Guard, 83, 208
National Suicide Prevention Lifeline, 135, 176(box)
Natural disasters, 66, 151
Navy Family Ombudsman, 37
Neighbors. *See* Friends
Nightmares, 17, 40, 69, 70, 98, 99, 110(box), 145(box), 188
   and posttraumatic stress disorder, 152, 154, 156
Numbness. *See* Emotions: emotional numbness

Obeying orders, 61
Operation Enduring Freedom/Iraqi Freedom (OEF/OIF), 25(box), 199(box). *See also* Afghanistan; Iraq
Opioids, 180, 229
Overcautiousness, 74, 77
Overprotectiveness, 119–120. *See also* Children: overprotection of

Pain, 25(box), 94, 161, 163, 168(box), 190
   chronic, 185
   mental pain, 137
   phantom limb pain, 188, 230
Panic, 70, 156, 229
   panic disorder, 184–185
Paraplegia, 190, 229
Parents of military personnel, 27, 29–30, 36, 42–43, 44–45, 45–46, 46–47, 49, 88, 108(box), 109, 117, 131, 162, 188, 189, 197
   as overlooked in reintegration process, 221–222
   support for, 129–130
Partners, 26, 28, 36, 40, 41–42, 44, 46–47, 64, 84, 88, 118, 124, 127, 131, 135, 160–162, 163, 205, 208, 215, 224
   Battlemind for, 62
   independence of, 10, 15, 77
   and injured service members, 197
   and posttraumatic stress disorder, 182–183
Passports, 222
Patience, 54, 79, 80, 81, 128, 130, 173
Patriotism, 5
Paxil, 167
PCP. *See* Primary care physician
PC-PTSD. *See* Primary Care PTSD Screen
PDHA. *See* Post Deployment Health Assessment
PDHRA. *See* Post Deployment Health Re-Assessment
Peacekeeping troops, 213, 218–219
Peer counseling, 164–165, 229
Persistent vegetative state (PVS), 193, 230
Pets, 4
Phantom limb pain, 189, 230
Phobias, 184, 231
Phone trees, 29, 37
Post Deployment Health Assessment (PDHA), 48, 50–51, 230
Post Deployment Health Re-Assessment (PDHRA), 51, 230
Post-deployment stage, 2, 13–18, 127, 230
   and children, 17
   honeymoon period, 13–14, 124, 223, 229
   impact by community on returning troops and families, 201–205
   impact on community of returning troops, 200–201
   and readjustment/renegotiation, 15, 28, 46, 63, 122, 230
   and reintegration, 15, 24, 44, 48, 49, 62, 64, 76, 79, 130, 136, 202, 205, 207, 216, 221, 223, 224

Post-deployment stage, *continued*
  and reservists, 14(box)
  See also Battlemind; Demobilization;
    Homecoming
Posttraumatic stress disorder (PTSD),
    17, 50, 55, 68, 79, 82, 90(box),
    144, 148, 150–170, 171, 184, 202,
    225(box), 230
  chronic, 165
  classes of, 163–164
  and co-occurring psychological
    problems, 156–157
  coping with, 168–170
  delayed onset, 163–164
  diagnosing, 151–153
  education about, 160, 164–165, 207,
    209–210
  and gender, 216
  likelihood of developing, 157, 218,
    219
  medications for, 164, 167, 194
  and minorities, 218
  National Center for Posttraumatic
    Stress Disorder, 208
  vs. normal stress reactions, 82,
    207
  vs. panic disorder, 184
  percentage of people having
    experienced, 149, 158(box)
  peer counseling for, 164–165
  and private contractors, 220
  recovery from, 158(box), 160,
    163–164, 168
  in remission with occasional relapses,
    163
  screening for, 144–145, 157
  and substance abuse, 181–182
  and sympathy, 158–159
  symptoms, 152, 153, 154, 167, 168,
    177, 218, 224
  and traumatic brain injury, 193, 194
  vs. traumatic grief, 109, 115
  treatments, 163, 164–168, 224

  understanding, 169–170 (*See also*
    Posttraumatic stress disorder:
    education about)
  See also under Family issues
Power of attorney, 5, 222
Pre-deployment stage, 2, 3–7, 117, 230
  impact on troops, 5–6
  impact on family, 6–7
  planning for deployment, 3–5, 8,
    27–28, 35
  and redeployments, 6
Prescription drugs, 180
Primary care physician (PCP), 144, 157,
    163, 177, 184, 186, 190, 198, 221
Primary Care PTSD Screen (PC-PTSD),
    144–145
Privacy laws, 142, 221
Private contractors. *See* Contractors
Problem solving, 139
Prostheses, 43, 189, 195, 232. *See also*
    Amputations
Psychoeducation, 164–165, 230
Psychotherapy, 164, 230. *See also*
    Therapy/therapists
PTSD. *See* Posttraumatic stress disorder
PVS. *See* Persistent vegetative state
PXs, 219, 230

Quadriplegia, 190, 230, 231

RDO. *See* Rear Detachment Officer
Rear Detachment Officer (RDO),
    38(box)
Recklessness, 175
Reconnecting with others, 116–135
  family members helping to reconnect,
    134–135
  reconnecting with children, 127–128,
    215
Recreation, 37
Redeployments, 6
Reintegration. *See under* Post-deployment
    stage

Relationships, 68, 72, 106, 109, 111, 115, 117, 118, 121, 122, 125, 126, 127, 130, 160, 176, 188
  and conversational time-outs, 131–132
  See also Deployment stage: effect on personal relationships; *under* Homecoming
Relaxation techniques, 69, 78, 94, 169, 184
Religion, 100–101, 105, 113(box), 169. *See also* Chaplains; Spirituality
Remorse, 96. *See also* Guilt feelings
Repression, 166
Resentment, 130
Reserve Component, 5, 230. *See also* Reservists
Reservists, 4, 5, 6, 20(box), 22, 31, 36, 51, 52, 198(box), 202, 204, 214
  Air Force Reserves, 48
  Military Reserve, 5, 14(box), 229
  Reserve Component, 5, 230
  Reserve Officer Training Corps, 198(box)
  special issues for, 14(box)
Responsibilities, 3, 7, 49, 55, 60–61, 63, 64, 71, 81, 91, 92, 111, 120, 124, 126, 131, 206
Risperidol, 167
Rituals, 113(box)

Seasonal tasks, 4
Sadness, 7, 26–27, 72, 73, 75, 89, 109, 123, 155, 168(box), 172
  and anger, 84
Seeking Safety therapy, 182
Selective serotonin reuptake inhibitors (SSRIs), 167, 230
Selective Service draft, 199, 230
Self-blame, 97. *See also* Guilt feelings
Self-forgiveness, 103
Sensationalism, 9
Separation issues, 6, 32, 117, 128

Serotonin, 167, 230
Sex, 53, 69, 72, 161, 188
  sexual assault, 151
  sexual dysfunction, 89
  sexual harassment, 88, 151
  See also Military sexual trauma
Shame, 89, 155, 160, 166
Simple phobia, 184
Single parents, 3
Sleep problems, 7, 17, 27, 40, 41, 49, 55, 69, 70, 78, 87, 94, 172, 188, 189, 192, 193, 202
  and posttraumatic stress disorder, 153, 155, 162–163
  See also Nightmares
Smoking, 178–179
Social phobia, 184
Spinal cord injury, 190
Spirituality, 100–101, 113(box). *See also* Religion
Spouses. *See* Partners
SSRIs. *See* Selective serotonin reuptake inhibitors
State Department of Veterans Affairs, 53, 140
Stereotypes, 216
Stigma. *See* Mental health: stigma surrounding mental health problems
Stimulant medications, 180
Stress, 16, 17, 24, 33, 39, 42, 43, 52, 53, 75, 101, 109, 117, 124, 126, 135, 171, 185, 188, 202, 204, 216, 218, 220, 221
  Acute Stress Disorder (ASD), 151(n)
  harmful coping strategies for, 141, 178
  normal reactions to, 55, 78–82, 118–123, 129
  race-related, 220
  stress inoculation training, 166–167, 231
  war zone stress reactions, 66–68, 185, 231
  See also Posttraumatic stress disorder

Stupor, 193, 231
Substance abuse, 16, 82, 90(box), 94, 99,
    111, 122–123, 141, 175–176,
    179–181, 204
  illegal drugs, 179–180
  and posttraumatic stress disorder, 156,
    162, 166, 176, 181–182
  treatments, 182, 224
  warning signs, 180–181
  See also Drinking alcohol
Suicidal thoughts, 82, 111, 171,
    173–175, 176
  National Suicide Prevention Lifeline,
    135, 176(box)
  suicide hotline, 74, 95(box)
  suicide watch, 99, 174
  warning signs, 175
Suicide bombers, 1, 22, 23, 38
Support issues, 8, 11, 15, 27, 32, 33, 35,
    38, 46, 62, 74, 75, 92, 101, 114,
    122, 126, 135, 139, 167, 170, 195
  in combat units, 10
  community support, 199–212
  and documentary films about war,
    211
  importance of, 16
  and injuries of service member, 188
  political support for war vs. support
    for troops, 30–31, 201
  support for families, 29, 30, 129–130,
    160, 190, 205, 212, 214, 220
  support services, 36–38
  vet-to-vet peer support groups, 165
Survival rates, 25(box)

TAP. See Defense Department: Transition
    Assistance Program
TBI. See Injuries: traumatic brain injury
Teachers, 204–205
Tension, 87, 145, 169, 184
Terrorism, 66, 152
  terrorist attacks of 9/11, 20
Tetraplegia. See Quadriplegia

Theater, 2, 231. See also Deployment
    stage
Therapy/therapists, 147–148, 164, 182,
    183
  brief psychodynamic therapy, 166, 227
  cognitive behavioral therapy (CBT)
    165, 166, 183, 194, 227
  cognitive processing therapy (CPT),
    165–166, 227
  couples therapy, 184
  group therapy, 167
  Seeking Safety therapy, 182
  talk therapy, 144, 165
  "thought-stopping" therapy, 166–167
  vocational rehabilitation therapists,
    189, 231
  See also Counselors
Tony K. case history, 20, 21–22, 26, 28,
    31, 32, 33, 34, 40–41
  angry at his own behavior, 86
  and buddy's death, 103–104, 110(box)
  homecoming, 70, 71–72, 75, 77, 90,
    91, 92, 98, 120, 121, 126,
    155–156, 172
Transportation assistance, 140
Traumatic brain injury, 143, 188,
    190–194, 226
Traumatic experiences, 66, 73, 99, 118,
    122, 158(box), 168(box), 185, 195,
    205, 215, 219, 221, 223
  trauma defined, 151
  Women's Trauma Recovery Program,
    217
  See also Grief: traumatic grief; Injuries:
    traumatic brain injury; Military
    sexual trauma; Posttraumatic stress
    disorder
Tricare, 139
Trust, 42, 63, 68, 73, 75–76, 89, 90(box),
    106, 130–131, 141, 168(box), 169
  and anger, 85
TSGLI. See Injuries: traumatic injury
    protection insurance

Uncertainty, 3, 32

Uniformed Services Employment and Reemployment Rights Act (USERRA), 202–203, 231

United Way, 207

U.S. Air Force Services Agency, 36

U.S. Army Judge Advocate General's Corp (JAG), 196

USERRA. *See* Uniformed Services Employment and Reemployment Rights Act

U.S. Food and Drug Administration, 167

VA. *See* Department of Veterans Affairs

VBA. *See* Department of Veterans Affairs, Veterans Benefits Administration

VBIED. *See* Improvised explosive devices: Vehicle Borne IED

Vegetative state, 193, 230

Vermont, 83
  Agency for Human Services, 208, 209
  community case study in, 210–213
  Military, Family & Community Network (MFCN), 209–211
  VT 211 telephone hotline, 210, 211

Vet Centers. *See under* Department of Veterans Affairs

Veteran's Service Organizations (VSOs), 140, 165

VHA. *See* Department of Veterans Affairs, Veterans Health Administration

Victimization, 85–86

Video games, 70, 88, 90

Vietnam War, 16, 25(box), 50, 158(box), 164, 201, 218

Violence, interpersonal, 66, 81, 86, 133(box), 135, 142, 182–183
  warning signs, 182–183

Vocational rehabilitation, 196
  therapists for, 189, 231

Volunteering, 8, 114, 207

VSOs. *See* Veteran's Service Organizations

Walter Reed Army Institute of Research/Hospital, 56, 190

War zone stress reactions. *See under* Stress

Weapons, 43, 44, 59, 119, 174, 187

While They're at War: The True Story of American Families on the Home Front (Henderson), 210

WIA. *See* Wounded in action

Wills, 4

Withdrawing. *See* Emotions: emotional detachment/withdrawal

Women, 98, 99, 158(box), 199
  getting help for women troops, 217
  in military, 20(box), 25(box), 215–216
  National Center for Violence Against Women, 135
  Women's Trauma Recovery Program, 217

Work. *See* Employment

World War II, 199

Worry, 7, 8, 11, 13, 26–27, 33, 34, 35, 117, 125, 183, 206, 222

Worthlessness, 109

Wounded in action (WIA), 191, 231. *See also* Casualties; Injuries

Zoloft, 167